Who Should Read This Book?

"**R**ead" may be the wrong word. "Engage" would be better, because this is not so much a book as it is a classic text, and Jewish classics are not read so much as they are engaged. Included here are a classic text of Jewish prayer, spanning 2,000 years of Jewish experience with the world and with God; and eleven thoughtful commentaries on that text, each one reaching back in a different way, again through 2,000 years of time. The question ought to be "Who should engage this book in personal dialogue?"

If you like to pray, or find prayer services baffling: Whether you are Orthodox, Conservative, Reconstructionist, or Reform, you will find that *My People's Prayer Book* tells you what you need to know to pray.

- The Hebrew text here is the most authentic one we have, and the variations among the Jewish movements are described and explained. They are all treated as equally authentic.

- The translation is honest, altogether unique, and outfitted with notes comparing it to others' translations.

- Of special interest is a full description of the Halakhah (the "how to") of prayer and the philosophy behind it.

If you are a spiritual seeker or Jewishly curious: If you have wondered what Judaism is all about, the prayer book is the place to begin. It is the one and only book that Jews read each and every day. The commentaries explain how the prayers were born, and synopsize insights of founding Rabbis, medieval authorities, Chasidic masters, and modern theologians. The layout replicates the look of Jewish classics: a text surrounded by many marginal commentaries allowing you to skip back and forth across centuries of insight.

If you are a teacher or a student: This is a perfect book for adult studies, or for youth groups, teenagers, and camps. Any single page provides comparative insight from the length and breadth of Jewish tradition, about the texts that have mattered most in the daily life of the Jewish people.

If you are a scholar: Though written in friendly prose, this book is composed by scholars: professors of Bible, Rabbinics, Medieval Studies, Liturgy, Theology, Linguistics, Jewish Law, Mysticism, and Modern Jewish Thought. No other work summarizes current wisdom on Jewish prayer, drawn from so many disciplines.

If you are not Jewish: You need not be Jewish to understand this book. It provides access for everyone to the Jewish wisdom tradition. It chronicles the ongoing Jewish-Christian dialogue, and the roots of Christian prayer in Christianity's Jewish origins.

My People's Prayer Book

TRADITIONAL PRAYERS, MODERN COMMENTARIES

Vol. 4 — *Seder K'riat Hatorah* (The Torah Service)

EDITED BY RABBI LAWRENCE A. HOFFMAN

CONTRIBUTORS

MARC BRETTLER

DAVID ELLENSON

JUDITH HAUPTMAN

LAWRENCE A. HOFFMAN

DANIEL LANDES

NEHEMIA POLEN

ELLIOT N. DORFF

ELLEN FRANKEL

JOEL M. HOFFMAN

LAWRENCE KUSHNER

RUTH LANGER

Jewish Lights Publishing
Woodstock, Vermont

My People's Prayer Book: Traditional Prayers, Modern Commentaries
Vol. 4 —*Seder K'riat Hatorah* (The Torah Service)
© 2000 by Lawrence A. Hoffman

Library of Congress Cataloging-in-Publication Data
My people's prayer book : traditional prayers, modern commentaries / edited and with introductions by Lawrence A. Hoffman.
p.   cm.
Includes the traditional text of the siddur, English translation, and commentaries.
Contents: vol. 4. *Seder K'riat Hatorah* (The Torah Service).
ISBN 1-879045-82-6 (hc)
1. Siddur. 2. Siddurim — Texts. 3. Judaism — Liturgy — Texts.
I. Hoffman, Lawrence A., 1942–   . II. Siddur. English & Hebrew.
BM674.39.M96   1997
296.4'5 — dc21   97-26836
                                                      CIP

First edition

10 9 8 7 6 5 4 3 2 1

Manufactured in the United States of America
Jacket design: Glenn Suokko
Text design: Reuben Kantor
Text composition: Douglas S. Porter

Published by Jewish Lights Publishing
A Division of LongHill Partners, Inc.
Sunset Farm Offices, Route 4
P.O. Box 237
Woodstock, Vermont 05091
Tel: (802) 457-4000   Fax: (802) 457-4004
www.jewishlights.com

Contents

CONTENTS

CONTRIBUTORS

About My People's Prayer Book

My People's Prayer Book is designed to look like a traditional Jewish book. Ever since the dawn of modern printing, Jews have arranged their books so that instead of reading in a linear fashion from the first line of the first page to the last line of the last one, readers were encouraged to linger on a single page and to consult commentaries across the gamut of Jewish thought, all at one and the same time. Every page thus contained a cross-cut of the totality of Jewish tradition.

That intellectual leap across many minds and through the centuries was accomplished by printing a text in the middle of the page and surrounding it with commentaries. Readers could scan the first line or two of the various commentaries and then choose to continue the ones that interested them most, by turning the page — more or less the way newspaper readers get a sense of everything happening on a single day by glancing at all the headlines on page one and then following select stories as they are continued on separate pages further on.

Each new rubric (or liturgical section) is, therefore, introduced in traditional style: the Hebrew prayer with translation in the middle of the page, and the beginning lines of all the commentaries in the margins. Commentaries are continued on the next page or a few pages later (the page number is provided). Readers may dwell for a while on all the comments, deciding which ones to pursue at any given sitting. They may want to compare comments, reading first one and then another. Or having decided, after a while, that a particular commentator is of special interest, they may instinctively search out the opening lines of that commentator's work, as they appear in each introductory page, and then read them through to arrive at a summary understanding of what that particular person has to say.

Introduction to the Liturgy

The Reading of Torah — Retelling the Jewish Story in the Shadow of Sinai

Lawrence A. Hoffman

Liturgy can seem confusing, more like a shapeless mass of verbiage than a carefully constructed whole; a jumble of noise, not a symphony; a blotch of random colors, hardly a masterpiece of art. But prayer *is* an art form, and like the other arts, the first step toward appreciation is to recognize the pattern at work within it.

There are three daily services: morning *(Shacharit)*, afternoon *(Minchah)*, and evening *(Ma'ariv* or *Arvit)*. For the sake of convenience, the latter two are usually recited in tandem, one just before dark, and the other immediately after the sun sets. All three follow the same basic structure, but the morning service is the most complete. It is composed of seven consecutive units that build upon each other to create a definitive pattern. Though the words of each unit have been fluid for centuries, the structural integrity of the service has remained sacrosanct since the beginning.

Services are made of prayers, but not all prayers are alike. Some are biblical quotations, ranging in size from a single line to entire chapters, usually psalms. There are rabbinic citations also, chunks of Mishnah or Talmud that serve as a sort of Torah study within the service. Medieval poetry occurs here too, familiar things like *Adon Olam* or older staples (called *piyyutim* — sing. *piyyut*) marked less by rhyme and rhythm than by clever word plays and alphabetic acrostics. And there are long passages of prose, the work again of medieval spiritual masters, but couched in standard rabbinic style without regard for poetic rules.

Most of all, however, the Siddur is filled with blessings, a uniquely rabbinic vehicle for addressing God, and the primary liturgical expression of Jewish spirituality.

Blessings (known also as benedictions, or, in Hebrew, *b'rakhot* — sing., *b'rakhah*) are so familiar that Jewish worshipers take them for granted. We are mostly aware of "short blessings," the one-line formulas that are customarily recited before eating, for instance, or before performing a commandment. But there are "long blessings" too, generally whole paragraphs or even sets of paragraphs on a given theme. These are best thought of as small theological essays on topics like deliverance, the sanctity of time and the rebuilding of Jerusalem. They sometimes start with the words *Barukh atah Adonai…* ("Blessed are You, Adonai…"), and then they are easily spotted. But more frequently, they begin with no particular verbal formula, and are hard to identify until their last line, which invariably does say, *Barukh atah Adonai…* ("Blessed are You, Adonai…") followed by a short synopsis of the blessing's theme ("…who sanctifies the Sabbath," "…who hears prayer," "…who redeems Israel," and so forth). This final summarizing sentence is called a *chatimah,* meaning a "seal," like the seal made from a signet ring that seals an envelope.

The bulk of the service as it was laid down in antiquity consists of strings of blessings, one after the other, or of biblical quotations bracketed by blessings that introduce and conclude them. By the tenth century, the creation of blessings largely ceased, and eventually, Jewish law actually opposed the coining of new ones, on the grounds that post-talmudic Judaism was too spiritually unworthy to try to emulate the literary work of the giants of the Jewish past. Not all Jews agree with that assessment today, but the traditional liturgy that forms our text here contains no blessings later than the tenth century.

The word we use to refer to all the literary units in the prayer book, without regard to whether they are blessings, psalms, poems, or something else, is *rubric.* A rubric is any discrete building block of the service, sometimes a single prayer (this blessing rather than that, or this quotation, but not that poem), and sometimes a whole set of prayers that stands out in contradistinction to other sets: The liturgy surrounding the reading of Torah, for instance (our topic here in Volume 4 of this series) is a large rubric, composed mostly of a variety of requests for personal well-being (like the individualized *Mi sheberakh,* a request that God show favor to someone who is sick; or *Y'kum purkan,* a similar petition on behalf of the whole congregation). There are blessings too, of course. As we saw in earlier volumes, the Rabbis commonly bracketed the reading of scripture with blessings before and after: the *Sh'ma,* for example, has such bracketing blessings (see Volume 1, *The Sh'ma and Its Blessings*), as do the psalms that make up the morning *Hallel* (see Volume 3, *P'sukei D'zimrah: Morning Psalms*). Here too the Torah is read, and so too (on Shabbat and holidays) is the *Haftarah,* a reading from the Prophets, but only with blessings being recited before and after. Relative to the entire Torah liturgy, the *Mi sheberakh, Y'kum purkan,* and the Torah or *Haftarah* blessings can be considered subrubrics, but sometimes, when considered relative to each other, they may be called rubrics as well. The term is flexible. It is just a convenient way to refer to a particular body of material without having to stipulate what kind of thing — a psalm? a blessing? a *piyyut?*— it is.

At the liturgy's core are two large rubrics to which Volumes 1 and 2 were devoted: the *Sh'ma and Its Blessings* and the *Amidah*— known also as the *T'fillah* or *Sh'moneh Esreh.* But on certain days (Shabbat, holidays, Mondays and Thursdays — market days in antiquity, when crowds were likely to gather in the cities) a third central rubric is added, and that is our topic here: the public reading of Torah. The *Sh'ma and Its Blessings* is essentially the Jewish creed, a statement of what Jews have traditionally affirmed about God, the cosmos, and our relationship to God and to history. The *Amidah* is largely petitionary. It is convenient to think of the *Sh'ma* as a Jewish conversation *about* God and the *Amidah* as a Jewish conversation *with* God. The Torah reading is a recapitulation of Sinai, an attempt to discover the will of God through sacred scripture, revelation anew of God's word, and a retelling of our sacred story. Since the *Sh'ma* and Its Blessings begins the official service, it features a communal Call to Prayer at the beginning: our familiar *Bar'khu.* We should picture these units building upon each other in a crescendo-like manner, as follows:

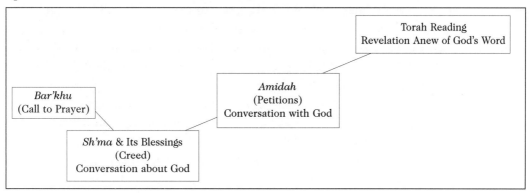

It is, however, hard for individuals who are normally distracted by everyday concerns to constitute a community given over wholeheartedly to prayer. Already in the second century, therefore, we hear of some Rabbis who assembled prior to the actual Call to Prayer in order to sing psalms of praise known as a *Hallel*, and even before that — at home, not the synagogue — it was customary to begin the day immediately upon awakening by reciting a series of daily blessings along with some study texts. By the ninth century, if not earlier, these two units also had become mandatory, and the home ritual for awakening had moved to the synagogue, where it remains today. The warm-up section of psalms is called *P'sukei D'zimrah* — meaning "Verses of Song" (See Volume 3, *P'sukei D'zimrah: Morning Psalms*) — and the prior recital of daily blessings and study texts (forthcoming in Volume 5) is called *Birkhot Hashachar* — "Morning Blessings." Since both of these rubrics now precede the main body of the service, gradually building up to it, the larger diagram can be charted like this:

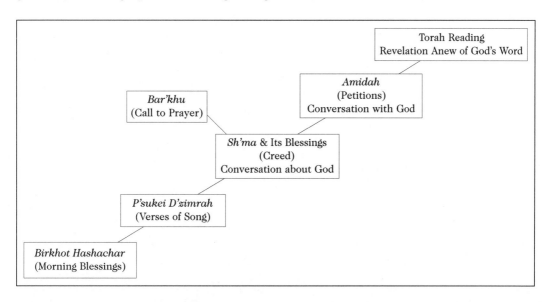

Two other expansions of this basic structure probably occurred in the first two centuries C.E., although our evidence for their being that early is less certain.

First, a Conclusion was added. It featured a final prayer called the *Kaddish,* which as yet had nothing to do with mourning, but merely followed the Torah reading, and therefore closed the service, by looking ahead to the coming of God's ultimate reign of justice. Eventually, other prayers were added to the Conclusion, including the *Alenu,* which had originally been composed as an introduction to the blowing of the shofar on Rosh Hashanah, but was moved here in the Middle Ages. Both the final *Kaddish* and the *Alenu* will appear in Volume 6 of this series.

But the *Kaddish* was eventually inserted in one form or another throughout the service, as a form of "oral punctuation," so to speak. People had no written prayer books yet, so a "whole *Kaddish*" signaled a full stop, a half *Kaddish* indicated a minor change in rubric, and so forth. In the liturgy surrounding the reading of Torah, for example, a half *Kaddish* separates the Torah from the *Haftarah* reading.

Second, the Rabbis, who were keenly aware of the limits to human mortality, advised all Jews to come to terms daily with their frailty and ethical imperfection. To do so, they provided an opportunity for a silent confession following the *Amidah,* but before the Torah reading. In time, this evolved into silent prayer in general, an opportunity for individuals to assemble their most private thoughts before God; and later still, sometime in the Middle Ages, it expanded on average weekdays into an entire set of supplicatory prayers called the *Tachanun* (again, the topic of a later volume in this series).

The daily service was thus passed down to us with shape and design. Beginning with daily blessings that celebrate the new day and emphasize the study of sacred texts *(Birkhot Hashachar),* it then continues with songs and psalms *(P'sukei D'zimrah)* which create a sense of spiritual readiness. There then follows the core of the liturgy: an official Call to Prayer (our *Bar'khu*), the recital of Jewish belief (the *Sh'ma* and Its Blessings), and communal petitions (the *Amidah*). Individuals then pause to speak privately to God in silent prayer (later expanded into the *Tachanun*), and then,

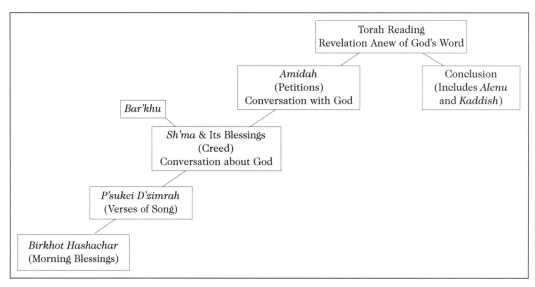

on select days, they read from Torah. The whole concludes with a final *Kaddish* to which other prayers, most notably the *Alenu,* were added later.

On Shabbat and holidays, this basic structure expands to admit special material relevant to the day in question, and contracts to omit prayers that are inappropriate for the occasion. On Shabbat, for instance, the petitions of the *Amidah* are excluded, as Shabbat is felt to be so perfect in itself as to make petitioning unnecessary. But an entire service is added, a service called *Musaf* (literally, "Addition"), to correspond to the extra sacrifice that once characterized Shabbat worship in the Temple. Similarly, as we saw, a prophetic reading called the *Haftarah* joins the Torah reading, and extra psalms and readings for the Sabbath are inserted here and there. The same is true for holidays when, in addition, numerous *piyyutim* are said, especially for the High Holy Days, when the sheer size of the liturgy seems to get out of hand. But even there, the basic structure remains intact, so that those who know its intrinsic shape can get beyond what looks like random verbiage to find the genius behind the liturgy's design.

THE READING OF TORAH

THE JEWISH "LECTIONARY": HOW READINGS ARE ORGANIZED

Reading scripture liturgically is common to religions with sacred texts. The official English word for the set of readings is "lectionary," and any given reading within it is a "lection." Hebrew terminology is far more complicated than that. Just as the native inhabitants of the Arctic Circle have many terms for "snow," so Jews who inhabit the world of Torah multiply words connected with Torah. The lexicon can prove bewildering, so I have listed its most important terms not only in the glossary, but in a short section at the end of this introduction (see p. 16).

There are three kinds of lectionaries: (1) fixed and continuous; (2) fixed but discontinuous; and (3) unfixed altogether.

The Torah readings are fixed and continuous — that is, we start with the beginning of Genesis and read continuously, week after week, until we get to the end of Deuteronomy. That fixed and continuous order is interrupted only for holidays, when the normal reading is replaced by the holiday reading. The next week, however, reverts to the fixed and continuous schedule. In order to make the entire lectionary end when it should (at the holiday of *Simchat Torah*), certain lections may be combined into one week's reading or separated into two weeks' worth of material. If many holidays fall on Shabbat during a given year, for instance, lections must be combined so that they can be squeezed into the remaining weeks. Alternatively, the Jewish calendar may stretch a year by an entire month. That is because it combines a solar year with lunar months. Each lunar month lasts between twenty-nine and thirty days (the time it takes for the moon to go around the earth). Since twelve such months (at twenty-nine and a half days each, on the average) yield only 354 days, a Jewish year is roughly eleven days short of the 365 ¼ days required for a complete solar year (the time it takes for the earth to go around the sun). In seven out of every nineteen years, therefore, the calendar calls for a leap year, when an extra month is added to compensate for the missing days that have piled up. On those occasions, since we have an entire extra month of Sabbaths, we divide lections to make sure we do not run out of portions to read.

In contrast to the Torah readings, the *Haftarah* portions are fixed but discontinuous — that is, the readings are assigned, but on any given week, we do not pick up from where we left off the week before. The reason for a given selection is not always evident. Sometimes the *Haftarah* mirrors the Torah portion. The Torah reading called *B'shalach,* for instance (Exod. 13:17–17:16), contains the song that is sung at the crossing of the Red Sea, so it is matched with Judges 4:4–5:31, which contains the song of Deborah. Sometimes the calendar drives the decision, as on the Sabbath between Rosh Hashanah and Yom Kippur, which is known as Shabbat *Shuvah* ("The Sabbath of 'Return'") and features a *Haftarah* from the prophet Hosea, who calls on Israel:

> Return, O Israel, to Adonai your God,
> for you have fallen because of your sin.
> Take words with you
> And return to Adonai.[1]

Ashkenazi and Sefardi congregations sometimes have different readings, leading us to believe that various alternatives were once available and that different methods of selection eventually crystallized into the normative Ashkenazi and Sefardi practices.

The *Haftarah* selections were probably completely unfixed originally. The earliest reference to what looks like a *Haftarah* comes from the New Testament's account of a visit by Jesus to a synagogue:

> When he came to Nazareth, where he had been brought up, he went to the synagogue on the Sabbath day, as was his custom. He stood up to read, and the scroll of the prophet Isaiah was given to him. He unrolled the scroll and found the place where it was written,
>
> > "The spirit of the Lord is upon me
> > because he has anointed me
> > to bring good news to the poor.
> > He has sent me to bring release to the captives
> > and recovery of sight to the blind,
> > to let the oppressed go free,
> > to proclaim the year of the Lord's favor."
>
> And he rolled up the scroll, gave it back to the attendant, and sat down. The eyes of all in the synagogue were fixed on him. Then he began to say to them, "Today this scripture has been fulfilled in your hearing."[2]

Our understanding of the origin of our *Haftarah* cycle depends on how we read this passage. When Jesus got up to read the *Haftarah,* was he handed the scroll of Isaiah already open to the lection that had already been set for the day? If so, the point of the story is that Jesus miraculously turned up in his home-town synagogue on precisely the day when the *Haftarah* predicted his messianic coming. In that case, we would have to conclude that already in the first century, the *Haftarah* cycle was fixed. More likely, however, the point of the story is that Jesus took the scroll and chose to read the section that he interpreted as heralding his claims to be the messiah. If so, the *Haftarah* readings were unfixed originally, allowing the reader to choose any portion whatever. Only later did standard readings become normative.

In all probability, the fixing of the *Haftarah* lectionary grew by fits and starts, with some *Haftarot* being set before others. The best examples are the *Haftarot* for the three weeks leading up to Tisha B'av (the anniversary of the Temple's destruction and therefore a major fast day traditionally) and the seven weeks following, both of which developed fixed *Haftarah* lectionaries dealing with theological themes emerging from the destruction. As the Rabbis saw it, God must have allowed, and perhaps even caused, the Temple to fall as punishment for Israel's sins. The first three weeks, therefore, anticipate the fall and are called "the three readings of retribution" *(t'lata d'puranuta)*. They culminate with the Shabbat prior to Tisha B'av, Shabbat *Chazon* ("The Sabbath of 'the Vision,'") which features Isaiah's premonitory vision of Jerusalem's fall and the expectation of ultimate recovery (Isa. 1:1–27):

> Ah sinful nation....
> When you lift up your hands,
> I will turn my eyes away from you.
> Though you pray at length,
> I will not listen.
> Your hands are stained with crime....
> I will turn my hand against you....
> Zion shall be saved in the judgment;
> Her repentant ones in the retribution.
> But rebels and sinners will be crushed.[3]

The following seven Sabbaths, which take us all the way to Rosh Hashanah, call for *Haftarot* that guarantee hope. They are the "seven weeks of comfort" *(shivah d'n'chemta)*. A fourteenth-century Spanish savant, David Abudarham, explains how the readings together constitute a dialogue between God and Israel in which God promises comfort and Israel expresses its doubt, given the devastation of the Temple that God caused:

> The Rabbis ordained that the seven *Haftarot* of comfort should begin with "Comfort, O comfort my people" (Isa. 40:1–26), meaning that the Holy One of Blessing said to the prophets, "Comfort my people." The congregation of Israel answers [the next week, week two, with the *Haftarah* beginning] "Zion said, Adonai has abandoned us" (Isa. 49:14–51:3), which is to say, "I am not appeased by the words of comfort spoken by the prophets." So [the next week, week three], God says..."Unhappy storm-tossed one, who will not be comforted...." (Isa. 54:11–55:12), meaning that the prophets tell God again, "The congregation of Israel will not be appeased by your words of comfort."[4] So [the next week, week four] God says again, "It is I, I Myself, who brings you comfort" (Isa. 51:12–52:12). Moreover [in week five] God says, "Shout O barren one, you who bore no child, shout aloud for joy" (Isa. 54:1–55:5), and then [in week six], God says "Arise, shine for your light has come" (Isa. 60:1–22). To this, the congregation of Israel replies [in week seven], "I will surely rejoice in Adonai" (Isa. 61:10–63:9), which is to say, "Now I have something to rejoice about. 'My whole being exults in God; for God has clothed me with garments of triumph'" (Isa. 61:10).[5]

7

Not only are the prophetic readings linked by calendar here; they are linked to each other, independently of their accompanying Torah portions. Jews attending synagogue in this critical time period before and after Tisha B'av get not only the ongoing "plot" of the Torah portions as they occur one after the other, but an intriguing "subplot" involving the love affair between Israel and God. The final reading, moreover, wherein Israel affirms the possibility of starting anew because of God's patent compassion, provides a wonderful introduction to Rosh Hashanah, which inevitably falls during the week following, since Rosh Hashanah introduces the new year with its ten days of repentance, during which sins are forgiven and, indeed, we do begin anew. We do not know for sure when these serialized *Haftarah* readings came into being, but as we saw, unfixed *Haftarot* are at least as old as the first century C.E.

Reading Torah is probably older still. Scholars who accept the idea that Torah evolved through time see the final document as a product of the fifth century B.C.E., possibly put together by Ezra, a priest who established the theocratic commonwealth that followed the return from exile. The traditional rabbinic view claims that the Torah in its entirety was given on Sinai. It followed, for the Rabbis, that Moses himself ordained the weekly Torah reading, although talmudic opinion suggested that Moses' edict held only for Shabbat and the holidays. It was Ezra who expanded the reading to Mondays and Thursdays, when market days brought many people into the city.[6]

Nehemiah, the governor of Jerusalem in Ezra's day, tells us that Ezra assembled all the people in the town square — men, women, and children — and read the Torah to them from dawn to midday.[7] But despite the talmudic tradition that regular readings were instituted then, Ezra's reading was probably a singular incident. It is not described as part of a liturgical service at all, for the simple reason that there was not yet such a thing as synagogue worship. Literature from about 100 B.C.E. to 100 C.E. describes public readings of Torah, but still not as part of the evolving synagogue service that was just coming into being in rabbinic circles and had yet to become a part of what happened in synagogues. (Jesus' reading, for instance, occurs on Shabbat, but we do not find him praying as part of the reading.) It may be that some kind of regularized synagogue reading was the norm even before the rest of the liturgy entered the synagogue. When the liturgy moved there, possibly in the second or third century, the Torah (and *Haftarah*) readings were fused with the worship service and became a highlight within it.

The earliest way of reading Torah was not the annual cycle that we enjoy today. Jews in the Land of Israel used what is called a triennial cycle — that is, a cycle (of readings) that lasted three years. The title is somewhat misleading, however, since the cycle actually took anywhere from three to four years to be completed, depending on the number of holidays that fell on Shabbat and postponed the normal readings. The annual system that we use today comes from Babylonia. Jews there used it, and we inherited it from them, along with all the other liturgical customs passed down through history by the Babylonian Talmud and its final codifiers, the Geonim (c. 750–1038). (See Volume 1 in this series, *The Sh'ma and Its Blessings,* pp. 7–9.)

In the annual cycle, the readings are long, since the entire Torah has to be divided up with just one year's worth of Sabbaths in mind. Reform Jews in Germany found the lengthy readings ponderous and aspiritual, since the only way to get through them was to read or chant them at breakneck speed without attending to the details of what the words say. Reform Judaism therefore adopted the practice of reading only a part of every reading on Shabbat. Eventually, a new kind of triennial reading system was born. In a desire to shorten the readings but also to finish Deuteronomy by Simchat Torah along with other Jews who were reading the entire portion every week, weekly sections were divided into thirds. Each year a different third would be read. In time, Conservative Judaism too adopted this system as an alternative to reading the entire portion. In practice, however, the new triennial system is rarely used by anyone. Most Conservative congregations read the whole portion, and most Reform synagogues feature a different selection from the reading, but not necessarily an entire third of what is traditionally chanted. Reform Jews are apt to hear a section chosen at the discretion of the rabbi or cantor, perhaps because the text for the sermon is taken from the section in question.

LECTIONARY IN PRACTICE: WHY READING TORAH MATTERS

Traditional opinion sometimes sees scriptural readings as horoscopes: they access the secrets of the universe, predicting the future. If, for example, the readings had been fixed in Jesus' day, then he had no choice but to read the biblical announcement of the deliverance that he claimed to represent — a sign of the truth of his message. In his day, of course — as we saw above — the *Haftarah* lectionary was still unfixed. Today, however, when both Torah and *Haftarah* are determined in advance, so that each week has its own unique "flavor," so to speak, there are some who think that the weekly readings actually affect the flow of current events the way horoscopes are thought to do. On any given day, someone born as a Leo may be well advised to invest in mutual funds, whereas a Capricorn should stay out of the stock market altogether. The Rabbis held this point of view. Astrology was a "hard science" in antiquity, and Jews have always accepted scientific findings as real. For the Rabbis, then, it seemed self-evident that Jews should take advantage of a season's astral opportunities. Every time of year, known as a *z'man* (z'-MAHN), was considered unique: auspicious for one thing but not for another. To this day, for instance, the holiday *Kiddush* (kee-DOOSH, or, commonly, KIH-d'sh), the prayer inaugurating the sacred occasion, speaks of *z'man cheruteinu* (z'MAHN khay-roo-TAY-noo) — "the time of our freedom" — at Passover, expressing the rabbinic belief that Passover is the natural time for deliverance. Just as Jews were saved from Egyptian bondage on Passover eve, so they would be saved from Roman oppression then.[8] The festival of Shavuot, by contrast, was not a time in which salvation could be expected. It was not "the time of our freedom" but "the time of the giving of Torah" *(z'man matan torateinu)*. That is why the early Christian community, still Jewish in mind-set, recorded Shavuot (or Pentecost, as they called it) as the time of new revelation. On Pentecost, "There came a sound like the rush of violent wind," at which time the disciples "were filled with the Holy Spirit."[9]

This perspective characterized the way the Rabbis saw certain months of the year. According to the Book of Esther, for example, the Jews had been saved from their archenemy Haman during the winter month of Adar. Adar, therefore, was a month to anticipate happiness. By contrast, the month of Av, which had included the Temple's destruction, was a time of impending disaster. Particular weeks as well shared the theme of the weekly readings. The Torah and *Haftarah* readings indicated the cosmic nature of the time in which they were read.

That is not why we read Torah today, however. We no longer believe that the assigned readings put us in touch with cosmic possibilities. On an elementary level, we read Torah simply because we have been commanded to do so — that is, Torah is central to Jewish tradition, to the point where it would be inconceivable not to read the Torah publicly, and the order of the readings, both Torah and *Haftarah,* is so old and established that it is virtually unimaginable to challenge it. We should differentiate the *reason* for reading Torah from the *benefit* of doing so. The *reason* we eat, for example, is that we are hungry; the *benefit* is that our bodies are nourished. So too, the *reason* we read Torah is that Jewish tradition prescribes it. The *benefit* is that we get in touch with the Jewish story of the centuries.

In many ways, religion can best be described as a story. Its historical accuracy is somewhat beyond the point. Did a man named Noah ever actually live? Did the Red Sea split apart just as the Bible describes? Were Adam and Eve real historical characters who inhabited an actual garden named Eden? To all these questions, biblical fundamentalists answer "Yes," even as religious skeptics answer "No." Serious, sophisticated, and thoughtful religious thinkers, however, see both responses as irrelevant. Much of life depends not just on the facts but on the story we tell about them.

Consider a trip you make to Israel — your first one ever, perhaps. You arm yourself with camera and film, and proceed, as all visitors do, to take more pictures than you thought possible. Upon returning home, you select the best of the photos and put them into an album called "My trip to Israel." The rest of the photographs are relegated to a trunk in the attic. You find, however, that your trip moved you to learn everything you could about the land of our ancestors, so you begin taking courses in Israel's history and geography. One day, you come across the newspaper report of Egyptian president Anwar Sadat's historic visit to Jerusalem, the first step in the peace process between Israel and its Arab neighbors. It turns out that Sadat stayed overnight in an ancient home in East Jerusalem, a photo of which is reproduced in grainy black and white on the front page of an old edition of the *New York Times.* You suddenly realize that you may have taken a picture of that house, but, not recognizing its historical importance, you probably relegated it to the second-rate pictures that got stored in the attic. You run to the attic and discover the picture, only to find out, simultaneously, that you now have a problem. Where do you put the picture now? It is too important to go back into the trunk; but you have no room in the album.

So you return to the album to see if you can squeeze it in. As you turn the pages that you haven't looked at for over a year, you come across a picture of a cactus. "Why did I ever take a picture of a cactus?" you wonder. At the time, it must have struck you as a moving example of desert growth, but by now your memory of its beauty has faded. Out goes the cactus; into the album, in its place, goes Sadat House. The next day, your Aunt Millie, whom you haven't seen in many years, arrives for a visit. You show her your album. When she gets to the picture of Sadat House, you point proudly to it, explaining how wonderful it was to have been there and to have taken its picture even though no one else knew that it was important at the time.

What album corresponds best to your trip? The album with the cactus, or the album with Sadat House? Or, perhaps, neither?

My example demonstrates the extent to which our stories about life change through time, and also how the changing stories alter the way we see reality. Our very lives are made of too many photographs for us to remember at any one time. We select some of them and file away others. We go to therapists when traumatic pictures prove hard to handle. Life is a photography scrapbook, in which a selective perception of who we are is filed away. All the more so is our connection with past generations something we formulate creatively. Feminists have taught us, for instance, that female ancestors got stored in the attic trunk; we are reclaiming them now and putting them into our album. Earlier generations had albums filled with pictures of Jewish persecution; we are learning to balance that part of Jewish history with pictures of Jewish cultural efflorescence. How we see ourselves depends on how we see our history, and how we see our history depends on how we read our story.

Reading Torah is the most important way we read our story. The major benefit of reading Torah is the way it teaches us to see ourselves in some ways but not in others. Members of Reform congregations that do not read the entire weekly passage will especially learn the Torah's accounts selectively. But even congregations that read every word of every weekly reading must inevitably emphasize one part of the reading over another. The story of Noah, for example, ends with Noah's sons confronting their father's drunkenness. But few people know this; we prefer to emphasize the flood and the rainbow. Reading Torah every week provides the master metaphors of the Jewish narrative through time. We learn to see our lives as recapitulations of the stories of our people — and not just the biblical stories, but the Rabbis' elaborations on those stories, called Midrash.

Human beings need metaphors. Life is always lived in the "as if" subjunctive mood. What indeed is marriage, for instance? A legal contract? An opportunity to file joint income tax returns? Or, perhaps, a covenant like the one Israel made with God at Sinai? Reading Torah provides the Jewish categories in which we think. It is the height of the worship service, because it allows us to walk away from prayer thinking differently about who we are and what life is all about.

THE TORAH SERVICE: PRAYERS SURROUNDING THE READING

Technically, the prayers surrounding the reading of Torah are not "a service." The word "service" is properly reserved for a set of prayers that includes an *Amidah: Shacharit* (the morning service); *Minchah* (the afternoon service); *Ma'ariv* (the evening service); *Musaf* (the additional service for Shabbat and holidays); and *N'illah* (the concluding service for Yom Kippur). In common parlance, however, it is usual to think of other things being separate services too: the Memorial Service for holidays, for instance — just a tiny part of the traditional liturgy's *Shacharit* service, but expanded and set aside as a unique "service" in and of itself in most liberal liturgies. We should therefore think of the Torah liturgy in this broader sense as a service in its own right, with its own character and content. Only gradually, and over the course of many centuries, did the Torah service come into being, and in a sense it is still evolving.

People called to read from the Torah are said to receive an *aliyah* (ah-lee-YAH, or, commonly, ah-LEE-yah; plural, *aliyot,* ah-lee-YOHT). The word has two possible connotations. Literally, it means "ascending," so it is taken to indicate the actual physical act of ascending the *bimah* (bee-MAH, or, commonly, BEE-mah), the "platform" where the Torah is read. But it did not mean that originally. Synagogues did not have raised platforms in antiquity. Also, the reader of the *Haftarah* is never described as receiving an *aliyah,* even though the *Haftarah* would have been read from the same place as the Torah. The *Haftarah* reader was called the *maftir* (mahf-TEER, but commonly, MAHF-teer), meaning "concluding reader," or sometimes *maftir banavi* (mahf-TEER bah-nah-VEE), "the one reading the concluding reading from the prophets."

Originally, the verbal form of *aliyah, oleh* (oh-LEH), meaning "one who ascends," was used in the idiom *oleh laminyan* (oh-LEH lah-min-YAHN), meaning "be included in the counting." The number of *aliyot* varies with the occasion: seven people for Shabbat morning, for instance, but only three for Monday and Thursday mornings. Originally, therefore, a person who received an *aliyah* was just someone who was included in the count of those called to the Torah. Nowadays, however, we tend to apply the word *aliyah* to the act of rising to stand near the Torah as it is read, and we think of ourselves — at least metaphorically — as replicating the act of receiving the Torah, climbing the *bimah* the way Moses climbed Mount Sinai.

The first prayers to be called for were blessings for the Torah and the *Haftarah* readings. In general, the Rabbis bracketed large liturgical citations of scripture with blessings. (The *Sh'ma,* for example, and the daily *Hallel*— see Volume 1, *The Sh'ma and Its Blessings,* pp. 19–20, and Volume 3, *P'sukei D'zimrah* [Morning Psalms], pp. 9–10). Here too, very early on, blessings before and after the readings of Torah and *Haftarah* were assigned. Originally, only people who could actually read from the Torah received an *aliyah;* the first person called would say the opening blessing, and the last person called would say the concluding one. Eventually, however, reading Torah was assigned to a professional (a *ba'al korei,* literally, "a master of reading") who specialized in the task, at which time there was nothing left for the people receiving an *aliyah* to do except look on while the *ba'al korei* did his job. So the blessings were now reassigned in such a way that all the people called to Torah said them both, one before and one after the reading for which they had been called. It is easier to read the *Haftarah* because, unlike the Torah, it can be read from a vocalized text. Therefore, no professional was assigned for the *Haftarah* reading, which continued to be read by a single member of the congregation who also recited the blessings before and after.

The dating of the rest of the Torah liturgy is difficult, because unlike older rubrics like the *Sh'ma* and the *Amidah,* the Torah service grew slowly over centuries and differently in different countries. Our first sign of a complex liturgy surrounding the removal and the return of the Torah in the ark comes from an eighth-century work called *Massekhet Sofrim* (mah-SEH-khet soh-FREEM). Another source from about the same period mentions the fact that Babylonian Jews ritualized only replacing the Torah in the ark, while Jews in the Land of Israel marked both taking it out and putting it back in with elaborate ceremony;[10] *Massekhet Sofrim* seems to be a report of the latter. The next benchmark is our first known comprehensive prayer book, *Seder Rav Amram,* a Babylonian work from the middle of the ninth century, which combines the earlier Babylonian ritual for replacing the Torah in the ark with a borrowed version of what Jews in the Land of Israel did. Finally, an eleventh-century French work called *Machzor Vitry* demonstrates the early Ashkenazi rite, which combines much of *Massekhet Sofrim* and *Seder Rav Amram* and adds material of its own, giving us very largely what we have today.

Nonetheless, additions continued to be made to the ritual, which was not fixed by halakhic regulations the way earlier rubrics were. The trauma of the Crusades, for instance, gave rise to a prayer requesting divine vengeance on the crusaders who had massacred Jews in the Rhineland (see p. 177), and by the sixteenth century, a standard prayer for the government had been added (see p. 163).

Perhaps the best known addition to the service is a set of prayers requesting God's blessing on those who receive an *aliyah* or on their family members. A standard blessing beginning with *Mi sheberakh,* "May the One who blessed [our ancestors]...." could be adapted for any number of instances. In this volume (p. 121), we have included only the version that requests a blessing for the person receiving an *aliyah,* but parallel blessings exist for other occasions. Traditionally, only men were called to the Torah, and they might request blessings for sick people in their family, for a wife who had just gone through childbirth, and so on. In Sefardi congregations, people received an additional blessing for the souls of members of their families who had died. This opportunity to request blessings for oneself and one's family was eventually regarded as the central benefit of being called to the Torah, so much so that it became common to pledge monetary donations to the community in return.

Moreover, the person called to the *Haftarah* began to request such a blessing. But for reasons of which we are unaware, the blessing was so inextricably linked to the Torah that it was not thought possible to generalize it to the *Haftarah* reader as well. The result was that the *Haftarah* reader was invited first to receive an *aliyah.* After the requisite number of people were called to the Torah (seven, on Shabbat), the *Haftarah* reader would be called as an extra *aliyah,* at which time the last three verses of the Torah would be reread. This extra *aliyah* was called *maftir,* the term by which the *Haftarah* reader was already known. The *maftir* would say the requisite Torah blessings and would receive a *Mi sheberakh;* then the Torah would be closed, and the *Haftarah* reading would take place.

Until the age of printing, it was relatively simple to multiply prayers during the Torah service. With the onset of printing, it became more difficult, since the set of printed prayers that people held in their hands was viewed by worshipers as sacrosanct. Nonetheless, even in our day, the liturgy surrounding the Torah is more apt to change than rubrics like the *Sh'ma* and the *Amidah* that were codified centuries earlier and outfitted with halakhic regulations describing in detail how they are said. After the founding of the State of Israel, for instance, a prayer for Israel was added. In the United States and Canada, the latest widescale alteration is the growing custom in many congregations of singing a *Mi sheberakh* for anyone who is sick in the congregation.

Because the prayers in the Torah service grew without regard to an overall plan or structure, the way we conceptualize the shape of the service is somewhat arbitrary. Nonetheless, it is helpful to group various prayers together into five discrete units and to see that there really is a natural flow to the way the Torah service unfolds. At first, the flow is difficult to grasp in its entirety, so we might do well to consider it in stages.

There are five units:
1. Introduction: removing the Torah from the ark
2. Reading Torah: the *aliyot*
3. The *Haftarah*
4. Prayers for the community
5. Conclusion: replacing the Torah in the ark

As we shall see, the most important theme is community. Receiving the Torah is the primal community event in Jewish history, after all, and it is replicated whenever we read Torah liturgically. Before looking further at that community theme, however, we can expand the basic structure to understand in greater depth how the Torah service makes its point.

The introductory (#1) and concluding (#5) prayers for taking the Torah out of the ark, and for returning it there, are like liturgical bookends:

• The introduction can be thought of as "setting the stage" for a sacred drama that is about to unfold. We are about to receive Torah as if standing again on Sinai. A series of short prayers alternately praise God's might and mercy, both of which are evident in the gift of Torah. A kabbalistic insertion combines these two attributes of God, after which we take the Torah in hand, as if from Sinai, and, holding it, affirm God in three proclamations, including the *Sh'ma*. Praising God further, we march the Torah to the reader's desk.

• The conclusion, too, is a combination of diverse material, with the twin theme of rejoicing in Torah and praising God, at which time, our drama of Sinai completed, the Torah scroll is restored to its place in the ark of God.

Following the Introductory prayers, we find prayers associated with the actual reading of Torah, that is, the *aliyot* (#2), and prayers associated with the *Haftarah* (#3).

• After a prayer that summons the people called for *aliyot*, we get the familiar Torah blessings that those who are summoned say before and after the reading. The liturgy also features additions for special cases (those who have escaped danger and a prayer for bar/bat mitzvah). Everyone called to Torah receives a *Mi sheberakh,* after which we hold the Torah on high and affirm "This is the Torah…"

- The *Haftarah* blessings are divided into a single blessing before the reading and several blessings thereafter.

Last, but in many ways most interesting, are the prayers for the community (#4) that follow the Torah and *Haftarah* readings.

- We pray (1) for those of antiquity as if they were still alive; (2) for our community today; (3) for the government; (4) for a new month of blessing (if it is the Shabbat prior to the new moon); and (5) for our martyrs.

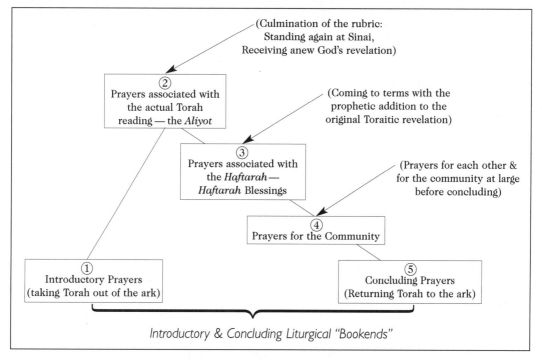

As I said, the entire Torah service is saturated with a celebration of Jewish community — not just the immediate community here and now but the Jewish People collectively, through all time. The communal focus is evident even in the choreography of the service. Traditionally, the Torah is read from the midst of the people, not from far away. It is carried from the ark to the *bimah,* which, according to traditional synagogue design, was either in the middle of the room (in Ashkenazi synagogues) or at the end opposite the ark (Sefardi practice). The introductory prayers are designed not just to take the Torah from the ark but also to carry it to the *bimah,* in a procession called a *hakafah* (hah-kah-FAH), meaning "going around [the room]." As the procession winds its way to the *bimah,* people approach the Torah, even kiss it. The Torah is being accepted by the community with all the love it can muster, just the way it must have been received when it first came down from Sinai. In his final peroration, Moses reminds Israel,[11]

Surely, this instruction which I enjoin upon you this day is not too baffling for you, nor is it beyond reach. It is not in the heavens that you should say, "Who among us can go up to the heavens and get it for us and impart it to us that we may observe it?" Neither is it beyond the sea, that you should say, "Who among us can cross to the other side of the sea and get it for us and impart it to us that we may observe it?" No, the thing is very close to you, in your mouth and in your heart, to observe it. See, I set before you this day life and prosperity, death and adversity.... Choose life — if you and your offspring would live — by loving Adonai your God.

Participating in the Torah service drums home the wisdom of Moses' last words. Torah is never far away from us. It is not even read far away. It is brought into the midst of the people, who choose life by welcoming it, honoring it, and observing its commandments. Reading Torah is an affirmation of the continuing pact between the community of Israel and God. It is a celebration of a four-thousand-year-old relationship that began when God chose Israel and Israel responded: *na'aseh v'nishma,* "We will do and we will hear." Reading Torah is the height of the morning liturgy because as a community, we come together "to do" the *mitzvah* of reading Torah and "to hear" its words together.

THE LECTIONARY LANGUAGE: *SEDRA, PARASHAH, MAFTIR, PEREK, HAFTARAH, ALIYAH, OLEH/OLAH, GABBAI, TROPE, HAGBAHAH, G'LILAH*

- The *Haftarah* reading is just called *Haftarah* (pronounced hahf-tah-RAH, or, commonly, hahf-TOH-rah).
- The Torah reading is called *sedra* or *parashah*. *Sedra* (pronounced SEHD-rah) is actually a modern mispronunciation of the original *sidra* (seed-RAH), an Aramaic word used in antiquity by Jews in the Land of Israel, for whom Aramaic was the vernacular. It is the Aramaic equivalent of the Hebrew *seder* (SAY-dehr), meaning "order," and reflects the fact that Torah readings go in a particular order. *Parashah* (pah-rah-SHAH, but commonly shortened to PAHR-shah) is the parallel Babylonian word for the same thing. Nowadays, *sedra* and *parashah* are used interchangeably. More than one Torah reading gets the anglicized *sedras* (SEHD-rahs) or *parashahs* (PAHR-shahs), but sometimes the proper Hebrew plural *parashiyot* (pah-rah-shee-YOTE) is used. Finally, it is common to link a form of the word *parashah* with the Hebrew for "week" *(shavu'a)* to refer to "the weekly portion," or *parashat hashavua* (pah-rah-SHAHT hah-shah-VOO-ah).
- A *parashah* (or *sedra*) is divided into sections. Each section is called a *perek* (PEH-rehk). Traditionally, on Monday and Thursday mornings (the *Shacharit* service) and on Shabbat afternoon (the *Minchah* service), only the first *perek* of the following week's *parashah* is read. Some non-Orthodox congregations take greater liberty with the readings, selecting something other than the first *perek* for weekdays.
- The reader is called a *ba'al korei* (bah-ahl KOH-ray), meaning "a master at reading." The people called to the Torah receive an *aliyah* (ah-lee-YAH or, commonly,

ah-LEE-yah). A man who is so called is an *oleh* (oh-LEH), and a woman (Orthodox congregations do not call women to the Torah, but other movements do) is an *olah* (oh-LAH). Reform congregations do not feel bound by the traditional numbers. They may call fewer than seven people to the Torah on Shabbat morning. The principle governing the decision to shrink the reading size and to limit the number of people getting an *aliyah* is the halakhic principle not to make worship burdensome to the worshipers. Traditionalist and nontraditionalist congregations differ from each other on how that principle is applicable to the Torah reading.

- In many synagogues, a ritual functionary called a *gabbai* (GAH-bah'i) supervises the process of handing out the honor of being called for an *aliyah*. The name comes from the Hebrew word meaning "to collect," because each *aliyah* was once auctioned off to or otherwise purchased by the person receiving it.

- The Torah and *Haftarah* are usually chanted, not just read. The chanting system is called trope. The *tropes* for Torah and *Haftarah* differ from each other, and the Torah trope changes for holidays and fast days, so that musically educated Jews recognize the holiday and its mood by the sound of the reading. Special tropes exist also for the five scrolls that are chanted liturgically on certain holidays (Esther for Purim, Ruth for Shavuot, Lamentations for Tisha B'av, Ecclesiastes for Sukkot, Song of Songs for Passover).

- Though only seven readers are traditionally required on Shabbat mornings, common practice is to call up eight. The extra *oleh/olah* (who also reads the *Haftarah*) generally rereads the last three verses of the *parashah,* although on holidays, the *maftir* is a different reading altogether, usually read from a second Torah scroll. That reading and the person called up for it are both called *maftir* (MAHF-teer), meaning "concluding reading."

- Sefardi congregations enclose their Torah scroll in a container called a *tik* (TEEK), which stands upright and can be opened or closed with a metal clasp. Ashkenazi congregations tie the Torah scroll with a sash and then cover it with a soft mantle made of cloth. When the reading is over, someone is given the honor of raising the Torah on high to let the congregation see the writing within it. That person is called *hagbahah* (HAHG-bah-hah) or sometimes (a shortened form) *hagbah* (HAHG-bah), meaning "raising [of the Torah]" on high. Ashkenazi congregations also invite someone to tie the scroll up and cover it. That person is called *g'lilah* (G'-LEE-lah), meaning "binding [the Torah]."

NOTES

1. Hosea 14:2–3.
2. Luke 4:16–21.
3. Isaiah 1:4, 15, 25, 27, 28.
4. Abudarham notes an alternative *Haftarah* here: "Awake, awake, clothe yourself with splendor, O arm of Adonai. Awake as in days of old" (Isaiah 51:9). Apparently, even in his day, different traditions existed, again indicating the original crystallization of different traditions here and there.
5. *Abudarham Hashalem,* Solomon Aaron Wertheimer, ed. (Jerusalem: Usha Press, 1963), pp. 302–303.

6. P.T. Meg. 4:1; M. Meg. 1:1; B.B. 22a.
7. Nehemiah 8:1–3.
8. See *Mekhilta,* ed. Horowitz; *Parashat Bo,* p. 52. Rabbi Joshua taught, "On that night they were redeemed and on that night they will be redeemed in the future."
9. Acts 2:2, 4.
10. *Chilluf Minhagim Bein Bavel V'erets Yisrael,* Joel Mueller, ed. (1878; reprint ed., Jerusalem: Makor Press, 1970), Section 49.
11. Deuteronomy 30:11–15, 19.

Celebrating the Presence of the Torah

The History and Meaning of Reading Torah

Ruth Langer

The most elaborate synagogue rituals accompany the public reading of Torah. While the rest of the liturgy is said mostly privately in one's place, the Torah ritual includes a public procession through the congregation, communal singing, the calling up of congregants to recite blessings over the Torah reading, and the dramatic lifting of the open Torah before it is ceremonially returned to the ark. The ritual was not written all at once. A fascinating history shows us how it grew to become central to the synagogue service: a reenactment of the Sinai revelation and, eventually, also of Jerusalem.

Nehemiah 8 provides the earliest record of a public ritual associated with reading the Torah. It occurred as part of the reconstitution of the Jewish state under Ezra after the return from Babylonian exile:

> When the seventh month arrived — the Israelites being settled in their towns — the entire people assembled as one in the square before the Water Gate, and they asked Ezra the scribe to bring the scroll of the Teaching of Moses with which Adonai had charged Israel. On the first day of the seventh month, Ezra the priest brought the Teaching before the congregation — men and women and all who could listen with understanding. He read from it, facing the square before the Water Gate, from the first light until midday, to the men and women and those who could understand; the ears of all the people were given to the scroll of the Teaching. Ezra the scribe stood upon a wooden tower made for the purpose. Ezra opened the scroll in the sight of all the people, for he was above all the people; as he opened it, all the people stood up. Ezra blessed Adonai, the great God, and all the people answered, "Amen, amen," with hands upraised. Then they bowed their heads and prostrated themselves before Adonai with their faces to the ground.

The Torah reading in our synagogue service is a later innovation, but the Rabbis used this biblical precedent as their model, teaching that Moses and Ezra had established the times and lengths of Torah readings.[1] We do not know when public Torah readings actually began, but by the late Second Temple period, they were common. Descriptions of synagogue gatherings by such writers as Philo of Alexandria (c. 20 B.C.E–50 C.E.), Josephus (c. 38 C.E.–after 100), and the New Testament evangelists all mention Torah reading, but interestingly enough, these readings are not part of a communal prayer service! A first-century dedicatory inscription discovered in Jerusalem records explicitly that a synagogue president named Theodotus "built the synagogue for the reading of the Torah and for the study of the commandments." There is no mention of prayer. The rest of rabbinic prayer was apparently later grafted onto this preexistent custom of communal Torah study.

At this point, the Torah was treated reverently, but there were no special prayers or ceremonies surrounding the reading. Unlike today's elaborate ritual, this felt more like just communal study of an important book. Even the Talmud records no specific liturgy surrounding the Torah reading, except the blessings — a circumstance that allowed later generations to see their Torah ceremonies as grounded only in custom, not law, and therefore amenable to their own creativity.

One possible explanation for the rise of Torah ritual only in the late- or even post-talmudic era is that only in the period of the Talmud (c. 200–550 C.E.) did the Torah scroll become a distinctive ritual object. Until this time, a normal book was a parchment scroll stored as a single roll or a series of rolls. The scroll would be unrolled for reading and then rolled back to the beginning when each reading was completed. In the period of the Talmud, however, technology became available to create parchment sufficiently thin to enable the inclusion of all five books of the Torah in a single scroll. Now, however, to eliminate the need to reroll such a huge scroll each time to the beginning, Jews outfitted their Torah with two poles (like our Torah scrolls today), so as to allow the Torah to remain rolled to wherever the current reading ended. Other peoples in the area, however, Christians included, adopted the more user-friendly "codex" (like our books), rather than a scroll, for their sacred literature. Thus, whereas in the first century the Torah looked like every other multivolume set of scrolls, by the sixth century its unique appearance as a double scroll suggested that it carried deep symbolic meanings.

Jewish authorities after the Talmud (called Geonim, c. 750–1034) then transformed the talmudic *descriptions* of Torah production into *prescriptions,* so that our Torah today looks the way it did 1,500 years ago.[2]

The application of other new technologies of book production, like paper and printing, to all other literature only enhanced the sense that the Torah is not just a book, but "The Book" connecting us directly to God. Not a few modern Jews imagine Moses at Mount Sinai holding their congregation's Torah scroll in his arms, complete with velvet mantle and silver ornaments — as if the liturgical response to seeing the Torah raised aloft, "This is the Torah that Moses placed before the children of Israel" (Deut. 4:44), refers not just to the contents of the scroll but also to its very form. The Torah service as we have it is a post-talmudic response to this sense of the Torah's uniqueness.

Early rabbinic literature describes Torah ceremonies that took place in the Jerusalem Temple, not the synagogue. The Mishnah (c. 200 C.E.) says,[3]

> How does the high priest recite his [Torah] blessings [on the Day of Atonement]?
> The officiant of the synagogue takes the Torah scroll and hands it to the president of the synagogue, and the president of the synagogue gives it to the adjutant high priest

and the adjutant high priest gives it to the high priest, and the high priest stands and receives it and reads Leviticus 16:1–34 and 23:26–32. Then he rolls the Torah and, embracing it in his bosom, says, "More than what I have read to you is written here." Then he recites Numbers 29:7–11 by heart, and recites eight blessings over [the Torah]: for the Torah; for the worship; for the thanksgiving; for the forgiving of sin; for the Temple; for Israel; for the priests; and for the rest of the prayers.

How is the king's portion performed? On the conclusion of the first festival day of Tabernacles, on the eighth year of the sabbatical cycle, they make a platform of wood for him in the courtyard of the Temple, and he sits on it…. Then the officiant of the synagogue takes the Torah scroll and gives it to the president of the synagogue, and the president of the synagogue gives it to the adjutant high priest, and the adjutant high priest gives it to the high priest, and the high priest gives it to the king, and the king stands and receives it and reads it sitting. King Agrippas stood and received it and read it standing, and the sages praised him…. The king reads from the beginning of Deuteronomy to *Sh'ma,* and *Sh'ma* (Deut. 6:4–9) and Deuteronomy 11:13–21, 14:22–29, 26:12–15, and the portion of the king (Deut. 17:14–20), and the blessings and curses until he completes the entire chapter (Deut. 28). The blessings which the high priest recites, the king also recites, except that he substitutes that of the festivals for the forgiving of sin.

The Mishnah is describing what may be authentic memories of the annual Yom Kippur ritual cleansing of the Temple, its officiants, and all Israel from sin, as well as the once-in-seven-years solemn assembly of the whole nation when the king himself read from Deuteronomy. The king's reading required the building of a simple wooden platform, probably in the large outer area of the Temple called the "Courtyard of the Women" — a ritual reenactment of the wooden tower at the Water Gate where Ezra first read Torah to the people. Erecting a special structure constituted a public announcement of an event of significance. But Temple rituals were usually much more colorful than these Torah readings. Sukkot, for instance, featured an elaborate nightly celebration called *Simchat Bet Hasho'evah,* "the water drawing festival," complete with numerous golden candelabra, torches, instrumental music, singing, and dancing.[4] By contrast, the very austerity of these Torah readings suggests that they were late interpolations into the Temple cult.

Nonetheless, the Temple precedent of reading Torah from a platform *(bimah)* became normative for synagogue practice. Archaeology teaches us that platforms were common, though not universal, features of the ancient synagogue. A platform stages the reading dramatically, but in addition, it increases the visibility of the reader and makes it easier for the congregation to hear.

What scroll do these Mishnaic reports describe? Probably they were small scrolls that could be held securely by the reader without using a desk or table. The high priest's scroll likely contained only Leviticus, and the king's, only Deuteronomy. Elsewhere, we hear also that when the high priest finished, all present began reading from their own personal scrolls,[5] which must also have been small enough to be comfortably carried and read while held by individuals.

Apparently, the high priest and the king did not preface their reading with a blessing, although after the reading, they recited a series of eight benedictions. However, we have no idea what these blessings contained, since the Mishnah lists only their topics, and talmudic traditions provide little additional detail. Probably, at this early period, only general forms and topics were fixed, and the person performing the ritual had the freedom to improvise within the established ideational and compositional structure.

Overall, these early Temple rituals stand out as mostly functional, lacking any obvious sense of celebration, particularly when compared with other rituals for these days. By contrast, Torah rituals became a major celebratory focus of the later synagogue service.

In the late Second Temple era, Torah reading was indeed the central activity of synagogues, but probably as an act of communal study, unaccompanied by extensive prayer. As late as the first century C.E., only the Dead Sea Scrolls of Qumran linked Torah reading with communal prayer,[6] and even there the prayer setting is ambiguous. Most Jews of this period clearly saw the public Torah reading as an act of study. A systematic cyclical reading of all of Torah did not emerge until after the destruction of the Temple, and its mechanics were still being clarified in the early second century. Indeed, the earliest readings were probably functional, reminding the community of its obligations pertaining to a particular holiday. But as the Torah was elevated in importance as the single object (in the absence of the Temple) best connecting the community with God's revelatory voice, didactic reading for the purposes of instruction faded in comparison with the symbolic concepts that reading Torah replicated Sinai and its continuation in Zion. While the Temple still stood, it had been the place to access God. Now reading Torah came to fill this gap, especially during the rabbinic prayer service: the primary place where public readings now occurred.

This heightened meaning is reflected in the liturgical blessings that came to frame the ritual Torah reading. Our familiar blessing texts first appear explicitly in post-talmudic literature, although the Talmud certainly knows that blessings were recited, even if it does not cite them. Both blessings allude to Sinai, and both conclude by praising God as the giver of Torah. The same themes are reiterated in the blessings surrounding the *Haftarah,* the prophetic reading. Originally, however, people were called up to the Torah not to recite the blessings but to do the actual reading — an expectation that persists among Yemenite Jews today. The first blessing was recited by the first reader before commencing the reading, and the last blessing was said by the last reader when the reading was over. Because of "the people coming and going" (as the Talmud puts it),[7] the custom was adjusted so that each person called to the Torah recited the full set. Whether or not communal irresponsibility was the real reason for the change, this adjustment only emphasized further the meaning that the blessings provided for the rite. Especially in Palestine, where readings were short, because Palestinians spread out the Torah readings in a cycle that lasted approximately three and a half years (unlike the Babylonian, and our, one-year cycle) the Torah ritual would contain almost as much blessing as scriptural text, often two blessings for every three verses.

In marked contrast to the rites of other religions, Jewish ritual rarely refers explicitly to its own "mythic" referents. The *Amidah,* for instance (the "Eighteen Benedictions" — see Volume 2 of this series), became especially significant because it replaced the biblically ordained sacrificial service.[8] But except in the additional service *(Musaf)* for Sabbaths and holidays, no explicit mention of this purpose appears in the prayer itself. Here the Torah ritual differed. Its implicit meaning became manifest once every single reader had to recite the Torah blessings. This effectively emphasized the growing symbolic role of Torah in the Jewish world. Torah embodied the Sinai revelation itself, and the sequential reading of the entire text reiterated the sacred history on which all of Judaism is built. Ritual Torah reading thus became an act of standing again at Sinai and also of rehearsing the master story of the Jewish People.

Non-verbal aspects of the ritual reinforced this meaning. People who read Torah or who are awarded Torah honors stand during the reading as an act of respect for the holiness of the text. In the Temple ritual, even high priests and kings, in spite of their own rank, stood when the Torah was handed to them. The high priest continued standing as he read it, and the Rabbis applauded King Agrippas for voluntarily humbling himself and standing. The Talmud asks:

> What is the biblical source [for standing]? Rabbi Abbahu said, "It is the verse [that records the words God spoke to Moses at Sinai], 'Stand here with Me [and I will tell you all the commandments and laws]' (Deut. 5:28)." Rabbi Abbahu also said…"It is as if even the Holy One, blessed be He, were standing."[9]

Reading the Torah while standing is more than a logistical necessity — more even than a sign of respect. According to this interpretation, readers who stand while proclaiming the text emulate not just the human Moses (who stood to receive it) but even God, the giver of Torah!

The architecture of the Palestinian synagogue also supports the heightened holiness of the Torah scroll. In the tannaitic (pre-third century) literature, the person leading the *Amidah* was called "one who descends in front of the ark." The ark had begun as a movable chest brought into the synagogue when necessary, but beginning in the third century, permanent niches on the Jerusalem-facing wall can be found. With this, any prayer that needed to be said facing Jerusalem was physically mediated by the Torah scroll. This became a universal feature of synagogues throughout the world, and the ark itself came to symbolize God's presence, both in Jerusalem and in the synagogue.

Other than the Torah blessings themselves, we have no talmudic record of any prayers that were recited in the course of the Torah service. By the twelfth century, however, the point from which we begin to have original prayer book manuscripts preserved in any variety, rich and varied liturgies have emerged to express this reenactment of Sinai and Zion.

Jewish literature during the intervening period (from the Talmud's completion, about the sixth or seventh century, to the twelfth century) does not really clarify the evolution of this liturgy. During that time, we have only a few descriptions of any detail, none of which suffices to answer all our questions, because they are too brief or too confused by later scribal interpolations to provide definitive evidence. Nonetheless, these interim accounts from the seventh to the twelfth century do give us at least incomplete views of an evolving liturgy.

One unique account of reading Torah (by a tenth-century writer named Nathan the Babylonian) records the service of installation for a new exilarch, the civil leader of Babylonian Jewry. Nathan includes the tantalizing report that after the *Haftarah,* an officiant "should continue by blessing the exilarch with the Torah scroll. Then…he blesses both of the [rabbinic] heads of the academies."[10] Here is the earliest record of what becomes universal practice in conjunction with Sabbath and holiday Torah readings: the blessing in one form or another of the heads of the community, both secular and religious. It may not be mere happenstance that these leaders are blessed (as Nathan puts it) "with the Torah scroll." The very presence of the scroll enhances the efficacy of the blessing. The scroll had become a marker of God's presence, so that prayers offered in proximity to it were considered to be especially powerful.

Today, too, we invoke blessings for the government, for the community, and for its leaders with the Torah present. We also ask God's blessings for individuals, remember our departed loved ones, and consecrate the new month in this setting. Something about the physical presence of the Torah scroll seems to enhance our most fervent prayers. Even when the Torah is not read, the scroll may be taken from the ark to add gravity to rituals — like the release of vows during *Kol Nidre* — or the ark may simply be opened for important prayers, whether communal or personal. Nathan the Babylonian's account gives only our first hints of the Torah's special power as a viaduct to God.

If we consider all our early sources up to the twelfth century, we can reconstruct a reasonable estimate of what the first medieval service for reading Torah looked like.[11] Its most obvious stylistic characteristic is that it chained together biblical verses to create a new liturgical composition: a literary genre known as a *florilegium* that was quite popular during the geonic period (c. 750–1034). This also suggests that our Torah service is post-talmudic.

What was being expressed by this early liturgy? Interestingly, there was as yet no reference to Torah at all, except in conjunction with the reading itself, and certainly no explicit reference to Sinai. The biblical verses presented primarily effusive praise of God, as did an accompanying ancient prose prayer, beginning, "May the name…" (see below, p. 85, v. 5), a prayer that added another theme: petitions for the coming of the messiah and the restoration of God's presence in Zion.

The theme of Sinai begins to appear, however, in a work called *Massekhet Sofrim,* which probably hails from eighth-century Palestine, even though various sections in it are interpolated by later editors living elsewhere. This text is important here because it becomes closely related to what eventually becomes the dominant Ashkenazi custom. It is the oldest text to include both the *Sh'ma* and the lifting of the Torah to display its text (although Ashkenazi Jews moved the latter to after the reading). After an extensive list of verses praising God's majesty, we read:

(The reader picks up the Torah and chants)

Hear O Israel, Adonai is our God, Adonai is One (Deut. 6:4).

(Then the people repeat this, after which he says)

Our God is one, our Lord is great: holy.
Our God is one, our Lord is merciful: holy.
Our God is one, our Lord is great: holy and awesome is His name.

Your beneficence is as high as the heavens, O God, for You have done great things; O God, who is like You (Ps. 71:19)? Adonai, Your name endures forever, Your fame, Adonai, through all generations (Ps. 135:13). Let everyone ascribe might to our God and ascribe glory to the Torah.

Proclaim Adonai's greatness, and let us exalt His name together (Ps. 34:4).

*(The reader must lift up the Torah during "Hear O Israel,"
and during the three declarations of God's unity,
and during "Proclaim Adonai's greatness.")*

(He lifts the Torah up high and says:)

Our God is one, our Lord is great, holy and awesome is His name for ever and ever.

(He begins to chant, saying:)

Adonai is God, Adonai is His name (1 Kings 18:39, Exod. 15:3).

*(The people answer after him twice, repeating and doubling his words.
Immediately, he unrolls the Torah scroll to show three columns,
and lifts it up and shows its writing to the people standing to his right and left,
and he turns it frontward and backward, for it is a commandment for
all the men and women to see the writing and to bow and say:)*

This is the Torah that Moses put before the children of Israel (Deut. 4:44).

(Additionally he says:)

Adonai's Torah is pure, reviving the soul; Adonai's testimony is sure, educating the simple; Adonai's laws are just, delighting the heart; Adonai's command is clear, lighting the eyes (Ps. 19:8–9).

The drama here is striking! The reader presents the Torah to the congregation just as Moses presented it at Sinai. He does this by holding the Torah high and proclaiming the *Sh'ma,* which rabbinic tradition links to the Ten Commandments that precede it almost directly in Deuteronomy. In today's Ashkenazi liturgy, too, this recitation of *Sh'ma* immediately after the Torah is taken from the ark on Sabbaths and holidays is a moment of supreme drama. Torah is being revealed to us, and we too declare our relationship to God's revelation with the recitation of this verse and with our (slightly simplified) response to it: "Our God is one, our Lord is great, holy (and awesome) is His name."

In the liturgy of *Massekhet Sofrim,* this drama occurs a second time when the reader returns to this line, again lifting the Torah up high. Then, the intensity increases as he chants words that the congregation repeats over and over: "Adonai is God, Adonai is his name." The educated congregation would have recognized these two phrases as coming from prime examples of God's revelation, Exodus 15:3 and I Kings 18:39: the Song of the Sea (Israel's prayerful response to deliverance from the Egyptians) and the response to Elijah's victory over the false prophets of Baal on Mount Carmel. Then, after tense excitement has built up, the scroll itself is opened and its text is displayed so that all the people — men and women — can see its very words. The onlookers respond with the explicit declaration that this scroll is precisely the Torah revealed at Sinai: "This is the Torah that Moses put before the children of Israel" (Deut. 4:44). While most rites eventually copy *Massekhet Sofrim* and add to their liturgy this lifting of the open Torah with its response, none preserve the full drama present here. Instead, early modern Ashkenazi Jews found it necessary to emphasize the meaning of this response, elaborating on it with additional verses, beginning with the phrase we today assume is part of the original: "dictated by God and transcribed by Moses" (Num. 9:23).

Sinai themes like this become increasingly important as the Torah service continues to develop, but they do not stand alone. The giving of the Torah at Sinai was a critical event in Jewish history, but its importance would have been lost had revelation and engagement with revelation ended there. In the biblical world, there were no explicit ritual commemorations of Sinai. Instead, the important parts of that event — the written revelation and the ongoing access to God — moved on to new locations, first to the desert tabernacle and eventually to the Jerusalem Temple. These were the living continuations of the Sinai experience.[12]

As the Ashkenazi Torah service developed in the later Middle Ages, it added explicit references to this aspect of Israel's experience of God, expanding its *florilegium*, its pastiche of biblical verses of praise, with the verse that first describes the ark's journey — and Israel's — away from Sinai (Num. 10:35), followed immediately by "For Torah shall come forth from Zion and Adonai's word from Jerusalem" (Isa. 2:3). With this addition, the older petitions for the rebuilding of Jerusalem already present in the service[13] gain more specific application to their liturgical setting.

Whereas Sinai was a seminal one-time event, the proclamation of Torah from Jerusalem was central to Jewish life for close to a millennium. When the Torah service remembers Jerusalem and prays for the Temple's restoration, it also reenacts, and thus continues, this proclamation of Torah. During this ritual, each synagogue becomes for the moment a bit of Sinai, but even more, it becomes a temporary Jerusalem: the place where Torah continues to be proclaimed and studied in each and every generation. In this, especially in later mystical conceptions, the Torah scroll and its ark become markers of God's presence in the midst of the synagogue congregation just as God was present in the Holy of Holies of the Jerusalem Temple. Celebration of the Torah is thus a celebration of God and of God's covenantal relationship with Israel.

NOTES

1. BK 82a; P.T. Meg. 4:1, 75a.
2. Menahem Haran, in a series of articles, has proposed this understanding. See, for example, his "Bible Scrolls in Eastern and Western Jewish Communities from Qumran to the High Middle Ages," HUCA 56 (1985): 21–62.
3. M. Sot. 7:7–8 (comp. M. Yoma 7:1).
4. M. Suk. 5:1–4.
5. Tos. Kip. 3(4):18.
6. 1QS 6.6–8.
7. Meg. 22a.
8. Ber. 26a/b.
9. Meg. 21a.
10. Ad. Neubauer, *Medieval Jewish Chronicles and Chronological Notes* (Oxford, 1895), vol. 2, p. 84.

11. Derived from *Massekhet Sofrim* 14:4–9 and *Seder Rav Amram Gaon*, and the medieval rites.

Upon removing the Torah from the ark, the leader calls out to the congregation:

Proclaim Adonai's greatness with me, and let us exalt his name together (Ps. 34:4).

The congregation responds:

Exalt the Eternal our God and bow down to his footstool; He is holy! Exalt Adonai our God, and bow down at his holy mountain, for Adonai our God is holy (Ps. 99:5, 9).

The leader and/or the congregation pray:

May the name of the King over the kings of kings be made great, holy, praised, glorified, exalted, and extolled above all in the worlds that He created — this world and the world to come — according to his will and to the will of those who fear Him and according to the will of the entire house of Israel. Let his majesty be revealed and seen among us speedily, and let Him rebuild his house in our days, and may He in his great mercy and with much lovingkindness favor our remnant and the remnant of all his people the House of Israel with favor, lovingkindness, mercy, life, and peace, and may He have mercy on us and on all his people the House of Israel for the sake of his great name, and let us say: "Amen."

The leader calls out:

Let us all ascribe greatness to our God and give honor to the Torah. Let the *kohen* approach. Let [name] the priest stand up.

The congregation responds:

Adonai's Torah is pure, reviving the soul;... (Ps. 19:8–11)
Adonai will give strength to his people, Adonai will bless his people with peace (Ps. 29:11).

Reading of the Torah (and Haftarah when appropriate)

After the reading, when returning the Torah to the ark, the leader proclaims:

Let them praise Adonai's name, for His name alone is exalted (Ps. 148:13).

The congregation responds:

His majesty is above earth and heaven. He is the strength of his nation, the praise of his faithful, of the children of Israel, the people near to Him. Halleluyah. (Ps. 148:13b–14)

12. See Joshua Berman, *The Temple: Its Symbolism and Meaning Then and Now* (Northvale, N.J.: Jason Aronson, 1995), Chapter 3, "Sinai and Sanctuary."

13. In the verses from Psalm 99 calling for bowing to God's footstool and holy mountain (i.e., the Temple), in the prayer "For everything..." and, in some rites, "Merciful Father, may it please you to make Zion prosper; rebuild the walls of Jerusalem."

The Theory and Halakhah of Reading Torah

Daniel Landes

THE TWOFOLD MEANING OF *KRI'AT HATORAH*

The Rabbis understand *Kri'at Hatorah* (the public reading of the Torah) as an enactment of great antiquity, stemming from Israel's journey through the desert. Since Torah is traditionally likened to life-sustaining water, they interpret the verse "They traveled three days in the desert, and they did not find water" (Exod. 15:22) to imply that what they really suffered from was going three days without Torah. According to the Talmud, "The prophets among them enacted the reading of Torah on Shabbat, have a hiatus on the first day after Shabbat, read again on the second day, have another hiatus on the third and fourth days, and read again on the fifth, in order that they should not go three days without Torah" (B.K. 82a). This enactment is also ascribed to Moses (P.T. Meg. 4:1 and 10:1).

The reading is likened both to the public study of Torah and to revelation.

First, it is a form of *talmud Torah* (Torah study). Indeed, the same Talmud passage says that Ezra "enacted that they should read [the Torah] in the same way every Shabbat afternoon *(Minchah)*" because of the *yoshvei k'ranot,* "those who dwell at the corners," which is interpreted to be either "those who have business in the market and don't get a chance to go to the study hall" (Rashi, Solomon ben Isaac, France, 1040–1105 to B.K. 82a), or wastrels "who gossip and banter at the street corners" (*Arukh,* eleventh-century Italy). *Kri'at Hatorah* is thus a public education course in Torah.

Additionally, however, the Rav (Rabbi Joseph B. Soloveitchik, Lithuania, Berlin, Boston-New York, the major Talmudic legalist and theologian of the middle and late twentieth century) understands *Kri'at Hatorah* as a reenactment of the theophany at Sinai; indeed, it is "a new giving of the Torah, the amazing standing under the mountain that burned with fire…. The experience of revelation returns and is repeated each time we take out the Torah" (see *"Uvikashtem Misham," Ish Hahalakhah* [Jerusalem, 1979], pp. 227–228). That is why the Maharam (Meir ben Baruch of Rothenberg, 1215–1293, Germany) held that one should stand during the reading. Rabban Gamaliel (first-century tanna) ruled that we may sit while studying, as a precaution against weariness, but the Maharam treated *Kri'at Hatorah* as revelation, which requires standing.

Then there is the *m'turgaman,* an official who, in ancient times — and still today, in Yemenite custom — translated the reading as it was taking place into the Aramaic vernacular. According to Maimonides (Moses ben Maimon, Egypt, 1135–1204), the *m'turgaman* must "stand, not leaning on a pillar or post, but up straight with awe and fear" ("Laws of Prayer," 12:11). His ruling follows from the Talmudic statement "Just as the Torah was given with awe and fear, so also we must treat it with awe and fear" (P.T. Meg. 4:1). Halakhah obligates only the *oleh* (the person receiving the *aliyah*), the *m'turgaman,* the Torah reader (the *ba'al korei*), and whoever is next to the Torah reader at the *Shulchan* (the Torah-reading table) to stand (*Shulchan Arukh,* by Joseph Caro, Turkey, Greece, and Israel, 1488–1575, O. Ch. 141). Nevertheless, it is a meritorious act (technically, a *hiddur,* a "beautification," of the *mitzvah*) for all to do so. This concept that reading the Torah reenacts Sinai is reflected also in the requirement of reading a minimum of ten verses in order to parallel the Decalogue (Meg. 21b).

This double understanding of *Kri'at Hatorah* as both Talmud Torah and revelation has several consequences. As Talmud Torah, the Torah reading takes place in a *minyan,* a community, and is a *chovat hatsibur,* a "communal obligation" (Moses ben Nachman, or Nachmanides, known as Ramban, 1194–1270, Spain — in his *Milchamot* to Meg. 5). Listeners must pay close attention to it, exerting their intellectual capacities to the fullest, so as to fulfill a serious commitment to study within a community. Hearing the reading need not be direct; that is, even a deaf person may have an *aliyah,* if he only hears via a hearing aid, for he is still certainly involved in the Talmud Torah experience (see *T'shuvot V'hanhagot* of Rabbi Moshe Sternbuch, contemporary authority, Johannesburg and Jerusalem, 2:83).

If, as study, *Kri'at Hatorah* is an intellectual exercise, as revelation it is experiential, demanding that we actually see the Torah removed from the *aron hakodesh,* the "holy ark" (the Talmud insists that only an insensitive person would refer simply to the "ark"). Its procession to the reader's desk is like the original transmission of the Torah to the Israelites at Sinai; we hear the reading as if it came from Moses. It is even appropriate that we tremble while reading the blessings during our *aliyah* (Moses Isserles, known as R'ma, 1530–1572, Cracow). That consideration explains the final decision in the question of whether people may study other parts of Torah during the reading. Some allow it, as long as at least ten people are listening to what is being read (Tos. Ber. 8a), especially if the person involved is a full-time Torah scholar (Isaac ben Jacob, Alfasi, Fez, 1013–1103; Maimonides, *Laws of Prayer* 12, and *Bet Yosef* 146 by Joseph Caro, Eretz Israel, 1488–1575). But the final judgment bans even the speaking of words of Torah after the Torah scroll has been opened (Elijah Gaon of Vilna, the Gra, Lithuania, 1720–1797), or at least once the reading has begun. This judgment applies between the *aliyot* (*Shulchan Arukh,* O. Ch.146), even if one has already heard the Torah reading elsewhere *(Pri Migadim),* since, after all, no one can speak at Sinai but God!

The twin conceptions of *talmud Torah* and revelation complement each other. For example, even those who find study difficult (because of a limited knowledge of Hebrew, perhaps) can have an *aliyah* because they too stood at Sinai. From the opposite point of view, as an aid to concentrated study, people may read along quietly with the Torah reader, even though they thereby interfere with the revelational aspect (*Magen Avraham,* by Abraham Gombiner, Poland, 1637–1683). When we raise the Torah to proclaim, "This is the Torah placed by Moses before the children of Israel" (Deut. 4:42), Torah study and the reenactment of revelation merge within community consciousness.

THE SANCTITY, DIGNITY, AND HONOR OF THE TORAH

According to philosopher and halakhic authority Saadyah Gaon (Baghdad, 882–942), the Torah is what defines the Jewish People. While the *sefer torah* (Torah scroll) is materially just parchment and ink, its contents are God's Torah and the credo of the Jewish People. For thousands of years, Jews have studied Torah, observed Torah, and, when required, martyred themselves for Torah. Our behavior toward the Torah scroll reflects our reverence for its substance.

Many of the laws and customs connected with the reading of Torah reflect our great respect and devotion for the Torah as well as our great love for its teachings. In this context, the reader of Jewish sources will encounter concepts like "cleanliness of mind, body, and clothing," and "modest dress." These are expressions of showing regard for the Torah by behaving and presenting ourselves in a manner that respects both the content of the Torah and the sanctity of the synagogue.

LAWS REGARDING THE TORAH WHILE IT IS BEING READ

Several laws reflect the respect due to the Torah, just as if it were a human being with whom we have a relationship and whose dignity we want to respect.

1. The Torah should be opened only for a minimal period of time. As soon as a reading and blessing are completed, it is rolled up.
2. The Torah should be unclothed for a minimal period only. If there is any interruption between *aliyot,* the Torah must be covered with its mantle.
3. If possible, the parchment of the Torah scroll should not be directly touched. A *ba'al korei* who uses a *yad* (pointer) should not actually touch it to the parchment. If the parchment accidentally gets stuck in one of the rollers, we try to cover our hand with a *tallit* before pulling at the parchment to dislodge it.
4. We approach the Torah scroll only with clean hands.
5. Nothing inappropriate may be said in front of the Torah.
6. If the Torah must be moved to another location, it should be accompanied by at least one person besides the person carrying it.

7. A Torah should not be moved to another location (that is, a different unconnected building) unless it will be read on at least three different occasions. Thus, for instance, a *shivah minyan* at the home of mourners to which a Torah scroll has been brought will customarily also have a Shabbat *Minchah* service, even though, technically, the mourners do not sit *shivah* on Shabbat and could go to the usual service at the synagogue. But this way, we know there will be at least three separate readings at that location.

LAWS REGARDING THE BLESSINGS

1. When public Torah readings were established, it was the custom for each *oleh* (the person given the *aliyah*) to read the Torah portion for which he had been called directly from the scroll. This is still the custom in many Sefardi communities. In many Ashkenazi communities, the *olim* read their portion on the holiday of Simchat Torah and, of course, at a bar mitzvah. Today, most communities have a reader *(ba'al korei,* or *ba'al k'riyah)* who acts as the representative or "voice" of the *oleh.* Technically, however, it is the *oleh,* not the reader, who is performing the *mitzvah* of reading publicly from the Torah, so the *oleh,* not the reader, says the blessing.

2. Since we take pains not to touch the actual parchment of the *sefer torah* (see M. Megillah 4), the *oleh* lightly touches the spot indicated by the reader as the place where the reading will begin, using the *tsitsit* of a *tallit* or the Torah's *gartel* (belt), and kisses it. Those not wearing a *tallit* usually touch the Torah with a Siddur, although the *yad* (pointer) or any other dignified "barrier" (such as a clean handkerchief devoted only to this purpose) may do.

3. The opening blessing is generally said while the Torah is closed or covered with the mantle, so as not to imply that the blessing is written within the Torah (Gloss by Moses Isserles [R'ma], Cracow, to *Shulchan Arukh,* O. Ch. 139:4). However, the Vilna Gaon said it with the Torah open, since it is the opening of the Torah that creates the obligation to say the blessing in the first place; likewise, the Rav held that rolling the Torah shut ends the obligation. If the Torah is open, however, the blessing is said with eyes closed or head turned to the side (*Shulchan Arukh,* O. Ch. 139; *Mishnah B'rurah,* 139:19).

4. During the blessing, we hold both of the *atzei chaim* (the handles of the wooden Torah rollers); during the reading, we hold the right-hand one. Some people do so with a corner of their *tallit.*

5. The *oleh* reads along quietly with the reader, so that the blessing just said will not be a blessing in vain — that is, an *oleh* who says a blessing over reading Torah should actually read it (*Shulchan Arukh,* O. Ch. 141:2); the Vilna Gaon (the Gra) used to read loudly enough that he could hear his own reading.

6. After the *aliyah,* we kiss the Torah, and when the Torah has been rolled shut, we say the final blessing.

7. All blessings must be recited loudly enough for the community to hear. The community should stand for at least the *Barkhu* and its response, *Barukh Ado-nai ham'vorach,* for that is considered a *davar shebik'dushah* ("a matter of holiness"). The *oleh* repeats *Barukh Ado-nai ham'vorach,* so as to be included himself in the category of those who bless God. The *oleh* bows slightly at the beginning of *Bar'khu* and stands upright again for God's name. When each person's introductory blessing is over, the community says "Amen," after which the reader recommences.

8. If called for an *aliyah,* we go up to the Torah using the most direct route and as quickly as possible.

9. A subject that often occasions some confusion is what to do with the *tallit,* which is customarily worn but is not absolutely required (at certain services, such as Shabbat *Minchah,* many communities have the custom not to wear one). Traditionally, one says a blessing before wrapping oneself in a *tallit,* but only if it is one's own. What does a person who has no *tallit,* and who borrows someone else's for the *aliyah,* do? The answer is that if the *tallit* is borrowed, the borrower does not recite the usual blessing over putting it on, since it is someone else's garment. A communal *tallit* may, however, occasion a blessing, since it is assumed to belong to everyone.

10. After concluding an *aliyah,* we return to our seat slowly and deliberately, so as not to imply that the experience was burdensome.

ORDER OF PRIORITY IN *ALIYOT*

1. In order to raise funds for the synagogue or the community, many communities auction off *aliyot* prior to the Torah reading (*Mishnah B'rurah* 137:4). This was once considered a display of the community's regard for the Torah. However, the Vilna Gaon forbade the practice, even though the money went to charity, as it looked like ordinary buying and selling.

2. A worthy Talmud scholar should receive an important *aliyah* such as *shlishi* (the third *aliyah*) or *maftir* (the last, or extra, one that generally goes to the person who is also charged with reading the *Haftarah*).

3. On festivals, we prefer to give *aliyot* to people who support the community (*Shulchan Arukh,* O. Ch. 136).

4. The general order for assigning *aliyot* to people is *kohen* ("priest," descendent of Aaron), *levi* ("a Levite," descendent of the tribe of Levi), *yisrael* ("an Israelite," that is, everyone else). Notwithstanding the general practice that scholars are given recognition first and foremost, in the case of reading Torah, even if a *kohen* is not learned and even if a great scholar is also present, the *kohen* has priority. This rule was instituted in antiquity to prevent conflict in the congregation, and we still abide by it.

5. Once the *yisrael* is called, all subsequent *aliyot* are *yisrael*. But if an *aliyah* is added to the required number, a *kohen* or a *levi* may be called for it (*Shulchan Arukh*, O. Ch. 135).

6. In general, people's own testimony to their being a *kohen* or *levi* is accepted.

7. When no *kohen* is present, a *levi* or a *yisrael* is called in place of a *kohen,* and a *yisrael* is called for all subsequent *aliyot*.

8. If a *kohen* has completed the first *aliyah* and no *levi* is present, the same *kohen* takes the *levi's aliyah* without being summoned, according to his priestly title.

9. In principle, mourners during the first week of bereavement do not study Torah, as the Torah is our chiefest joy and, as such, is inappropriate for people in deepest mourning (M.K. 21a). It follows, therefore, that mourners are not called to the Torah. But a *kohen* or a *levi* who is in mourning *may* be called to the Torah on Shabbat, which is itself a joyous occasion, if there is no other *kohen* or *levi* available to fulfill the public need. It is preferable, however, that the mourning *kohen* or *levi* leave the congregation for a moment, until the blessing of their "turn" has been said, and the reading has commenced. However, *all* mourners may be called for *hagbahah* and *g'lilah* (raising the Torah on high and tying it up, when the reading is over), since these acts do not involve the actual reading of Torah (Gesher HaChayim, 21:5–7, of Rabbi Yechiel Michal Tuckacinsky, Jerusalem, early twentieth century).

10. People who have special life-cycle events are called up according to the following system of priority:
    a. A wedding on that day (for a weekday Torah reading)
    b. A wedding during the coming week (for a Shabbat Torah reading)
    c. A child who has reached the age of obligation for *mitzvot*
    d. The birth of a child
    e. A wedding during the previous week (for a Shabbat Torah reading)
    f. *Yahrzeit* on that Shabbat or during that week
    g. Being the parent of a *b'rit milah* (a circumcision); or the *mohel* (a circumcisor); or the *sandek* (the person who holds the baby during the circumcision) in the coming week (for a Shabbat Torah reading)

THE TORAH READING AND ITS CORRECTION

1. The Torah reader should be fully prepared, knowing the proper pronunciation, syntax, and inflection (and, therefore, meaning) of every word of every verse. Even experienced readers should review the reading in advance.

2. Mistakes in pronunciation, inflection, or chanting should be corrected immediately.

3. The following applies when a reader has skipped over a verse or even a word, or misread a word or phrase in such a way that the mistaken pronunciation or cantillation changes the meaning of the text (for example, *shilum* ("payment") instead of *shalom* ("peace").

a. Readers who are not corrected immediately, or who do not hear the correction, or who ignore it must return to the place where the mistake was made, read the whole verse correctly, and then continue to the end of the *aliyah* (*Mishneh B'rurah* 142:3).

b. Even if the mistake is discovered only after the *oleh* has already recited the final blessing, the next *oleh* recites the first blessing, and the reader starts over again from the verse where the mistake was made (*Mishnah B'rurah* 142:1).

c. If the mistake in pronunciation or cantillation has not changed the meaning of the text, it is not necessary to return to the mistake and reread it correctly, although it is a good idea to do so (*Mishnah B'rurah* 142:1).

d. In all other circumstances, if the *oleh* at the time of the error has already recited the second blessing, the reader may continue as usual without going back to correct the error. However, the reader should be notified privately that a mistake was made (*R'ma* 142 and *Eshel Avraham*).

4. A *gabbai* (plural, *gabbai'im*) or "overseer" of the reading stands on both sides of the reader and follows the reading in printed books. *Gabai'im* should be expert in Torah reading and must review each week's Torah reading in advance.

MISTAKES IN THE *SEFER TORAH*

Precise rules for every letter and every line were laid down in the tenth century by experts known as *masoretes*. Scrolls are written by a *sofer* ("scribe"), who should be pious, expert in the rules, and skilled at writing. Nonetheless, mistakes sometimes occur.

1. If a mistake is found during the reading, the best expert present is consulted to determine the mistake's severity, as an imperfect *sefer torah* may not be used for public proclamation.

2. The reading may continue in the case of the following minor errors (*t'a'yot kalot*):

a. If only part of a letter is erased, but its general outline is unmistakable, even to a child who knows the alphabet but not the word.

b. If the ink of a word or even of a few sentences has reddened with age, but is read easily.

c. If a word is written *malei* ("in full," that is, with a *vav* or *yod*) instead of *chaser* ("in short form," that is, without a *vav* or *yod*), or the opposite, as long as the meaning of the word is clear.

d. If a letter that was to be written extra large or small has been written normally, or if the masoretic dots that crown certain words are missing.

e. If two letters are crowded together, but are nevertheless distinguishable.

In all these cases, the reading proceeds, and after Shabbat, a *sofer* makes the necessary corrections.

3. There are, however, "complete mistakes" (*t'a'yot g'murot*) that render the scroll invalid for public proclamation (*pasul*), and necessitate finding another scroll from which to complete the reading. If a complete mistake is found, the scroll is

marked as invalid, usually by tying its belt *(gartel)* around the outside of the mantle. Complete mistakes include the following:

a. A missing letter or word.

b. The inversion of letter-order in a word, even if the meaning is clear.

c. The partial erasure of a letter, whether at the top, at the bottom, or in the middle, such that a child could not easily recognize the letter.

d. A space within a word that makes it look like two words.

e. Extra ink that makes the letter look like another letter (e.g., a closed *heh* that looks like a *chet*).

f. Two letters crowded together so that they look like one.

4. Communities should have a steady relationship with a *sofer.* Otherwise, a *sefer torah* can fall into such disrepair that fixing it becomes almost overwhelmingly expensive. A community has a right to expect that the word of God will be proclaimed from a fully fit, kosher Torah scroll. Would a synagogue board be fulfilling its duties if it did not fix a leaking roof or if it overlooked a cracked boiler? The *sefer torah* demands no less from us.

5. In the case of a complete mistake, the reading continues from a second, kosher, scroll, in the following way:

a. Each *aliyah* must contain at least three verses. If, therefore, three verses in the *aliyah* have already been read when the mistake is discovered, the reading stops, and the *oleh* recites the final blessing, ending the *aliyah.* The Torah is then bound from the outside (without *hagbahah,* the ritual of holding the Torah aloft for all to see) and returned to the Holy Ark. The congregation stands while the second *sefer torah* is brought, without fanfare, to the reader's desk. The next *aliyah* starts with the verse where the mistake was found, thereby completing the reading that would normally have constituted the prior *aliyah,* but then continues to the end of the next reading, thus preserving the number of *aliyot.*

b. If three verses have not been read, or if an interruption at the mistaken verse would destroy the sense of the reading, the *oleh* does not recite the final blessing but remains in place, without speaking and in full concentration. The Torah is bound and put away, and the second Torah scroll is quietly brought, opened, and rolled to the spot. The reader continues from the place where the mistake was found. Upon completion of the *aliyah,* the *oleh* recites the final blessing.

c. If the entire Torah portion has been read, and the mistake is found at the end, the *maftir* is read without blessings before or after.

d. Sometimes the *maftir* is not a repetition of the last few lines of the reading, but is another reading altogether, specially selected from a second scroll. In such a case, the first scroll is put away as above, and the *maftir* is read from the second scroll.

If there is no second, kosher scroll available, the reading may take place even from a scroll in which a "complete mistake" is found. But the *aliyot* are handled differently.

a. If the *oleh* has not recited the final blessing when the mistake is located, the reader finishes the *aliyah*. The *oleh* does not recite the final blessing at that point, but remains in place until the entire reading is completed. Other *olim* are called to the Torah as usual, but they do not recite any blessings. At the end of the entire Torah section, the *oleh* in whose *aliyah* the complete mistake was found recites the final blessing (for when that *oleh* was called to the Torah, the scroll was still kosher!).

b. If the *oleh* has recited the final blessing (and, therefore, no more blessings may be recited over the invalid *sefer torah*), the reader reads the rest of the weekly portion without stopping or interruption.

6. The reader, *oleh,* or *gabbai* should not be afraid of finding or announcing concern over a mistake or imperfection in the Torah scroll. If it turns out to be a slight mistake, then a beauty mark has been found in our beloved Torah. If it is a complete mistake, then what has been discovered can be repaired. Pointing it out bespeaks care and concern for the community and the Torah, and confidence in both of them.

ADDITIONAL LAWS OF READING

1. It is customary to have at least three people at the reader's desk during the reading. Normally, *olim* remain in place during their own *aliyah* as well as during the next one, to ensure the proper number.

2. The number of *aliyot* may be increased on Shabbat alone, for it already is distinguished by the largest number of *aliyot,* and adding a few more will not prove burdensome to the congregation. On Mondays and Thursdays, for example, congregants may be rushing to work, and care should be taken not to alienate people from the Torah reading. This problem presumably does not exist on Shabbat, when we do not go to work and have more time to be in synagogue (*Mishnah B'rurah* 135:2). This rule is so crucial that we do not waive it even on secular holidays or during vacations, even though congregants may then have free time.

3. Except for emergencies, we remain in the room from the time the Torah is taken out until it has been returned.

4. Many maintain that one need not stand during the reading (*Shulchan Arukh,* O. Ch. 142; the Gra); others require it (R'ma) but allow sitting between *aliyot.* In any case, standing during the reading constitutes a *hiddur mitzvah* (a "beautification of the commandment").

HALAKHAH FOR *HAGBAHAH* (RAISING THE TORAH) AND *G'LILAH* (BINDING THE TORAH)

1. The Ashkenazi custom is to raise and bind the Torah after the reading. Sefardi congregations which use Torah scrolls in a case (called a *tik* — pronounced TEEK) that remains upright during the reading, raise and close the Torah before the first reading. For both rites, *hagbahah* is considered a great honor.

2. *Hagbahah* in Ashkenazi congregations is done by retaining the Torah in its open state, then opening it further to show three columns of the Torah to the congregation. It is turned in all directions (right, left, facing the person holding it, and then facing the other way) so that all can see (*Shulchan Arukh*, O. Ch. 134).

3. People not strong enough to lift the Torah and control it while showing it should not be called for *hagbahah*; if called, they should not accept the honor.

4. While the Torah is being displayed, we strive to see its letters. We bow when saying *Zot hatorah*, and say those words with joyful enthusiasm. Anyone outside the room should reenter for this occasion.

5. During the raising and binding, we try not to touch the holy *klaf* (parchment) with our hand. If it is necessary to touch it, we cover our hand with a *tallit*.

6. *G'lilah* includes tying the Torah, placing the mantle (the cover) over the scroll, and replacing the *yad* (pointer), breastplate, and *keter* (crown) or *rimonim* (the ornaments that fit over the Torah rollers).

7. If closely supervised, children may do *g'lilah*, in order that they may develop love of the Torah.

HALAKHAH FOR READING *HAFTARAH*

1. The *Haftarah* is recited by someone who is first given an *aliyah* called *maftir*. *Maftir* is usually a repetition of the last three verses of the weekly Torah portion. The person called to say the blessings over those verses concludes the *aliyah* and then remains at the reader's desk to recite the *Haftarah* (*Shulchan Arukh*, O. Ch. 292). The person called should not already have had another *aliyah*, especially if the *maftir* is from a second Torah scroll, as this might connote some suspicion about the first scroll (*Mishnah B'rurah*, O. Ch. 144:4). If, however, there is no one else who can recite the *Haftarah*, a second *aliyah* is permissible.

2. Ideally, the *Haftarah* should be read from a scroll written on parchment, but nowadays, reading from a printed book is commonplace. Reading from a complete Tanakh (Bible) is preferred over reading from the *Chumash* (just the books of Torah, to which the *Haftarah* portions are appended) or a separate booklet altogether (see commentaries to *Shulchan Aruch*, O. Ch. 284).

3. The *Haftarah* blessings may begin after the Torah scroll has been retied but not yet completely dressed, but preferably we wait until the *g'lilah* has been completed so that the people performing *hagbahah* and *g'lilah* can listen (*Sha'arei Ephraim* 10:25).

4. The blessings are recited loudly, with the scroll or book containing the *Haftarah* evident on the reader's table.

5. If the *Haftarah* is read from a scroll, everyone listens in silence. If it is read from a book, people follow along quietly in their own books, for the reader cannot entirely fulfill the obligation of the community unless reading from a scroll (Chatam Sofer). In either case, the reading must be clearly audible to all (*Mishnah B'rurah* 284:11 and 12 and the *Be'ur Hahalakhah; Sha'arei Ephraim* 9:33).

6. A child who can read properly may read any *Haftarah* except those of the four special Sabbaths that precede Purim and Passover, called *Sh'kalim, Zachor, Parah,* and *Hachodesh.* [Ed. note: The Mishnah calls these the *Arba Parashiyot,* meaning the "four [special] readings." They consist of extra Torah portions tacked on to the normal one that is read on the day in question, and drawn from sections of the Torah taken out of the usual order. The Sabbath in question gets its name from the special Torah reading.

   Shabbat *Sh'kalim* ("The Sabbath of 'Shekels'") generally falls two weeks before Purim. The reading (Exod. 30:11–16) describes the poll tax of half a *shekel* tax commanded for the desert sanctuary. Its *Haftarah* (2 Kings 12:1–17) describes how King Jehoash (late ninth century B.C.E.) raised money for the Temple.

   Shabbat *Zachor* ("The Sabbath of 'Remember'") immediately precedes Purim. It features Deuteronomy 25:17–19, the commandment to remember always how Amalek, Israel's archenemy, attacked from the rear and cut down the stragglers among the Israelites on their way to the Land of Israel. Its accompanying *Haftarah,* 1 Samuel 2–34, describes King Saul's war against the Amalekites of his day, and an ensuing reproach from the prophet Samuel for not utterly destroying Agag, the Amalekite king.

   Shabbat *Parah* ("The Sabbath of 'the Cow'") falls after Purim and introduces a theme of Passover, ritual purity. Its reading (Numbers 19:1–22) describes the biblical ritual of the red cow *(parah adumah)* by which the ashes of a slaughtered cow are used to effect purification after contact with a corpse. Its attendant *Haftarah* (Ezekiel 36:16–38) describes God's promise to the Babylonian exiles that they will be cleansed of all impurity and find the spirit of God newly inculcated within them as they prepare to return to their homeland.

   Finally, Shabbat *Hachodesh* ("The Sabbath of 'This Month'") falls after Shabbat *Parah* and announces the Hebrew month of Nisan: "This month shall [mark for you the beginning of months]" (Exod. 12:1–20). The biblical calendar began with Nisan because Passover falls then. Shabbat *Hachodesh* is, therefore, a call to prepare for Passover. Its *Haftarah* (Ezek. 45:16–46:18) features Ezekiel's call to the exiles to prepare for the Passover they will offer when they return home from captivity.]

7. The *Haftarah,* like the Torah reading, requires a *minyan* (a quorum of ten).

Introduction to the Commentaries

How to Look for Meaning in the Prayers

Lawrence A. Hoffman

THE ART OF JEWISH READING

I remember the day I looked at a manuscript of a prayer book that no one could identify. It had been smuggled out of Russia, then the Soviet Union, and was obviously the liturgy for Rosh Hashanah, but who had written it? And when? It was handwritten, so the style told us much, but in addition, someone had written marginal notes in another handwriting, and yet a third person had written comments to the comments — a third unknown scholar of years gone by whose name we wanted to rescue from oblivion.

Standing before the massive volume, I reflected on the sheer joy of studying a traditional Jewish text. I had seen printed versions before, but never a handwritten instance. What a wonderful habit we Jews developed once upon a time: writing a text in the middle of the page and then filling up the margins with commentaries. Every page becomes a cross-cut through Jewish history. Jewish Bibles come that way; so do the Talmud, the Mishnah and the codes. We never read just the text. We always read it with commentaries, the way other people have read it.

To be a Jewish reader, then, is to join the ranks of the millions of readers who came before us, leaving their comments in the margins, the way animals leave tracks in the woods. Go deep into the forest, and you will come across deer runs, for example: paths to water sources, carved out by hundreds of thousands of deer over time. The deer do not just inhabit the forest; they are part of the forest; they change the forest's contours as they live there, just as the forest changes them, by offering shelter, food, and water. There is no virgin forest, really; it is an ecosystem, a balance between the vegetation and the animals who live there.

So, too, there are no virgin texts. They too are ecosystems, sustaining millions of readers over time. When we read our classic texts, we tread the paths of prior readers in search of spiritual nourishment. *My People's Prayer Book* is therefore not just the Siddur text; it is the text as read by prominent readers from among the people. You are invited to share our path and even to break new ground yourself, passing on to others your own marginal notes, should you wish.

The preparation of this volume of *My People's Prayer Book* was particularly challenging because the Torah ritual varies so much from rite to rite, and because the ritual for Shabbat differs substantially from the parallel set of prayers for Mondays and Thursdays. Since our other volumes in this series have so far dealt with the liturgy for weekdays, we might easily have limited ourselves to that. But the Torah liturgy for weekdays is sparse relative to the richness of the Shabbat parallel. Still, there are some weekday characteristics that do not appear on Shabbat. So we combined the two. Basically, this is the Shabbat ritual with some weekday variations.

Even so, however, in order to conserve space and make this volume accessible, we omitted some prayers not common to most rites that we deemed marginal or that were weekday options (when we used the Shabbat alternative). For example, the Shabbat ritual concludes with Psalm 29; the weekday ritual uses Psalm 24. We have included the former, not the latter.

Also, the half *Kaddish,* which is recited prior to "This is the Torah" *(Zot hatorah)* in some congregations, does not appear in this volume. Because the *Kaddish* is such a significant prayer and reappears elsewhere, it will be addressed instead in Volume 6 of this series.

THE HEBREW TEXT AND TRANSLATION

As with the other volumes, for the Hebrew text we have chosen the Ashkenazi edition favored by the renowned liturgical historian, the late E. D. Goldschmidt, perhaps the greatest master of liturgical text who ever lived. Born in Germany, later a refugee from the Nazis, Goldschmidt moved to Israel, where he assiduously collected and compared thousands of manuscripts for the Siddur, to arrive at an authoritative version as free of scribal and printing error as possible.

Goldschmidt omits some of the material that most synagogues in North America know best. But the Torah liturgy varies a great deal from place to place, so even though Goldschmidt's selections may be true to the "authentic" Ashkenazi rite of the centuries, we felt that we should add to it any familiar prayers we now say that Goldschmidt omits. To arrive at these, we consulted Philip Birnbaum's *Hasiddur Hashalem,* a classic American Orthodox Siddur that has enjoyed wide use since its inception in 1949.

The Torah service contains two Aramaic prayers, the translation for which was done by the editor. But the bulk of the service is the Hebrew of the Goldschmidt text (altered somewhat by what we found in Birnbaum's Siddur), which was then translated by Joel Hoffman, who consulted regularly and at length with Marc Brettler, to reproduce not only the content of the original Hebrew but also its tone, register, and style, and to bring to modern readers the same experience (to the greatest extent possible) that the original authors would have conveyed with their words. In terms of content, we assume that by and large, words have meaning only to the extent that they contribute to sentences and concepts — as, for example, "by and large," which has nothing to do with "by" or "large."

We try to reproduce a tone and register similar to the original text: formal, but not archaic; prose or poetry, depending on the Hebrew. Where the Hebrew uses obscure words, we try to do the same, and where it uses common idiom, we try to use equally common idiom.

In addition, as much as possible, parallel structure and other similar literary devices found in the Hebrew are replicated in the English translation. We have not doctored the text to make it more palatable to modern consciousness. Blatant sexisms are retained, for instance, wherever we think the author intended them. We depend upon our commentaries to bridge the gap between the translation of the original and our modern sensibilities.

THE COMMENTARIES

The heart and soul of *Minhag Ami* is its choice of commentaries that surround the prayerbook text. Translator Joel M. Hoffman explains his choice of words, provides alternatives, and compares his own translation with a selection of the most popularly used prayer books in the English-speaking world. Marc Brettler comments particularly on the way the Bible is embedded in the Siddur. Elliot N. Dorff and Ellen Frankel provide theological reflections on what the prayers might mean, should mean, could mean, cannot mean, or have to mean (even if we wish they didn't). Judith Hauptman adds insight from the world of the Talmud, and the rabbinic tradition that it spawned. Daniel Landes gives us an introductory essay and a commentary on the Halakhah of prayer, the rules and traditions by which this sacred liturgical drama has traditionally been carried out. Lawrence Kushner and Nehemia Polen supply a kabbalistic commentary, adding wisdom from the world of Chasidic masters. David Ellenson surveys liberal prayer books of the last two hundred years to see how their writers agonized over attempts to update this book of Jewish books for modern times. Ruth Langer provides an introductory essay that explores the grand metaphoric message of the Torah ritual, which is more than what it seems to be on its surface. My own contribution is a summary of what we know about the historical development of the liturgy: when prayers were written, what they meant in the context of their day — and to some extent, what later generations saw in them. I also provide some of the interesting textual variants between one tradition and another.

Some of the commentaries require some comments in advance.

Translator Joel M. Hoffman had to make a judicious selection of translations to compare with his own. For an Orthodox version, he relied on Philip Birnbaum's classic (1949) *Daily Prayer Book: Hasiddur Hashalem* ("Birnbaum") but looked also at *Siddur Kol Ya'akov* ("Artscroll," 1984). American Reform was represented by the *Gates of Prayer* (*"GOP,"* 1975) and revisions since; Conservative Jews will find their *Siddur Sim Shalom* (*"SSS,"* 1985) and Reconstructionists will see their *Kol Han'shamah* (*"KH,"* 1994) cited. He compared British liturgy too: *Forms of Prayer* (*"FOP,"* 1977) from the Reform Synagogues of Great Britain; and both *Service of the Heart* (*"SOH,"* 1967) and *Siddur Lev Chadash* (*"SLC,"* 1995) from the Union of Liberal and Progressive Synagogues. For biblical citations, he consulted the Jewish Publication Society Bible (*"JPS"*), but compared it with the New Revised Standard Version of 1989 (*"NRSV"*), and *The Five Books of Moses,* by Everett Fox ("Fox," 1995).

My own historical commentary had to deal with the fact that the Goldschmidt translation is only for Ashkenazi Jews — more specifically, the Ashkenazi version common in eastern Europe, often under the influence of Elijah ben Solomon of Vilna, known as the Vilna Gaon (1720–1797). To balance the picture, I cite Sefardi practice also, though hardly doing it justice. The Torah service, especially, has a great deal of variation between Ashkenazi and Sefardi custom, and citing every alteration would have added little of theological or historical substance.

It should be noted that the word *Sefardi* has two distinct meanings.

Nowadays, it usually describes Jews whose liturgy was influenced by Chasidism and the specific brand of Kabbalah initiated by Isaac Luria (the "Ari"), in sixteenth-century Palestine. Goldschmidt compiled a scientific edition of this variant too, and I used that to represent "Sefardi practice." But "Sefardi" can also mean the old Spanish-Portuguese custom carried by Jews from Spain in 1492 and then brought to the Netherlands, whence it moved to England (among other places) and eventually to America as well. When I want to draw attention to this Spanish-Portuguese custom, I call it that, using as my guide the standard work published in England at the turn of the twentieth century by Moses Gaster, *The Book of Prayer and Order of Service According to the Custom of the Spanish and Portuguese Jews.* I try also to cite early prayer books of our tradition and commentators from the Middle Ages, as well as the Genizah Fragments, manuscripts telling us how Jews prayed in the Land of Israel prior to the Crusades.

David Ellenson was asked to fill in the gap caused by the fact that even the standard Ashkenazi and Sefardi versions hardly represent the majority of Jews today. As Jews have evolved, so have our modern movements, each with its own version of what our forebears once considered normative. The last two hundred years have witnessed the composition of countless Jewish prayer books, and Ellenson surveys the most prominent of these for instances where the traditional text evoked debate.

For historical reasons, many are Reform, beginning with the *Hamburg Temple Prayer Books* of 1819 and 1841, the very first efforts to make the content of the classical liturgy comport with modern ideas. Ellenson's survey of the nineteenth century also included *Seder T'filah D'var Yom B'Yomo* (1854; republished, 1870) by Rabbi Abraham Geiger, the preeminent leader of German Reform.

For early American liturgies, he turned to Rabbis Isaac Mayer Wise and David Einhorn. Wise's *Minhag America* (1857) was the most popular prayer book of its day, and Einhorn's *Olath Tamid* (1856) became the prototype for the *Union Prayer Book* (*"UPB"*), which was adopted in 1895 as the official liturgy for North American Reform Jews. In 1975, *Gates of Prayer* (*"GOP"*) replaced the *UPB*, and in 1996 the latest in a series of gender-inclusive editions of *GOP* appeared. All three of these official movement books are cited here.

Among the non-American prayer books of late, Ellenson made extensive use of *Ha'avodah Shebalev ("HS"),* adopted by the Israeli Progressive Movement in 1982, and *Siddur Lev Chadash ("SLC"),* published by the Union of Progressive and Liberal Synagogues in London in 1995.

These Reform prayer books are supplemented by several Conservative and Reconstructionist volumes. The former include various prayer books produced since 1958 by the Rabbinical Assembly of the Conservative Movement, but especially the 1985 *Siddur Sim Shalom,* along, now, with its revised version of 1998. Since Conservative worship is in Hebrew, however, and since the Hebrew is generally unchanged while the vernacular equivalent is usually a literal translation of it, Ellenson has less to say about Conservative prayer books than he does of Reform volumes, where both Hebrew and English tend to vary widely. However, he has made careful use of the latest Conservative Siddur to appear in Israel: *Siddur Va'ani T'fillati ("SVT," 1998).* Precisely because Hebrew is the vernacular in Israel, this prayer book offers insight into contemporary issues of belief within Israeli Conservative Judaism. The Reconstructionist Movement, which, like Reform, has tended toward considerable liturgical creativity, is represented primarily by *Kol Haneshamah ("KH"),* published in 1996, but from time to time Ellenson discusses earlier work, especially by Mordecai Kaplan, the founder of the movement.

Ellenson gives priority to denominationally associated prayer books because they have been most widely disseminated, but he does include some others, notably *The Book of Blessings,* authored in 1996 by Jewish feminist Marcia Falk. He uses liberal prayer books more than he does Orthodox ones, because liberal prayer books were changed more, as their authors tried to remain true to their liturgical heritage, without doing an injustice to modern ideas about God, the universe and human nature. Orthodox volumes are cited here, but references to them are limited.

Daniel Landes' halakhic introduction and commentary were included not just to explain how prayers should be said. Even without that abiding practical concern, they would have found their way here because Halakhah (Jewish law) is essential to Judaism. Frequently misunderstood as mere legalism, it is actually more akin to Jewish poetry, in that it is the height of Jewish writing, the pinnacle of Jewish concern, sheer joy to create or to ponder. It describes, explains, and debates Jewish responsibility, yet is saturated with spiritual importance. Jewish movements can be differentiated by their approach to Halakhah, but Halakhah matters to them all.

A short overview of its history and some of its vocabulary will be helpful in advance.

The topic of Halakhah is the proper performance of the commandments, said to number 613, and divided into positive and negative ones, numbering 248 and 365, respectively. Strictly speaking, commandments derived directly from Torah *(mid'ora'ita)* are of a higher order than those rooted only in rabbinic ordinance (called *mid'rabbanan),* but all are binding.

The earliest stratum of Halakhah is found primarily in the Mishnah, a code of Jewish practice promulgated about 200 C.E. The Mishnah is the foundation for further rabbinic discussion in Palestine and Babylonia, which culminated in the two Talmuds, one from each center, and called the Palestinian Talmud (or the Yerushalmi), and the Babylonian Talmud (or the Babli). While dates for both are uncertain, the former is customarily dated to about 400 C.E., and the latter between 550 and 650.

With the canonization of the Babli, Jewish law developed largely by means of commentary composed to the Talmuds and of responsa, applications of talmudic and other precedents to actual cases. These are still the norm today, but they were initiated by authorities in Babylonia called Geonim (sing., Gaon) from about 750 to shortly after 1025. By the turn of the millennium, other schools had developed in North Africa particularly, but also in western Europe. Authorities in these centers are usually called Rishonim ("first" or "early" [ones]) until the sixteenth century, when they become known as Acharonim ("last" or "later" [ones]).

The first law code is geonic (from about 750), but it was the Rishonim who really inaugurated the trend toward codifying, giving us many works, including three major ones that are widely cited here: The *Mishneh Torah,* by Maimonides (Moses ben Maimon, 1035–1104), born in Spain, but active most of his life in Egypt; the *Tur,* by Jacob ben Asher (1275–1340), son of another giant, Asher ben Yechiel, who had moved to Spain from Germany, allowing Ashkenazi and Sefardi practice to intertwine in his son's magnum opus; and the *Shulchan Arukh,* by Joseph Caro (1488–1575), who is technically the first generation of the Acharonim, but who wrote influential commentaries on both the *Mishneh Torah* and the *Tur* before composing what would become the most widely used Jewish legal corpus ever.

The halakhic commentary in this volume draws on all of the above. References to the *Tur* and the *Shulchan Arukh* usually are to the section called *Orach Chayim,* "The Way of Life," which contains most of the Halakhah on prayer, and is shortened here to "O. Ch." The other references are either to standard halakhic works or to the authorities who authored them. In keeping with Jewish tradition, we refer to the authorities by acronyms that are formed by combining their title (usually, Rabbi) and their names, or by other titles that history has bestowed upon them. A list of the most cited books and authorities follows:

Abudraham (David Abudraham [late thirteenth-fourteenth century], Spain)

Bach (short for Bayit Chadash, commentary to the *Tur* by Joel Sirkes [1561–1640], Poland)

Ben Ish Chai (The Chakham Joseph Chaim [1832–1909], Baghdad)

Chida (Chaim Joseph David Azulai [1724–1806], Jerusalem)

Gra (The Vilna Gaon, Rabbi Elijah of Vilna [1720–1797], Lithuania)

Har Zvi (Zvi Pesach Frank [d. 1961], Jerusalem)

Iggrot Moshe (Moshe Feinstein [1895–1986], Russia and New York)

Maharil (Jacob ben Moses Moelin [1360–1427], Germany)

Magen Avraham (commentary to the *Shulchan Arukh* by Abraham Gombiner [1637–1683], Poland)

Mishnah B'rurah (by Israel Meir HaCohen Kagan [1838–1933], Poland)

Rashi (Solomon ben Isaac [1040–1105], France)

Rashba (Solomon ben Abraham Adret [1235–1310], Spain)

R'ma (Moses Isserles [1530–1575], Poland)

Riva (Isaac ben Asher [d. 1130], Germany)

Rivash (Isaac ben Sheshet Perfet [1326–1408], Spain)

Sefer Charedim (R. Eleazar ben Moses Azikri [1533–1600], Safed, Israel)

Sefer Chasidim (Judah Hachasid [d. 1217], Germany)

Taz (short for *Turei Zaha,* commentary to the *Shulchan Arukh* by David ben Samuel Halevi [1586–1667], Poland)

Torat Habayit (commentary by Moses ben Nachman, better known as Nachmanides [1194–1270], Spain)

We have gone out of our way to provide a panoply of scholars, all students of the prayerbook text, and all committed to a life of prayer, but representative of left, right, and center in the Jewish world. They represent all of us, all of *Am Yisrael,* all of those God had in mind when God said to Ezekiel (34:30) "They shall know that I, Adonai their God, am with them, and they, the House of Israel, are My people." Unabashedly scholarly and religious at one and the same time, *Minhag Ami,* "A Way of Prayer for My People," will be deemed a success if it provides the spiritual insight required to fulfill yet another prophecy (Isa. 52:6), that through our prayers,

> My people *[ami]* may know my name
> That they may know, therefore, in that day,
> That I, the One who speaks,
> Behold! Here I am.

1 *Introduction*

Removing the Torah from the Ark

A. SETTING THE STAGE: ON ONE HAND, GOD'S GREATNESS

I. "THERE IS NO GOD LIKE YOU" (*EIN KAMOKHA*)

[Prayer leader approaches ark; congregation rises.]

[1] There is no god like You, Adonai, and there are no works like yours. [2] Your kingdom is a kingdom for all times, and your reign endures through every generation. [3] Adonai is King; Adonai has always been King; and Adonai will always be King. [4] Adonai will grant his people strength; Adonai will bless his people with peace.

II. "FATHER OF MERCY" (*AV HARACHAMIM*)

[5] Father of mercy, favor Zion with your goodness. [6] Rebuild the walls of Jerusalem. [7] For it is in You alone that we put our trust, our King, high and exalted God, eternal Lord.

III. "WITH THE MOVING OF THE ARK" (*VAY'HI BINSO'A HA'ARON*)

[The ark is opened; congregants rise.]

[8] With the moving of the ark, Moses would say: [9] Arise, Adonai, so that your enemies be scattered, and those who hate You flee from before You. [10] For Torah shall come forth from Zion, and Adonai's word from Jerusalem. [11] Blessed is the One who gave Torah to his people Israel in holiness.

[Prayer leader approaches ark; congregation rises.]

אֵין כָּמְוֹךָ בָאֱלֹהִים אֲדֹנָי. וְאֵין כְּמַעֲשֶֽׂיךָ: ²מַלְכוּתְךָ מַלְכוּת כָּל־עֹלָמִים. וּמֶמְשַׁלְתְּךָ בְּכָל־דּוֹר וָדֹר: ³יְיָ מֶֽלֶךְ יְיָ מָלָךְ. יְיָ יִמְלֹךְ לְעֹלָם וָעֶד. ⁴יְיָ עֹז לְעַמּוֹ יִתֵּן. יְיָ יְבָרֵךְ אֶת־עַמּוֹ בַשָּׁלוֹם:

⁵אַב הָרַחֲמִים הֵיטִיבָה בִרְצוֹנְךָ אֶת־צִיּוֹן ⁶תִּבְנֶה חוֹמוֹת יְרוּשָׁלָֽיִם: ⁷כִּי בְךָ לְבַד בָּטָֽחְנוּ מֶֽלֶךְ אֵל רָם וְנִשָּׂא אֲדוֹן עוֹלָמִים:

[The ark is opened; congregants rise.]

⁸וַיְהִי בִּנְסֹֽעַ הָאָרֹן וַיֹּֽאמֶר מֹשֶׁה ⁹קוּמָה יְיָ וְיָפֻֽצוּ אֹיְבֶֽיךָ וְיָנֻֽסוּ מְשַׂנְאֶֽיךָ מִפָּנֶֽיךָ: ¹⁰כִּי מִצִּיּוֹן תֵּצֵא תוֹרָה וּדְבַר־יְיָ מִירוּשָׁלָֽיִם: ¹¹בָּרוּךְ שֶׁנָּתַן תּוֹרָה לְעַמּוֹ יִשְׂרָאֵל בִּקְדֻשָּׁתוֹ:

49

BRETTLER (BIBLE)

[1] *"There is no god like You"* The Torah service begins with a reference to God, not the Torah, and God remains the focus here. The Torah is not even mentioned until much later, at which time we get an identification between God and Torah; this is a fundamental tenet of this section of our prayers. The biblical context of the opening text, which is from Psalm 86:8, is God's role in heeding the prayer of the individual (vv. 1-7), but it is followed by the idea that God, as creator, will be heeded by all (vv. 9-10). It is difficult to date this psalm and its reference to *elohim,* (pagan) "gods," so it is hard to know whether the biblical psalm recognized

(p. 52)

DORFF (THEOLOGY)

[1] *"There is no god like You, Adonai"* The Torah service begins by declaring the absolute dominion of God. Since the reading of the Torah is, among other things, a reenactment of the revelation at Mount

(p. 54)

ELLENSON (MODERN LITURGIES)

[1] *"There is no god like You..."* The Hamburg Temple prayer books of 1819 and 1841 took great liberties with the received Ashkenazi liturgy for the Torah service and reconfigured elements drawn from the traditional Ashkenazi and Sefardi orders of service for their own Torah rite. They appropriated (p. 55)

FRANKEL (A WOMAN'S VOICE)

[1] *"There is no god like You"* "There is no god like You" introduces the Torah service by voicing two paradoxes that frequently recur in the traditional Jewish prayer book: first, the concept of a supreme being who is simultaneously universal and parochial; second, the schizophrenic identity of a people rooted in a particular land and at the same time wandering rootless in diaspora. In affirming these paradoxes, we embrace our historical legacy as Jews.

The dominant metaphor in the Torah service is that of (p. 57)

A. SETTING THE STAGE: ON ONE HAND, GOD'S GREATNESS

[Prayer leader approaches ark; congregation rises.]

[1] There is no god like You, Adonai, and there are no works like yours. [2] Your kingdom is a kingdom for all times, and your reign endures through every generation. [3] Adonai is King; Adonai has always been King; and Adonai will always be King. [4] Adonai will grant his people strength;

HAUPTMAN (TALMUD)

[1] *"There is no god like You"* Typical of this liturgy, the Torah service opens with a prayer that has no talmudic warrant. All the liturgy surrounding the reading seems quite late. Nonetheless, reading a portion of the Torah each week is an ancient part of our service. The specific rules of how it is to be done were developed by the Rabbis, and a number of biblical passages lay the foundation for it. The idea of a regular, public Torah reading is first found in the book of Deuteronomy (31:11, 12). Moses tells the priests and Levites that (p. 58)

KUSHNER & POLEN (CHASIDISM)

8–9 *"With the moving of the ark, Moses would say: Arise, Adonai, so that your enemies be scattered, and those who hate You flee from before You"* [Num. 10:35] The Torah reading does not fit naturally into the liturgy. Instead, it seems to be grafted disjunctively onto it from somewhere else. It is neither prayerful nor, like other biblical passages, woven into the flow of the prayers. It abruptly shifts the rhythm of worship from meditation, supplication, and thanksgiving into the study hall. What is going on here? *(p. 60)*

[Prayer leader approaches ark; congregation rises.]

אֵין כָּמוֹךָ בָאֱלֹהִים אֲדֹנָי. וְאֵין כְּמַעֲשֶׂיךָ: מַלְכוּתְךָ מַלְכוּת כָּל־עֹלָמִים. וּמֶמְשַׁלְתְּךָ בְּכָל־דּוֹר וָדֹר: יְיָ מֶלֶךְ יְיָ מָלָךְ. יְיָ יִמְלֹךְ לְעֹלָם וָעֶד. יְיָ עֹז לְעַמּוֹ יִתֵּן.

LANDES (HALAKHAH)

1, 5 *"There is no God like You.… Father of mercy"* These first two prayers present the theological preamble to the Torah reading. The first asserts God's uniqueness in providing for all the world's peoples, since it speaks of God as universal King throughout all time and space. The second balances the universalism by the particularistic promise of Jewish redemption in Zion: God will "favor Zion" and "rebuild Jerusalem."

8 *"With the moving of the ark"* The dramatic opening of the holy *(p. 61)*

L. HOFFMAN (HISTORY)

THE FIRST OF FIVE UNITS THAT SETS THE STAGE FOR THE SACRED DRAMA THAT THE TORAH LITURGY REPRESENTS: RELIVING REVELATION AT SINAI THROUGH THE UNVEILING OF GOD'S WORD, THE TORAH. THE INTRODUCTION IS DIVIDED INTO FIVE PARTS. THIS FIRST PART (1A) SETS THE STAGE BY PROCLAIMING GOD'S GREATNESS.

1 *"There is no God like You"* Mentioned first in the eighth-century work *Massekhet Sofrim*, where the *maftir* (the person who reads the *Haftarah*) is given the honor of saying it and the liturgy that follows, including the *Sh'ma* and the other verses of divine acclamation. Why *(p. 62)*

J. HOFFMAN (TRANSLATION)

1 *"There is no god like You"* As in Birnbaum. Artscroll offers the more literal "There is none like thee among the gods," but then the second half would read "There is nothing like your works," which is barely English.

2 *"For all times"* Artscroll's "spanning all eternity" is a nice poetic variation.

2 *"Reign"* Or "dominion."

2 *"Endures"* Literally, "is in," but that is barely acceptable English.

3 *"Always"* We add the word "always," absent but implied in the Hebrew, to make the English flow better.

5 *"Favor Zion with your goodness"* As in *Siddur Sim Shalom*, an *(p. 62)*

Adonai will bless his people with peace.

5 Father of mercy, favor Zion with your goodness. 6 Rebuild the walls of Jerusalem. 7 For it is in You alone that we put our trust, our King, high and exalted God, eternal Lord.

[The ark is opened; congregants rise.]

8 With the moving of the ark, Moses would say: 9 Arise, Adonai, so that your enemies be scattered, and those who hate You flee from before You. 10 For Torah shall come forth from Zion, and Adonai's word from Jerusalem. 11 Blessed is the One who gave Torah to his people Israel in holiness.

יְיָ יְבָרֵךְ אֶת־עַמּוֹ בַשָּׁלוֹם:

⁵אַב הָרַחֲמִים הֵיטִיבָה בִרְצוֹנְךָ אֶת־צִיּוֹן ⁶תִּבְנֶה חוֹמוֹת יְרוּשָׁלָיִם: ⁷כִּי בְךָ לְבַד בָּטָחְנוּ מֶלֶךְ אֵל רָם וְנִשָּׂא אֲדוֹן עוֹלָמִים:

[The ark is opened; congregants rise.]

⁸וַיְהִי בִּנְסֹעַ הָאָרֹן וַיֹּאמֶר מֹשֶׁה ⁹קוּמָה יְיָ וְיָפֻצוּ אֹיְבֶיךָ וְיָנֻסוּ מְשַׂנְאֶיךָ מִפָּנֶיךָ: ¹⁰כִּי מִצִּיּוֹן תֵּצֵא תוֹרָה וּדְבַר־יְיָ מִירוּשָׁלָיִם: ¹¹בָּרוּךְ שֶׁנָּתַן תּוֹרָה לְעַמּוֹ יִשְׂרָאֵל בִּקְדֻשָּׁתוֹ:

BRETTLER (BIBLE)

other gods in reality, or just in theory. (See comment to Volume 1, *The Sh'ma and Its Blessings*, p. 130.)

² *"Your kingdom"* From Psalm 145:13, the *Ashre*. (See Volume 3, *P'sukei D'zimrah*, p. 117.) This verse expresses the central theme of that prayer, the kingship of God, which is a core biblical image. Though God's kingship may be viewed as a projection of human dominion, it differs in that divine reign is fundamentally superlative. The Davidic dynasty, according to some texts (e.g., 2 Sam. 7:13–16), is *ideally* supposed to be eternal, but God is envisioned here as *actually* reigning forever.

³ *"Adonai is King; Adonai has always been King"* A composite of biblical verses. "Adonai is king" is found several times (e.g. Ps. 10:16). The second sentence, "Adonai has always been King," is characteristic of the enthronement psalms, which describe God as (becoming) king (e.g., 93:1; 96:10; 97:1; 99:1) and plays a central role in the *Kabbalat Shabbat* service, while sentence three, "Adonai will always be King," is a shortened version of the conclusion of the Song of the Sea (Exod. 15:18; see Volume 3, *P'sukei D'zimrah*, p. 168). No single biblical verse states that God is and both has been, and will be, king, so this idea is conveyed liturgically through the combination of these verses, in a section that is otherwise composed of exact biblical quotations.

[4] *"Adonai will grant his people strength"* The end of Psalm 29 (v. 11) concludes this little unit, moving the focus from God to Israel. The thought of the verse is remarkable, though quite typical in the psalms: God expresses his great power by bringing peace to Israel. This verse bridges God and Israel; that too, of course, is the function of the Torah.

[5] *"Father of mercy"* An invocation of God through one of his attributes; such invocations are a typical way of beginning a prayer. The depiction of the merciful *father* is based on Psalm 103:13, where God is likened to a father (rather than a mother) having compassion on his children.

[5] *"Favor Zion with your goodness"* A request for the restoration of Jerusalem, a prominent liturgical theme (see Volume 2, The *Amidah*, pp. 140–141), taken from Psalm 51:20, most likely written between the destruction of the First Temple (586 B.C.E.) and the completion of the Second Temple (516 B.C.E.). The context of the verse is especially apropos to the postsacrificial liturgy, as the previous verse says: "True sacrifice to God is a contrite spirit; God, You will not despise a contrite and crushed heart."

[7] *"For it is in You alone that we put our trust"* A postbiblical sentence, in biblical style. It incorporates various biblical ideas, including the importance of trusting God alone (e.g., Ps. 115:9–11). As the motivation for the preceding "rebuild the walls," however, it is quite remarkable in that it suggests that God's motivation for restoring Israel is Israel's recognition of God's sovereignty. By contrast, most biblical motivations in prayers build either upon God's desire to hear praises (e.g., Ps. 57:10) or on God's *chesed* or lovingkindness (e.g., Num. 14:19, Ps. 6:5). Yet, the Torah service is about to begin, so the *relationship* between God and Israel, epitomized through the Torah, is invoked. God is also referred to in superlatives, returning us to the beginning of the larger unit, "There is no god like You," nicely rounding off this introduction.

[8, 9] *"With the moving of the ark.... Arise, Adonai, so that your enemies be scattered"* From Numbers 10:35, recited when the ark of covenant was carried in the wilderness. The Bible pictures the ark, in later periods, being brought into battle (e.g., 1 Sam. 4:46), so that the presence of God might accompany the warriors. This explains the war imagery of the verse, which also returns us to the main theme of the previous section: God's power and incomparability as king.

In its liturgical context, "ark" refers to the housing of the Torah scrolls, and must be seen in the broader context of the biblical quotation that follows ("Torah shall come forth from Zion").

[10] *"Torah shall come forth from Zion"* From the famous eschatological vision in Isaiah 2:3 and Micah 4:2, which focuses on the worldwide supremacy of the Jerusalem Temple, where God is the ultimate judge, who will (in contrast to the military image of the verse just above this one in the prayer) ban war from the world (Isa. 2:4: "And they shall beat their swords into plowshares"). In the original prophecy, *torah* referred to "instruction" rather than to a specific book or set of books. It rounds out the introductory prayer by introducing two more key concepts: the ideal future and the centrality of *torah* to all of humanity.

¹¹ *"Blessed is the One who gave Torah"* Following the pattern of the two earlier prayers, here too we have a collection of biblical citations concluded by a post-biblical composition. Since there is no appropriate biblical verse that connects the Torah, Israel, and God, the editor has composed such a text, but in biblical style. The sentence also properly returns the focus from the universalistic eschatological future of the previous verse to the particularistic present, with Israel at the focus.

¹¹ *"In [his?] holiness"* Perhaps not accidentally, the pronoun of *bikdushato* is ambiguous. It may refer to either God, who is intrinsically holy, or Israel, who was holy when it received the Torah (Exod. 19:10), or to both, binding them together.

DORFF (THEOLOGY)

Sinai, it is appropriate that we start by acknowledging the reign of the sovereign whom we are about to encounter.

⁶ *"Rebuild the walls of Jerusalem"* Having noted the power of God, we pray that God use that power to initiate messianic times by rebuilding Jerusalem. The interweaving of the themes of Torah and Jerusalem continues in the verses that we sing as we rise to open the ark: Make "those who hate You flee" precisely so that "Torah shall come forth from Zion, and Adonai's word from Jerusalem." In the messianic vision of these verses, Jews not only reoccupy Jerusalem but study and teach Torah there. The Jewish messianic dream is not only national or political; it is inherently religious.

¹¹ *"Blessed is the One who gave Torah to his people Israel in holiness"* The Torah that we are about to remove from the ark and read is not experienced primarily as the decrees of a powerful monarch; it is rather seen as a gift for which God is to be praised and thanked. In philosophical terms, the laws of the Torah are "heteronomous," not "autonomous" — that is, they come from a source outside us (God), not from ourselves. They are nevertheless *not* perceived as arbitrary and severe, but as a boon from a gracious God.

This theme is emphasized in the last line chosen for this introductory prayer. God grants us the favor of the Torah "in his holiness" — that is, through the divine nature, which is wholly separate and different from our own. God is different from us, first, in being extraordinarily powerful and awesome. But God differs also in knowing the structure and the ways of the world far better than we ever can, so that God's Torah articulates laws that we appreciate as both just and good. In the Torah that we are about to read, God's distinctive character, or "holiness," is manifest in both these senses.

ELLENSON (MODERN LITURGIES)

classical sources in novel ways to promote a prayer book reform of evolution, not revolution.

Because of its seminal influence upon subsequent Reform liturgy, it is worth our seeing precisely how the Hamburg prayer books recast this part of the service. They removed the first three paragraphs of the classical service altogether, for several reasons. To begin with, they found several passages in these paragraphs ideologically troublesome. For example, "There is no god like You" implied the doctrine of henotheism, rather than strict monotheism — that is, that even though Israel has its sole God, other gods do exist for other peoples. The Jewish nationalism of "Favor Zion with your goodness" was another problem. And the ethic of vengeance that they saw in "Arise Adonai, let your enemies be scattered…" posed a third challenge.

The most compelling factor, however, was the Hamburg editors' desire to establish a compelling liturgical identity over against the dominant Ashkenazi community of which they were a part. Throughout Jewish history, denominational or sectarian groups have changed their liturgy to create their own unique identity in opposition to the establishment. Chasidim, for instance, replaced "Abundant peace" *(Shalom rav),* the normative final blessing in the *Amidah* of the afternoon *(Minchah)* service, with "Grant us peace" *(Sim shalom),* the parallel prayer from the morning liturgy. This same sociological mechanism is undoubtedly operative here. By changing their introduction to the Torah service, the Hamburg Reform synagogue established itself as separate from the traditionalist Ashkenazi community that surrounded it.

The Hamburg reformers took as their beginning liturgy Psalm 24:7–10, a reading that is traditionally recited by Ashkenazi Jews at the *end* of the service for the return of the Torah to the ark on pilgrimage festivals that fall on weekdays. Reform Jews will still recognize these verses, which have been part of their *Union Prayer Book* and are still found in *Gates of Prayer* in the following truncated version:

> *Lift up your heads O gates* (S'u sh'arim rasheikhem…)*!*
> *Lift yourselves up, O ancient doors!*
> *Let the King of glory enter.*
> *Who is this King of glory?*
> *The Lord of hosts.*
> *He is the King of glory.*

Psalm 24:7–10 was followed by (1) the traditional, "Blessed is He who gave the Torah to his people Israel in his holiness," (2) Psalm 34:4, "Declare the greatness of God with me, and let us exalt his Name together," (3) a series of other biblical verses (1 Chron. 29:1; Deut. 33:4; Deut. 4:44; and Prov. 3:18), (4) the traditional call to the Torah, "Let us declare the greatness of our God, and give honor to the Torah," and (5) Psalms 18:31 ("The way of God is perfect; the word of Adonai is pure; He is a shield to all who trust in him").

The Hamburg decision has proved lasting. The passages drawn from Psalm 24:7–10 have become a staple for countless liberal prayer services, including Wise, *UPB,* the

1967 *British Service of the Heart,* and an alternate service in *GOP.* Most nineteenth-century Reform prayer books, including Geiger, *Olath Tamid,* and the 1895 *UPB,* omitted the traditional opening paragraphs from this part of the service, and only Wise, a liturgical conservative, retained the classical first paragraph in his *Minhag America.* The key point is not that later Reform prayer books slavishly followed the model created by Hamburg. Rather, the Hamburg rite granted them license to depart from the received Ashkenazic service and inspired their liturgical creativity.

In recent years, *GOP* and *Lev Chadash,* as well as *Ha'avodah Shebalev,* have readopted the traditional Ashkenazi reading, "There is no god like You, Adonai," as the opening passage in their Sabbath Torah service. This restoration of the classical liturgy bespeaks the traditional trajectory that marks so much of present-day Reform Judaism.

Kol Haneshamah (Reconstructionist) and the 1998 egalitarian edition of the Conservative *Sim Shalom* actually transliterate the Hebrew here, thereby following a precedent established in *GOP.* This use of transliteration by all three movements today indicates that North American Jews who attend liberal synagogues are highly homogeneous and acculturated. They may turn to tradition as a source of meaning, but their knowledge of Hebrew, regardless of denominational affiliation, is often weak or nonexistent.

[5, 6] *"Favor Zion with Your goodness. Rebuild the walls of Jerusalem"* The Zionist content of these lines caused all nineteenth-century Reform prayer-book editors to remove these passages. Britain's Liberal movement's *Lev Chadash* still omits them, but *GOP* has restored these words as a sign of present-day North American Reform Judaism's positive attitude toward the Jewish state nowadays. Israel's *Avodah Shebalev* of course includes these prayers, and *Kol Haneshamah* (Reconstructionist) comments on them: "How different these words must have sounded before there was a sovereign living State of Israel! No longer do we merely dream of a distant rebuilding. The walls are rising before our eyes. Like our ancestors, we must now be concerned with building both the earthly Jerusalem and the heavenly Jerusalem."

[9] *"Arise, Adonai, so that your enemies be scattered, and those who hate You flee"* Many liberal prayer books have omitted this passage from Numbers 10:35, feeling that the call for the elimination of enemies — even God's enemies — reflects an ethic of resentment and vengeance that is inappropriate in the modern world. The Reconstructionist *Kol Haneshamah* includes this verse but offers, as an alternative reading, Psalm 118:19: "Open to me, O you gateways of justice; Yes, let me come in and give thanks unto Yah."

[10] *"For Torah shall come forth from Zion, and Adonai's word from Jerusalem"* The Hamburg Temple prayer books removed this passage altogether, objecting to its identification of Zion as the locale for revelation. They believed that continuous revelation was available to all generations, wherever they might live. Abraham Geiger shared this opinion but adopted another solution. He kept the Hebrew but (as he did generally when he retained traditional Hebrew prayers for symbolic associations but objected to their literal content) employed the vernacular to say what he really believed.

As an uncompromising foe of Jewish nationalism, Geiger wrote, "Jerusalem and Zion are places whence instruction went forth, and to which holy memories are attached. But, on the whole, they are to be celebrated more as a spiritual idea, as the nursery of the Kingdom of God, than as a certain geographical locale connected with a special divine providence for all times." His "translation" replaces the future (*teitzei*, "shall go forth") with the past (*ist ausgegangen*, "went forth") to demonstrate his conviction that Zion was only the place "whence instruction [once] went forth, and to which holy memories are attached." However, Israel surely was not the "geographic locale connected with a special divine providence for all times."

——◆——

FRANKEL (A WOMAN'S VOICE)

kingship. God is proclaimed as supreme ruler of the world; the Torah, as God's effigy in our midst. Adorned in a royal mantle, crown, and scepter; paraded around in a royal processional; its hem kissed in obeisance; and accorded absolute deference, the Torah represents for us the last vestige of ancient priesthood and dynasty. Here, in this opening prayer of only fifty words, references to God's kingship predominate. Six words derive directly from *melekh*, "king." Several others —*memshalt'kha*, "your kingdom"; *Adon/Adonai*, "Lord/my Lord" (one of the names of God); *oz*, "strength"; *el ram v'nisa*, "high and exalted God" — underline the idea of God's sovereignty over the earth and its peoples. Yet, we are reminded that God's throne is not found everywhere among all the world's kingdoms; rather, its only appropriate resting place is Zion, which is why the prayer beseeches God to "rebuild the walls of Jerusalem." For though God once reigned as king, still reigns, and will reign eternally, no matter what happens to human fortunes, still the Jewish People will feel secure — "in You alone…we put our trust" — only when God reassumes the throne in the Jerusalem. Is it any wonder that holy wars continue to rage over that empty chair?

The other paradox, inextricably twined with the first, has to do with how we see ourselves as God's subjects. If God governs from one special place, then we Jews need to go to that place to pay homage and receive our instructions. So when we proclaim in this passage that Adonai will always be king, we are being somewhat ingenuous. In reality, we would prefer that God "favor Zion" and rebuild the very real mortar-and-stone walls of Jerusalem. For as much as we praise God's indisputable mastery over *all* the earth, proclaiming, "There is no God like You," we nonetheless remind God that because we are *amo*, "God's own people," we must not be overlooked among the nations. Given that special status, we ask God for strength and — even more important — for peace, which makes strength superfluous.

In this dance of universal and particular, of diaspora and promised land, of faith and insecurity, we are reminded of a truth that resolves these polarities: that we — God and humanity, God and Israel — depend upon each other, for as my teacher Rabbi Hershel

Matt, *z"l,* once wrote: "Just as there can be no parent without a child (and vice versa) and no teacher without a pupil, so there is no king without subjects who acknowledge and accept his kingship."

[8] *"With the moving of the ark"* How freighted with symbolic baggage is the ark — and what an ambiguous symbol it is! The original ark invoked in this verse housed within it both the first tablets of the Law (shattered by Moses when he found the people worshiping the golden calf) and the second (which Moses brought down whole). Crowned by the *kapporet,* the mercy seat, the ancient ark symbolized God's holiness *(k'dushah),* but when the people faced danger, it also served as an ensign of war, scattering Israel's enemies.

In grafting together in one prayer two well-known biblical passages, the first from Numbers and the second from Isaiah, the Rabbis acknowledged the ark's dual role. For in the past, when the people wandered, vulnerable and irresolute, through the desert, they needed proof that God would protect them. Proclaiming, "Arise, Adonai, so that your enemies be scattered, and those who hate You flee from before You," they turned the ark into a battering ram and God into their secret weapon. But in Isaiah's messianic vision of Israel's future, the source of the second quotation, the ark turns back into an instrument of peace. Following Isaiah's proclamation that *mitzion tetsei torah,* "God's teaching will go forth from Zion," the prophet declares in the next verse (not cited in this prayer) that the nations "shall beat their swords into plowshares and their spears into pruning hooks." On that day, the ark will no longer be needed to march us out to war. So, when we end this passage by blessing God for the gift of Torah, we also echo the petition we voiced in the opening prayer: that God will bless our people with peace.

———◆———

HAUPTMAN (TALMUD)

once every seven years they are to gather all the people — the men, the women, and the children — and read the entire Torah aloud to them so that they learn to fear God and keep the *mitzvot.* Although this public reading is intended to be infrequent, it is still designed to have a profound religious effect upon those who hear it.

The Bible makes historical reference to two public Torah readings several hundred years apart. The Book of Kings reports that when King Josiah heard that a scroll of Torah had been found in the Temple during renovations (2 Kings 22:8), he arranged for it to be read to all of Israel (23:2). The book of Nehemiah (8:1-8) tells us that on the first day of Tishrei, on Rosh Hashanah, Ezra the scribe read the entire Torah aloud to all of the people — the men, the women, and the children. The reading lasted from the light of day until noon. In both of these instances, the verses relate, people repented because of what they heard. It therefore seems reasonable to conclude that these events played a role in establishing the Torah reading as a standard, central feature of Jewish worship.

The Talmud stipulates many rules about reading the Torah in public. Believing that three days should not go by without hearing words of Torah (B. K. 82a), the Rabbis scheduled readings on Shabbat (morning and afternoon), Mondays, and Thursdays, with the full portion read on Shabbat morning only. The Mishnah details the readings for special occasions, the age and gender qualifications of a reader, and the need for appropriate dress (Meg., Chaps. 3 and 4). It also designates a *kohen* as the first reader and a *levi* as the second (M. Git.5:8), so that, as the Gemara later explains, people do not come to blows (Git. 59b).

But in all the Talmud we find no mention of a Torah service, as we know it today — no elaborate ritual that is associated with removing the Torah from the ark and returning it there. A post-Talmudic tractate, Soferim, provides the earliest description of such a Torah service (14:8–14). Many of its elements have remained constant to this very day, in particular the verses and prayers we recite when performing these activities. One fascinating detail recorded in Soferim is that after the reading of the *Haftarah,* the Torah is raised and shown to men and women alike (14:14). This suggests that women, as well as men, attended Sabbath services on a regular basis. Such a finding was not expected in a society in which women have fewer prayer obligations than men. Added to the Torah service at a later time were several personal prayers written in the first person singular — a most unusual occurrence in the Siddur. This period of time in the service was understood to be an especially propitious one for connecting with God and making requests of Him.

[8] *"With the moving of the ark"* Two verses bracket the Torah service: this one from Numbers 10:35 and "With its resting...." (10:36), which is recited upon returning the Torah to the ark. They form a literary device called an *inclusio* — that is, they constitute a rhetorical envelope of two biblical citations, one at the beginning and one at the end, with which the entire Torah service is framed. The verses fit this occasion well, because in the Bible they make reference to moving the ark containing the tablets from one place to another as the Israelites themselves moved from camp to camp.

But the two verses are hard to understand. The first (v. 35) says that when the ark was about to be moved, Moses challenged God to advance and scatter his enemies. The second (v. 36) says that when the ark was going to be set down, Moses would ask God to return and rest. The liturgy refers to traditional commentary on these verses. The first verse is said to imply that when the ark was moved, God's presence on the ark receded (Rashbam, Rabbi Samuel ben Meir, France, 1085–1174); but in the second verse, when the ark came to rest, it returned (Obadiah Sforno, Italy, c. 1470–c. 1550). As a result, Israel too would be at rest — that is, not under attack — when the ark rested, but in danger from attack when the ark (and God too) moved. So when the ark moved, Moses would challenge God not just to leave but to attack Israel's enemies. When it came to rest again, God would be invited back to his seat of honor upon it.

These two verses are marked off in the Torah scroll with a set of inverted letters, two *nuns,* signifying, perhaps, their independence from the verses that precede and follow.

INTRODUCTION

KUSHNER & POLEN (CHASIDISM)

Perhaps the purpose of reading the Torah within the liturgy is not so much about hearing and studying the weekly lection as about something else entirely. Consider, for example, the following mystical traditions surrounding the scroll of the Torah itself. According to the Zohar (II, 90a–b):

> Rabbi Eleazar taught: In these ten utterances [commandments] are embodied all the commandments in the Torah, decrees and punishments, cleanness and uncleanness, branches and roots, trees and plants, heaven and earth, sea and the depths. For the Torah is the Name of the Holy One. Just as the name of the Holy One is embodied in the ten utterances, so the Torah also is embodied in the ten utterances. These ten utterances are the Name of the Holy One. And the whole Torah is one Name, the actual holy Name of the Holy One.

So the commandments of the Torah are actually God's Name. In the introduction to his commentary on the Torah, Rabbi Moses ben Nachman, or the RaMBaN (d. 1270), the great thirteenth-century Spanish commentator and mystic, develops this theme:

> We have a tradition [in the Zohar II 87a] that the Torah is composed entirely of divine Names and that from another perspective the words separate themselves into Names. Imagine for example that the spaces separating the first three words of the first verse in Genesis can be moved so as to spell an entirely different, yet equally true, statement.... And it is this way with the whole Torah.

Not only the commandments, but the whole text is one long mystical Name of God. Other Kabbalists go even further. Moshe Idel ("Infinities of Torah in Kabbalah," in *Midrash and Literature,* ed. Geoffrey H. Hartman and Sanford Budick, Yale University Press, 1986, p. 145) cites the kabbalistic text *The Book of [Divine] Unity* which fuses the sign with what it signifies:

> All the letters of the Torah, by their shapes, combined and separated, swaddled letters, curved ones and crooked ones, superfluous and elliptic ones, minute and large ones, and inverted, the calligraphy of the letters, the open and closed pericopes and the ordered ones, all of them are the shape of God...since if one letter is missing from the Scroll of the Torah, or one is superfluous...that Scroll of the Torah is disqualified, since it has not in itself the shape of God.

More than even the Name, the Torah here is understood as the shape of God. But the fourteenth-century kabbalist Menachem Recanati makes it explicit. Gershom Scholem (*On the Kabbalah,* 44) cites him as saying, "The letters [of God's Name and of the Torah] are the mystical body of God, while God, in a manner of speaking, is the soul of the letters." The Torah, in other words, is more than the record of God's revelation. It is a manifestation of the presence of the Holy One, the shape of the divine — yes, even, as it were, "the body of God."

In this light we can now understand the passage from Numbers 10:35, chosen to accompany the procession of the Torah scroll through the congregation just prior to its reading. "With the moving of the ark, Moses would say: Arise, Adonai, so that your enemies be scattered, and those who hate You flee from before You" (Num. 10:35).

In his commentary *B'er Mayim Chayim* (p. 48), Rabbi Chayim of Tchernovitz explains that the reason for the insertion of this verse at this place in the liturgy is that it is being used as a kind of battle cry against the forces of evil, or, as they are called in Lurianic Kabbalah, the *k'lipot*. And the scroll of the Torah — a manifestation of, as it were, the presence of God — leads us in battle. Indeed, we realize that the main event may not be the reading but the actual march itself! In our procession with the scroll of the Torah, we are in effect carrying the physical presence of God out into the congregation and into the world! The great German talmudist Rabbi Jacob ben Moses Moellin (d. 1427), known also as the MaHaRiL, who was certainly no mystic, goes even further. He calculates the number of times the Torah is taken out and read before the congregation in one year — over fifty times on Shabbat morning, over fifty times during Shabbat *Minchah* (afternoon), over fifty times on Mondays and over fifty on Thursdays, eighteen on Rosh Chodesh (the new moon), twice on Rosh Hashanah and twice on Yom Kippur, nine festival readings, and so forth — and he comes up with a total of 248. And 248 is the traditional number of the body's limbs. Moellin concludes that this is because "Everyone wants to see [God's] limbs!" (*Magen Avraham* to *Shulchan Arukh,* O. Ch. 134, 2).

Something like this may also be in play with other rituals surrounding the public reading of Torah. Sefardim do *hagbahah* (the lifting of the open scroll for public inspection) *before* the actual reading. And in some Sefardi congregations, before the Torah is read, it is even carried through the congregation open in its case! Indeed, there is reason to conclude that the current practice of preaching and interpreting the Torah within the liturgy might better be saved for a separate occasion such as *s'udat sh'lishit,* the third Sabbath meal, as is the custom among the Chasidim.

◆

LANDES (HALAKHAH)

ark, accompanied by the singing of this prayer, affirms the major rabbinic dictum of faith that the Torah was given by God to Israel. We therefore stand here to receive the Torah again from Sinai. Since the entire ritual of taking the Torah from the holy ark, delivering it to the people, and reading from it is a reenactment of Sinai, frivolous conversation or leaving the synagogue before the Torah has been returned to the Holy Ark is an act of great insensitivity. We go out of our way to indicate our appreciation of standing at Sinai — for instance, by standing when the holy ark is opened, even though technically there is no real need to do so. Nonetheless, we stand anyway to show our gratitude (Israel, Meir Hakohen Kagan, the Chafetz Chayim, *Sha'ar Tzi'on* 146:18).

[1] *"Blessed is the name"* Some authorities say that this is to be recited even on weekdays when the Torah is read (*Pri Migadim* 34:6 and *Mishnah B'rurah* 1334:13). Others advocate reciting it only on Shabbat (Chayim Yosef David Azulai, the Chidah,

1724–1806, Jerusalem, following Isaac ben Solomon Luria, the Ari, 1534–1572, Israel), and that is the general custom.

———◆———

L. HOFFMAN (HISTORY)

the *maftir* says it we do not know. The traditional interpretation is that such an honor makes up for the fact that the *maftir* is given a *Haftarah* reading, not the more weighty honor of reading from the Torah. (Alternatively, see below, "Hear O Israel.")

Tradition *(Siddur Otsar Hat'filot)* suggests that we approach the ark at these words, but before reciting them, we repeat what Jacob said when he awoke from his desert dream to see angels ascending and descending from heaven: "How awesome is this place! This is none other than the abode of God, and that is the gateway to heaven." The ark, then, is conceived as the gateway to heaven because it holds God's word, the Jew's gateway to God.

———◆———

J. HOFFMAN (TRANSLATION)

attempt to reconcile the most likely interpretation of the content with the beauty of the Hebrew. More literally, the Hebrew reads "according to/in your will, do good to/for Zion." Another possibility is "make Zion better."

[7] *"For"* Birnbaum: "truly." While in isolation the Hebrew word *ki* might mean either, here it is clearly a relation of cause and effect.

[9] *"So that"* Or perhaps just "let."

[9] *"Who hate You flee"* The words for "those who hate You" *(m'san'ekha)* and "flee" *(yanusu)* sound similar to "moving" *(n'so'a)* above, forming a verbal pun in Hebrew, stronger in Hebrew than it seems in the English transliteration. Magic played an important role in all ancient cultures, so perhaps the pun connecting the time *(n'so'a)* with what will happen at that time *(yanusu m'san'ekha)* contributed to the plausibility of the argument.

————————◆ ◆ ◆————————

B: Setting the Stage: On the Other Hand, God's Mercy

I. The Thirteen Attributes (*Adonai, Adonai*)

[On festivals that occur on weekdays, add the following:

¹Adonai, Adonai, merciful and gracious God, endlessly patient, most kind and truthful, preserving kindness to the thousandth generation, forgiving iniquity, transgression, and sin, cleansing.

¹יְיָ יְיָ אֵל רַחוּם וְחַנּוּן אֶרֶךְ אַפַּיִם וְרַב חֶסֶד וֶאֱמֶת: נֹצֵר חֶסֶד לָאֲלָפִים, נֹשֵׂא עָוֹן וָפֶשַׁע וְחַטָּאָה וְנַקֵּה:

II. "May the words of my mouth" (*Yihyu l'ratson*)

²May the words of my mouth and the meditation of my heart find favor before You, Adonai, my rock and my redeemer.

²יִהְיוּ לְרָצוֹן אִמְרֵי פִי וְהֶגְיוֹן לִבִּי לְפָנֶיךָ יְיָ צוּרִי וְגוֹאֲלִי:

III. "I offer my prayer" (*Va'ani t'fillati*)

³I offer my prayer to You, Adonai, at this time of favor; God, in your great mercy; answer me with your saving truth.]

³וַאֲנִי תְפִלָּתִי לְךָ יְיָ עֵת רָצוֹן, אֱלֹהִים בְּרָב־חַסְדֶּךָ, עֲנֵנִי בֶּאֱמֶת יִשְׁעֶךָ:]

BRETTLER (BIBLE)

[1] *"Adonai, Adonai…"* Often called the thirteen attributes, from Exodus 34:6-7, given as God's response to Moses' request to see God's *kavod,* or "glory" (33:18). This is not, however, the complete list of attributes, which continues "yet He does not remit all punishment, but visits the iniquity of parents upon children and children's children, upon the third and fourth generations." The liturgy quotes selectively, invoking only God's "positive" attributes, not the problematic notion of intergenerational punishment. In fact, this is accomplished with great violence to the biblical text! The list here ends *venakeh,* "cleansing," but in the Bible, that word is part of a larger single phrase, *venakeh lo y'nakeh,* meaning "he certainly does   (p. 66)

DORFF (THEOLOGY)

[1] *"Adonai, Adonai, merciful and gracious God"* On the High Holy Days and the three biblical festivals (Pesach, Shavuot, and Sukkot) when we mark the seasons of the year, we insert a biblical passage that invites God's mercy. In ancient societies, the seasonal progress of the year and, even more, the passage from one year to the next were not seen as automatically guaranteed. Instead, at each turning point — especially in going from year to year — people negotiated an extension of their lease on life with the gods. Since human beings can never fulfill God's expectations of us, we too ask God to be merciful in excusing our trespasses so that we can continue to live through this transitional time. On the festivals, when we are merely going   (p. 66)

FRANKEL (A WOMAN'S VOICE)

[1] *"Adonai, Adonai, merciful and gracious"* On festivals and the High Holy Days, we recite an extra passage known as "the Thirteen Divine Attributes." In its original biblical context, the passage constitutes God's answer to Moses' request to see God's glory. This moment comes soon after the apostasy of the golden calf. Returning to the mountaintop to receive a second set of commandments after shattering the first, Moses pleads with God to have mercy on the people and forgive their sin.

B: SETTING THE STAGE: ON THE OTHER HAND, GOD'S MERCY

[On festivals that occur on weekdays, add the following:

[1] Adonai, Adonai, merciful and gracious God, endlessly patient, most kind and truthful, preserving kindness to the thousandth generation, forgiving iniquity, transgression, and sin, cleansing.

Why do we reserve this passage only for holy days? Why at these times do we need to remind God of these particular attributes? Perhaps it is because on these occasions, charged with less familiar laws and practices, we face greater opportunities to make mistakes, to do too much or too little, to be so carried away with our own observance that we worship a golden calf instead of God. Anticipating these lapses, we ask God to show us now the special divine attribute of *rachamim,* a mother's forgiving compassion.

———◆———

KUSHNER & POLEN (CHASIDISM)

[1] "Adonai, Adonai, merciful and gracious God, endlessly patient, most kind and truthful" [Exod. 34:6] One of the core tenets of all spirituality is the paradoxical suspicion that, in the words of the late professor Alexander Altmann, "God is in the self, but the self is not God" ("God and the Self in Jewish Mysticism," *Judaism*, 3:2 [1954]). We sense the same divine presence both in the world around us *and* within ourselves. Naturally, then, when Moses ascends Sinai and gets as close to God as any human being has ever come, we might expect an insight into our

[On festivals that occur on weekdays, add the following:

יְיָ יְיָ אֵל רַחוּם וְחַנּוּן אֶרֶךְ אַפִּיִם וְרַב חֶסֶד [1]
וֶאֱמֶת: נֹצֵר חֶסֶד לָאֲלָפִים, נֹשֵׂא עָוֹן וָפֶשַׁע וְחַטָּאָה
וְנַקֵּה:

soul's relationship with God. Indeed, as Moses is sheltered in a cleft of the rock while the divine presence passes by, God proclaims, "Adonai, Adonai, merciful and gracious God...." Noting the repetition of "Adonai," Levi Yitzhak ben Meir of Berdichev (d. 1810) offers the following insight into our relationship with God:

> The soul is a part of God. And therefore when the soul calls out to God in prayer, part of God is, as it were, calling out to God's own self. So, when our text says that God passed by Moses' face, it means that Moses was overcome by reverence and filled with fear and love. And just this is the reason that the word "Adonai" is   (p. 68)

L. HOFFMAN (HISTORY)

THE SECOND PART OF THE INTRODUCTION CONTINUES TO SET THE STAGE. IT BALANCES A CONSIDERATION OF GOD'S GREATNESS (FROM 1A) WITH A PARALLEL AFFIRMATION OF GOD'S MERCY, SEEN AS A MANIFESTATION OF GOD'S LOVE FOR ISRAEL. THE GIFT OF TORAH REQUIRES BOTH: GOD'S GREATNESS TO BE ABLE TO IMPART REVELATORY WISDOM, AND GOD'S LOVE FOR ISRAEL, BY WHICH GOD DOES IN FACT IMPART IT. THE FIRST PARAGRAPH IS ESPECIALLY SIGNIFICANT, AS IT IS THE THIRTEEN ATTRIBUTES OF GOD.

[1] "Adonai, Adonai" The thirteen attributes from Exodus 34 and again in Numbers 14. In Exodus, Moses climbs the   (p. 68)

J. HOFFMAN (TRANSLATION)

[1] "Most" "Most" in the sense of "very." The Hebrew literally reads, "abundant in."

[1] "Forgiving" The original Hebrew might not mean "forgiving," but that's clearly what the Rabbis wanted it to mean. But the Rabbis carefully omitted a word from this biblical quotation. Their version is "forgiving [nosei] iniquity, transgression, and sin, certainly cleansing." The original version, from Exodus, reads "forgiving [nosei] iniquity, transgression, and sin, and certainly not cleansing, recalling the iniquity of parents upon children and grand-children, to the third and fourth generation." In this original context, the Hebrew word *nosei*, literally "carrying," might mean "carrying forward," as from generation to generation. But   (p. 69)

² May the words of my mouth and the meditation of my heart find favor before You, Adonai, my rock and my redeemer.

³ I offer my prayer to You, Adonai, at this time of favor, God, in your great mercy; answer me with your saving truth.]

²יִהְיוּ לְרָצוֹן אִמְרֵי פִי וְהֶגְיוֹן לִבִּי לְפָנֶיךָ יְיָ צוּרִי וְגֹאֲלִי:

³וַאֲנִי תְפִלָּתִי לְךָ יְיָ עֵת רָצוֹן, אֱלֹהִים בְּרָב־חַסְדֶּךָ, עֲנֵנִי בֶּאֱמֶת יִשְׁעֶךָ:

BRETTLER (BIBLE)

not forgive (cleanse)!" The tradition of quoting only the "good" part of this description is older than the liturgy; Jonah, for example, justifies his flight from God by doing the same thing (Jon. 4:2). God, he says, is "compassionate and gracious…slow to anger, abounding in kindness, renouncing punishment." These types of selective quotations should be seen as creative rather than problematic.

² *"May the words of my mouth and the meditation of my heart find favor"* Again, a post-biblical prayer is given further authority by concluding it with a biblical verse (Psalm 19:15). The highly personal references in this verse, "words of *my* mouth and the meditations of *my* heart" make it especially appropriate as an ending for this highly personal prayer, which begins in the first person and now ends in the first person also.

³ *"I offer my prayer to You…at this time of favor"* From Psalm 69:14, mirroring the previous Siddur verse ("May the words of my mouth and the meditations of my heart find favor *[ratson]*") in both vocabulary and sentiment. Here, the worshiper looks for an *et ratson* — an efficacious time when God is especially attentive, as opposed to resting or ignoring humanity (Ps. 13:2; 44:24). The second half of Psalm 69:14, "O God, answer me," may reflect an original petition by the pray-er to a priest or a cultic prophet who answered the pray-er in God's name, announcing God's intention to heed the request. In its new liturgical context, the anticipated answer is the heeding directly by God of the petitioner's requests.

——◆——

DORFF (THEOLOGY)

from one season to the next, this passage is recited only here; on the High Holy Days, it is recited many times, for then we mark the passage from one year's lease on life to the next. Normally the passage is sung three times.

This passage, from Exodus 34:6–7 (and summarized in Num. 14:18), is called by the Rabbis "the thirteen attributes of God" (B. *Rosh Hashanah* 17b). To get the number thirteen, the Rabbis interpret the twin mention of "Adonai, Adonai" at the beginning of the verse as two separate attributes, namely, that "I am Adonai [who acts mercifully] before a person sins, and I am Adonai [who extends mercy] after a person sins." The third word, "God" *[el]*, then, is said to refer to the God of power and justice, so that the prayer pictures God as balancing mercy and justice. Moreover, the Rabbis understand the three words that describe violation of God's will as three different kinds of sin: iniquity *(avon)* is premeditated sin, transgression *(pesha)* is refusal to perform a positive duty, and sin *(chata'ah)* is sin committed unintentionally. Thus, the thirteen attributes are (1) Adonai, (2) Adonai, (3) God; (4) compassionate; (5) gracious; (6) slow to anger; (7) abounding in kindness (8) and faithfulness; (9) extending kindness to the thousandth generation; (10) forgiving iniquity, (11) transgression, and (12) sin; and (13) remitting [all punishment].

The remarkable thing about the liturgical use of this passage is that the Rabbis deliberately misread it by cutting it off in the middle when they reproduce it in the Siddur. In the Bible, it continues, "Yet he does *not* remit (cleanse) all punishment, but visits the iniquity of parents upon children and children's children, upon the third and fourth generation." The Rabbis' creative reading actually changes the meaning of the last word to mean the exact opposite of what the Torah says. The Torah employs a grammatical mechanism used to add emphasis: placing the infinitive form of a verb before the finite form. The Hebrew original is *nakeih lo y'nakeh,* literally, "remit" [the infinitive] "he will not remit," or, idiomatically, "He will certainly not remit [punishment for our sins]." In the prayer book, however, the Rabbis omit the last two words, *lo y'nakeh* ("He will not remit"), and preserve only the first one, the infinite *nakeh,* "remit," so that it comes out saying that God *will* wipe the slate clean! What theological audacity!

One could say that the Rabbis did this simply because the latter part of the verse does not speak of God's mercy, the theme they wanted to insert in the liturgy here — but that would ignore the Bible's insistence that God's mercy is not boundless, that God will balance mercy with justice in exacting punishment for sins. The biblical verse articulates the doctrine known as "vertical retribution," according to which God is actually being merciful in not exacting punishment immediately but rather postponing it to following generations. This is similar to what we feel about credit cards: we see it as a kindness when we can buy things without paying money right away, but the payment must ultimately be paid. The biblical verse, of course, involves the troubling doctrine that it will not be the sinners who pay but their children — a system that Jeremiah (31:29–30) and Ezekiel (18:1–4) prophesied would end in such a way that "The person who sins, only he will die." The Rabbis avoid this entire intra-biblical controversy about the way that God's justice is meted out simply by eliminating the last clause of the verse. Clearly they still believed in God's justice, but in prayer we are to appeal exclusively to God's mercy, even if we must excise part of a biblical verse and thereby change its meaning completely.

[3] *"I offer my prayer to You"* This verse, recited (or, often, sung) three times, reinforces the theme that because transition periods are dangerous, the festivals are times when we must ask that God save us. That was certainly true in the ancient understanding whereby transitions from one season to another were assumed to require divine approval. Even now, though, we find transitions hard, so a prayer for God's assistance in helping us over the hump is appropriate. For instance, those who have suffered the loss of relatives or friends since the last time this holiday was celebrated will find this holiday bringing them to mind. We ask God to ameliorate the sense of emptiness that we feel at their absence.

———◆———

KUSHNER & POLEN (CHASIDISM)

repeated. The first mentioning of "Adonai" is actually the aspect of God within Moses calling to its other, universal presence (Itturay Torah, *II, 268*).

[3] *"I offer my prayer to You, Adonai, at this time of favor"* [Ps. 69:14] Yehuda Aryeh Leib of Ger, in his classic *Sefas Emes* (I "5635" and IV "5639"), deliberately misreads the supplication in our verse. The "time of favor," he suggests, is not referring to a favorable time *to God* but rather a favorable time to the one who offers the prayer! And the best time, the most favorable time, to pray for something is when you already have it. The goal, in addition to wanting what you already have, is to experience what you already have now as a divine gift. Surely this would be a most favorable time to offer one's prayer!

———◆———

L. HOFFMAN (HISTORY)

mountain a second time to get another set of tablets, and there God's attributes are revealed to him. They are not quite as merciful as the liturgy suggests, however. The liturgy thus subverts the original meaning entirely, making the negative positive (see Elliot N. Dorff's commentary).

Still, the Rabbis had precedent for seeing the list of attributes as essentially compassionate rather than punitive, since Numbers 14 uses them that way. There, the scouts return from spying out the land of Canaan. God becomes furious when ten of them give a bad report on the Israelites' chances of conquering the "giants" whom they behold there. To convince God not to destroy the people, Moses cites the attributes he had learned in Exodus, thereby using God's own teaching against their divine teacher. As the Rabbis saw it further, these attributes begin with a two-fold use of the tetragrammaton *(Adonai),* which, by rabbinic calculus, is God's attribute of mercy (see Dorff's commentary).

Thereafter, these thirteen attributes become critical for rabbinic liturgy. The Talmud reports a divine conversation with Moses whereby Moses worries about what will happen to Israel after the Temple has been destroyed and sacrifices of atonement are no longer possible. Won't Israel have to die for its sins? God "covenants" with the thirteen attributes, making them Israel's defense attorney on high. As a model, God dons a *tallit* and tells Moses that on Rosh Hashanah, the beginning of every new year, the prayer leader should do likewise, and recite the attributes. Our High Holy Day liturgy thus features these attributes, especially on Yom Kippur, where they initiate the *s'lichot* section, the section of prayers filled with biblical verses that reflect God's mercy (*p'sukei d'rachamei,* "verses of compassion"), and poems *(piyyutim)* on the theme of God's forgiveness.

The extension of the attributes to the festival liturgy is a kabbalistic innovation introduced by Isaac Luria, sixteenth-century Safed.

———◆———

J. HOFFMAN (TRANSLATION)

in its revised rabbinic context, "forgives" certainly fits better. So the translation here conveys what the Rabbis wanted the text to mean.

[1] *"Cleansing"* The final word, *v'nakei,* is the first word of a three-word phrase in the original Hebrew (see above), but even that three-word phrase, just like the one-word rabbinic abridgement ("...and cleansing"), seems like it's missing something. We intentionally mimic the incomplete feeling of the Hebrew.

[2] *"Meditation of my heart"* This translation (which appears in Artscroll, Birnbaum, and *Gates of Prayer*) has become so well known that we retain it here. But while literally accurate, it is somewhat misleading, because the Hebrew *lev* (literally, "heart") functions metaphorically much differently than the English "heart," in that that the Hebrew suggests both emotions and intellect, while the English generally suggests emotion to the exclusion of intellect. (For a full discussion, see Volume 1, *The Sh'ma and Its Blessings,* pp. 100, 102.) A more accurate translation might read "May my spoken words and my inner thoughts," but while that translation captures the content of the original Hebrew, it fails to capture the metaphor of using two human organs, the mouth and the heart, to represent the external and the internal.

[3] *"I offer my prayer to You"* This famous line (also read as part of the morning blessings) is difficult to understand and to translate, particularly in this context. The original meaning of the first phrase is "But as for me, my prayer is to you" (as in Artscroll's "As for me, my prayer"). But in the prayer here, the biblical quotation is taken out of context, so it means something like "It is I who offer my prayer to you."

69

[3] *"Time of favor [et ratson]"* The question is whether the speaker is praying for a time of favor or at a time of favor. Opting for the latter, Birnbaum gives us "I offer my prayer at this time of grace," and preferring the latter, Artscroll reads "May my prayer be at an opportune time." We prefer Birnbaum's reading and suggest a translation of "At this time of favor."

The original Hebrew punctuation (as given to us by the trope, admittedly many hundreds of years after the Hebrew was written) groups *Elohim, b'rov-chasdecha* with *Adonai et ratson,* suggesting that we have two phrases, beginning with *Elohim* and *Adonai* (two words for God) in parallel construction. We thus get "God in your great mercy; Adonai, at this time of favor" as the twin preconditions of the hope, "Answer me with your saving truth." However, this translation is at odds with other translations.

◆ ◆ ◆

C. SETTING THE STAGE: KABBALISTIC INSERTION ON GOD'S GREATNESS AND GOD'S MERCY

1. "BLESSED IS THE NAME"
(B'RIKH SH'MEIH)

[1] Blessed is the name of the Master of the universe. [2] Blessed is your crown and your place. [3] May You love your people Israel forever. [4] Reveal the salvation of your right hand to your people in your sanctuary. [5] Lead us to discover the goodness of your light, and accept our prayer in mercy. [6] May it be your will to prolong our lives in happiness.

[7] May I too be counted among the righteous, so that You show compassion toward me and watch over me and mine and all who are a part of your People Israel. [8] You are the One who feeds and sustains all. [9] You are the One who rules over kings, for dominion is yours. [10] I am the servant of the Holy Blessed One, before whom and before the glory of whose Torah I bow at all times. [11] I trust not in man and I rely on no angels, but in the God of heaven who is a God of truth and whose Torah is true and whose prophets are true and who performs many acts that are good and true. [12] In Him do I trust, and to his holy precious name I speak praise. [13] May it be your will that You open my heart to your Torah and fulfill the wishes of my heart and the heart of all your People Israel, for good, for life, and for peace. Amen.

בְּרִיךְ שְׁמֵהּ דְּמָרֵא עָלְמָא.[1] בְּרִיךְ[2] כִּתְרָךְ וְאַתְרָךְ. יְהֵא רְעוּתָךְ עִם עַמָּךְ[3] יִשְׂרָאֵל לְעָלַם. וּפֻרְקַן יְמִינָךְ אַחֲזִי[4] לְעַמָּךְ בְּבֵית מַקְדְּשָׁךְ. וּלְאַמְטוֹיֵי לָנָא[5] מִטּוּב נְהוֹרָךְ. וּלְקַבֵּל צְלוֹתָנָא בְּרַחֲמִין. יְהֵא רַעֲוָא קֳדָמָךְ דְּתוֹרִיךְ[6] לָן חַיִּין בְּטִיבוּתָא. וְלֶהֱוֵי אֲנָא פְּקִידָא[7] בְּגוֹ צַדִּיקַיָּא. לְמִרְחַם עָלַי וּלְמִנְטַר יָתִי וְיָת כָּל דִּי לִי וְדִי לְעַמָּךְ יִשְׂרָאֵל. אַנְתְּ הוּא זָן לְכֹלָּא וּמְפַרְנֵס לְכֹלָּא.[8] אַנְתְּ הוּא שַׁלִּיט עַל כֹּלָּא. אַנְתְּ הוּא[9] דְּשַׁלִּיט עַל מַלְכַיָּא. וּמַלְכוּתָא דִּילָךְ הִיא. אֲנָא עַבְדָּא דְקֻדְשָׁא בְּרִיךְ[10] הוּא דְּסָגְדְנָא קַמֵּהּ וּמִקַּמָּא דִּיקַר אוֹרַיְתֵהּ בְּכָל עִדָּן וְעִדָּן. לָא עַל[11] אֱנָשׁ רָחִצְנָא. וְלָא עַל בַּר אֱלָהִין סָמְכְנָא. אֶלָּא בֵּאלָהָא דִשְׁמַיָּא דְּהוּא אֱלָהָא קְשׁוֹט. וְאוֹרַיְתֵהּ קְשׁוֹט. וּנְבִיאוֹהִי קְשׁוֹט. וּמַסְגֵּא לְמֶעְבַּד טַבְוָן וּקְשׁוֹט. בֵּהּ אֲנָא רָחִץ. וְלִשְׁמֵהּ[12] קַדִּישָׁא יַקִּירָא אֲנָא אֵמַר תֻּשְׁבְּחָן. יְהֵא רַעֲוָא קֳדָמָךְ דְּתִפְתַּח לִבִּי[13] בְּאוֹרַיְתָא. וְתַשְׁלִים מִשְׁאֲלִין דְּלִבִּי וְלִבָּא דְכָל עַמָּךְ יִשְׂרָאֵל לְטַב וּלְחַיִּין וְלִשְׁלָם: אָמֵן.

BRETTLER (BIBLE)

[1] *"Blessed is the name"* From the Zohar, but the majority of its themes are already found in the Bible. For example, "blessing God's name" in the sense of proclaiming that the name, and thus God, are blessed, occurs biblically (see Pss. 63:5; 96:2; 113:2; 145:1, 21).

[4] *"Reveal the salvation of your right hand"* Biblical society was predominantly right-handed, so much so that the judge, Ehud (see Judg. 3:15–21) is introduced as "a left-handed man" because he was the exception to the rule. Anthropomorphically speaking, God's right hand is the strong one. The same idea is found in other biblical texts that have entered the liturgy: The Song of the Sea, for instance

(p. 74)

DORFF (THEOLOGY)

[1] *"Blessed is the name"* This selection from the Zohar, read in many synagogues on Shabbat, emphasizes the sovereignty of God and the hope that God will have mercy on us and sustain us. We ask God to do that, for we "trust not in human beings and…rely on no angels, but in the God

(p. 75)

ELLENSON (MODERN LITURGIES)

[1] *"Blessed is the name…"* No Reform prayer book has included this passage from the classical mystical work the Zohar, probably because of the antimystical sentiment that marked nineteenth-century Reform Judaism and which, to some extent, is still a living legacy in Reform circles today. (p. 75)

FRANKEL (A WOMAN'S VOICE)

[1] *"Blessed is the name"* For those unfamiliar with Hebrew, this passage probably seems no more or less accessible than those surrounding it. But for those at home in Hebrew, this prayer poses a special challenge. For this prayer — like the familiar *Kaddish*— is written in Aramaic, a cognate language to Hebrew, but just different enough to frustrate easy comprehension. Ironically, centuries ago Aramaic was the common language of Jews (and early Christians), so the *Kaddish* (which goes back to the first century) was probably

C. SETTING THE STAGE: KABBALISTIC INSERTION ON GOD'S GREATNESS AND GOD'S MERCY

[1] Blessed is the name of the Master of the universe. [2] Blessed is your crown and your place. [3] May You love your people Israel forever. [4] Reveal the salvation of your right hand to your people in your sanctuary. [5] Lead us to discover the goodness of your light, and accept our prayer in mercy. [6] May it be your will to prolong our lives in happiness.

designed to be especially accessible to the broader community of Israel. However, *B'rikh sh'meih* comes from the Zohar, a book composed in the Middle Ages when only a scholarly elite used Aramaic. Without a translation on the facing page, few Jews understand what it says.

Yet, despite the linguistic barriers, *B'rikh sh'meih* remains a popular fixture in the traditional Torah service, particularly its final two sentences, beginning with the phrase *bei ana rakhetz,* "in [God] I put my trust." One explanation for its popularity (p. 76)

KUSHNER & POLEN (CHASIDISM)

[1,2] *"Blessed is the name of the Master of the universe. Blessed is your crown and your place"* [II Zohar 206a; *Vayakhel* 225 (*Sulam* ed.)] According to the Zohar (II 206a), we read that

> Rabbi Simeon said: When the scroll of the Torah is removed [from the ark] to be read to the congregation, the heavenly gates of mercy are opened and love is aroused in the world above. [Here] a person must say the following, "Blessed is the name of the master of the universe, blessed is your crown and your place. May You love your people Israel forever..." [cf. Wisdom of the Zohar, III, 1037].

L. HOFFMAN (HISTORY)

"BLESSED IS THE NAME" (B'RIKH SH'MEIH): A MEDIEVAL KABBALISTIC ADDITION THAT PRAISES GOD FOR THE COMBINED TRAITS OF GREATNESS AND MERCY, RECAPITULATING THE THEMES OF 1A AND 1B.

[1] *"Blessed is the name"* An addition from the Zohar, the thirteenth-century kabbalistic compendium (*Vayakhel* 224; *Sulam* ed.) reputed to be the mystical teachings of Rabbi Shimon bar Yochai, a second-century authority, and his circle. The sixteenth-century mystic Isaac Luria introduced the custom of including it in the public service. At first it was said as a private meditation, but after 1600 it became standardized as public prayer.

According to the Zohar:

> Rabbi Shimon said: When the scroll of the Torah is removed [from the ark] to be read to the congregation, the heavenly gates of mercy are opened and love is aroused in the world above. [Here] a person must say the following, "Blessed is the name of the master of the universe, blessed is your crown and blessed is your place. May You love your people Israel forever..."

[1] בְּרִיךְ שְׁמֵהּ דְּמָרֵא עָלְמָא. בְּרִיךְ [2] כִּתְרָךְ וְאַתְרָךְ. [3] יְהֵא רְעוּתָךְ עִם עַמָּךְ יִשְׂרָאֵל לְעָלַם. [4] וּפֻרְקַן יְמִינָךְ אַחֲזִי לְעַמָּךְ בְּבֵית מַקְדְּשָׁךְ. [5] וּלְאַמְטוֹיֵי לָנָא מִטּוּב נְהוֹרָךְ. וּלְקַבֵּל צְלוֹתָנָא בְּרַחֲמִין. [6] יְהֵא רַעֲוָא קֳדָמָךְ דְּתוֹרִיךְ לָן חַיִּין בְּטִיבוּתָא.

Opening the ark thus not only reveals the scroll of the Torah but effectively reveals the divine. It makes God *physically* present. The words "your place" can be taken literally. God dwells, as it were, *in* the Torah. Drawing on this tradition, the Baal Shem Tov [*Siddur Baal Shem Tov*, p. 153, citing *Likkutei Dibburim*, vol. II, col. 226] taught, "If [even] a simple, ordinary Jew, in faithful devotion and purity of heart, recites this Aramaic passage, 'Blessed is the Name of the Master of the Universe, blessed is your crown and your place. May (p. 76)

The prayer thus seems to be connected to the potential of God's love that is held to be auspiciously present as we open the ark to receive the Torah. Indeed, in kabbalistic theology, that is exactly the case because we are replicating the Sinaitic revelation, which is the supreme act of love toward the Jewish People. At the same time, revelation presupposes God's transcendent, even frightening, might: When the (p. 76)

7 May I too be counted among the righteous, so that You show compassion toward me and watch over me and mine and all who are a part of your People Israel. 8 You are the One who feeds and sustains all. 9 You are the One who rules over kings, for dominion is yours. 10 I am the servant of the Holy Blessed One, before whom and before the glory of whose Torah I bow at all times. 11 I trust not in man and I rely on no angels, but in the God of heaven who is a God of truth and whose Torah is true and whose prophets are true and who performs many acts that are good and true. 12 In Him do I trust, and to his holy precious name I speak praise. 13 May it be your will that You open my heart to your Torah and fulfill the wishes of my heart and the heart of all your People Israel, for good, for life, and for peace. Amen.

7וְלֶהֱוֵי אֲנָא פְּקִידָא בְּגוֹ צַדִּיקַיָּא. לְמִרְחַם עָלַי וּלְמִנְטַר יָתִי וְיַת כָּל דִּי לִי וְדִי לְעַמָּךְ יִשְׂרָאֵל. 8אַנְתְּ הוּא זָן לְכֹלָּא וּמְפַרְנֵס לְכֹלָּא. 9אַנְתְּ הוּא שַׁלִּיט עַל כֹּלָּא. אַנְתְּ הוּא דְשַׁלִּיט עַל מַלְכַיָּא. וּמַלְכוּתָא דִּילָךְ הִיא. 10אֲנָא עַבְדָּא דְקֻדְשָׁא בְּרִיךְ הוּא דְּסָגִדְנָא קַמֵּהּ וּמִקַּמָּא דִיקַר אוֹרַיְתֵהּ בְּכָל עִדָּן וְעִדָּן. 11לָא עַל אֱנָשׁ רָחִצְנָא. וְלָא עַל בַּר אֱלָהִין סָמִכְנָא. אֶלָּא בֵּאלָהָא דִשְׁמַיָּא דְּהוּא אֱלָהָא קְשׁוֹט. וְאוֹרַיְתֵהּ קְשׁוֹט. וּנְבִיאוֹהִי קְשׁוֹט. וּמַסְגֵּא לְמֶעְבַּד טַבְוָן וּקְשׁוֹט. 12בֵּהּ אֲנָא רָחִץ. וְלִשְׁמֵהּ קַדִּישָׁא יַקִּירָא אֲנָא אֲמַר תֻּשְׁבְּחָן. 13יְהֵא רַעֲוָא קֳדָמָךְ דְּתִפְתַּח לִבִּי בְּאוֹרַיְתָא. וְתַשְׁלִים מִשְׁאֲלִין דְּלִבִּי וְלִבָּא דְכָל עַמָּךְ יִשְׂרָאֵל לְטָב וּלְחַיִּין וְלִשְׁלָם: אָמֵן.

BRETTLER (BIBLE)

(Exod. 15:12), proclaims, "Thy right hand, O Adonai, crushes the foe" (see Volume 3, *P'sukei D'zimrah*, p. 169). Psalm 118:15–16 similarly declares, "The right hand of Adonai is triumphant."

5 *"The goodness of your light"* The Bible portrays God's radiant face as a blessing, as we see from the priestly benediction (Num. 6:25–26) (see Volume 2, *The Amidah*, p. 179). Similarly, Psalm 67:2 asks God to "shine his face upon us," and Psalm 80:4 promises that if God "shines his face on us we will be saved." Jewish mystical texts, which tend toward anthropomorphism, regularly show similar interest in aspects of the divine body.

9 *"You are the One who rules over kings"* A reflection of the rabbinic term *melech malchei ham'lachim*, "king, king of kings," which first occurs, though in Aramaic *(malka melech malkaya)*, in Daniel 2:37.

[10] *"I am the servant"* In contrast to God, who, as we just saw, "rules over kings," we are just God's servants. This too is a stereotypical biblical image, especially in laments where supplicants call themselves God's "servant." In Psalm 69:18, for instance, the psalmist pleads, "Do not hide your face from your servant." Psalm 86:16 says, "Turn to me and have mercy on me; grant your strength to your servant and deliver the son of your maidservant."

[11] *"A God of truth [kshot]"* Emphasis on "truth" as a crucial divine attribute comes from Daniel 4:34, "So now I, Nebuchadnezzar, praise, exalt, and glorify the King of Heaven, all of whose works are just." The Aramaic word for "just" here is *k'shot,* the same word that we have in our prayer. Similarly, but in Hebrew, God's attributes in Exodus 34:6 include *emet,* "truth." Psalm 25:5, for instance, asks, "Guide me in your truth and teach me." Understandably, the prayer next categorizes God's "Torah which is true" and "the prophets who are true." A true God has true laws, as in Psalm 19:10, "The judgements of Adonai are true."

[12] *"To his holy precious name I speak praise"* The prayer ends with a repetition of the introductory theme praising God's holy name. The ending also provides a perfect bridge to the recitation of the *Sh'ma* and the two lines that follow it, which come next.

[13] *"For good, for life, and for peace"* These three attributes are associated with wisdom or Torah. Proverbs 3:2 promises, "[My torah] will bestow on you length of days, years of life and peace"; verse 14 adds, "The goodness of its value in trade is better than silver."

◆

DORFF (THEOLOGY)

of heaven who is a God of truth and whose Torah is true and whose prophets are true." This paragraph, with possibly some anti-Christian overtones, sets the stage for reading the Torah and the selection from the Prophets called the *haftarah,* the books that we identify as our source of truth and divine guidance. The worshiper thus asks God to "open my heart to your Torah" so that I may learn God's truths and values.

◆

ELLENSON (MODERN LITURGIES)

This legacy has not been limited to Reform Judaism. It is evident in all the other movements as well. While retaining elements of this prayer, the arch-rationalist Mordecai Kaplan offered several options to it in his 1945 Sabbath prayer book. *Va'ani T'fillati* (Israeli Conservative), too, also provides an alternative meditation calling for an end to the bloodshed and strife. Finally, some Orthodox congregations informed by the sensibility of the Mitnagdim, the opponents of the Chasidim, omitted this passage as too mystical as well. This attitude was common to the Lithuanian academies *(y'shivot)* of the past century.

———◆———

FRANKEL (A WOMAN'S VOICE)

is the ancient, mournful melody in which it is sung in most Ashkenazi synagogues, a slow dirge that aptly fits its message: we humbly and gratefully submit to God's will in the hope that God will grant the wishes of our heart. Perhaps its enigmatic words actually add to its power, the way darkness brightens the candle's flame.

———◆———

KUSHNER & POLEN (CHASIDISM)

You love your people Israel forever…,'" God fulfills his request, if not all of it, then, at least in some respect, in part.

[13] *"Open my heart to your Torah" [II Zohar 206a; Vayakhel 225 (Sulam ed.)]* We read in Deuteronomy 10:16, "And you shall circumcise the foreskin of your heart." Commenting on this, Rashi says that it refers to a kind of encapsulation or obstruction of the heart and its covering. Puzzled by the apparent redundancy of Rashi's mentioning both a "covering" and an "obstruction," the Baal Shem Tov (or BeSHT) explained it thus.

There are two kinds of spiritual impediments that must be removed from the heart. One refers to the thickening caused by sins. But this, in turn, creates a second kind wherein a person, already desensitized by his or her perverse behavior, now, in addition, refuses to even listen to the chastisements and loving rebuke of friends. This second form, suggests the BeShT, is what Rashi means by "covering." Just this is the foreskin that must be cut away in order for the heart to be open to holiness, and this is why we pray, "Open my heart to the Torah" (*Sefer Baal Shem Tov, Ekev,* p. 216, par. 29, s.v. *"u-maltem,"* from a letter by Barukh of Medzhibozh).

———◆———

L. HOFFMAN (HISTORY)

Torah was given, "Mount Sinai was all in smoke, since Adonai had come down upon it in fire; the smoke rose like the smoke of a kiln, and the whole mountain trembled violently" (Exod. 20:18). "Blessed be the name" therefore conjoins reference to God's regal might with God's gracious love.

[2] *"Your place"* Since this follows "your crown," commentators often assume "your place" must be "the place of your dominion," possibly the throne on which God sits, an image going back to mystical speculation of the second or third century. Alternatively, it might be the Torah itself (see Kushner and Polen's commentary)!

[3] *"May You love"* Literally, "May your will be with…" The Aramaic *r'uta* is the same as the Hebrew *ratson,* which can mean "will," "pleasure," or "love." Here, we translate "love," since, in context, it is God's love for Israel that is at stake.

[7] *"May I too be counted"* Until now, the prayer has emphasized God's might. Though the previous two sentences ask God to "reveal the salvation of your right hand…in mercy.… Prolong our lives in happiness" (an apparent reference to God's love), it is still God's power to show love that is at stake here. Appropriately, God is referred to as the God of all Israel (it is "our lives" that are to be saved), not the God of the individual.

That changes now. The individual now relates to God personally, asking "May *I* too be counted" among those who are saved by God's love. The final line, which is sung by the congregation, sums up the individual worshiper's needs: "May it be your will that You open my heart to your Torah and fulfill the wishes of my heart and the heart of all your People Israel, for good, for life, and for peace." At the end, then, the individual returns to a concern for the group. Having been included among the saved, the worshiper prays that others too may enjoy "the wishes of [their] heart" (see the following comment).

[13] *"May it be your will that You open my heart to your Torah and fulfill the wishes of my heart and the heart of all your People Israel, for good, for life, and for peace"* There is a connection here. As the ark is being opened at this point, we pray, "Open my heart to your Torah" — that is, the Torah that we are about to read. God's merciful love comes through Torah. Only by opening our hearts to it do we receive the benefits that follow: "good," "life," and "peace."

The original source contains yet another petition that is missing from almost all rites, although it is included here and there, usually in brackets by editors who seek to restore it to the liturgical version of the prayer because they notice it is "missing." The Zohar asks, "Grant me male [!] children to do your will."

◆ ◆ ◆

D. AFFIRMING GOD WHILE TAKING THE TORAH

I. "HEAR O ISRAEL"
(SH'MA YISRA'EL)

[Prayer leader takes the Torah and turns to face the congregation.]

1 Hear O Israel, Adonai is our God; Adonai is one.

[Prayer leader takes the Torah and turns to face the congregation.]

שְׁמַע יִשְׂרָאֵל יְיָ אֱלֹהֵינוּ יְיָ אֶחָד:[1]

II. "OUR GOD IS ONE"
(ECHAD ELOHEINU)

2 Our God is one. Our Lord is great. His name is holy.

אֶחָד אֱלֹהֵינוּ גָּדוֹל אֲדוֹנֵנוּ קָדוֹשׁ שְׁמוֹ.[2]

III. "PROCLAIM ADONAI'S GREATNESS"
(GADLU)

[Prayer leader turns back to face the ark and bows while saying the following:]

3 Proclaim Adonai's greatness with me, and let us exalt his name together.

[Prayer leader turns back to face the ark and bows while saying the following:]

גַּדְּלוּ לַיְיָ אִתִּי. וּנְרוֹמְמָה שְׁמוֹ יַחְדָּו:[3]

BRETTLER (BIBLE)

[1] *"Hear O Israel"* From Deuteronomy 6:4 (see Volume 1, *The Sh'ma and Its Blessings,* pp. 87–88).

[2] *"Our God is one"* A non-biblical sentence sandwiched in between two biblical verses. It continues the theme with which the previous verse ended: God is one! It then uses snippets of biblical verses to further describe this God. Psalm 147:5 says, *"Our Lord is great [gadol adoneinu] and full of power"*; Isaiah 57:15 proclaims, "Thus said He who, high aloft, forever dwells, and *whose name is holy."* The theme of God's greatness will now be repeated in the next two lines of the liturgy.

(p. 82)

DORFF (THEOLOGY)

[1] *"Hear O Israel"* Earlier in the liturgy, when all three paragraphs of the *Sh'ma* are recited, this line is chanted together while congregants and prayer leader face the ark. Here, in the Torah service, it is done antiphonally. The prayer leader holds the Torah and (facing the congregation) sings the verse; then the community repeats it. The same thing happens with the second sentence here ("Our God is one..."). The responsive face-to-face rendering of these lines makes them dramatically declarative: we *as a community* affirm the convictions contained in them.

Curiously, the liturgy here omits any reference to the Torah. At this point

(p. 82)

FRANKEL (A WOMAN'S VOICE)

[1] *"Hear O Israel"* Lifting the Torah from the ark and standing before the congregation, the prayer leader calls upon us to "pledge allegiance" by reciting the *Sh'ma,* our declaration of fealty. Even as we salute the Torah, the physical symbol of divine presence in our midst, we bear witness to God's uniqueness and indivisibility. So tied are we to our senses as the sole conduits of both heaven and earth that we need to remind ourselves constantly that God stands here before us in name *(shem)* alone. The Torah is only a placeholder.

(p. 82)

D. AFFIRMING GOD WHILE TAKING THE TORAH

[Prayer leader takes the Torah and turns to face the congregation.]

[1] Hear O Israel, Adonai is our God; Adonai is one.

[2] Our God is one. Our Lord is great. His name is holy.

[Prayer leader turns back to face the ark and bows while saying the following:]

[3] Proclaim Adonai's greatness with me, and let us exalt his name together.

HAUPTMAN (TALMUD)

[1] *"Hear O Israel"* Although the *Sh'ma* and Its Blessings have already been read in the early part of *Shacharit,* we now recite at least the first verse of the *Sh'ma* again. At this dramatic moment in the service it seems appropriate to repeat our confession of faith and our belief in the oneness of God, the giver of Torah. Could this repetition be triggered by the need to publicly repudiate the basic tenets of other religions? Yes, the ongoing emphasis on the oneness of God and the truthfulness of his prophets suggests that the

(p. 83)

LANDES (HALAKHAH)

1, 1 *"Hear O Israel…greatness, power, glory, victory, and majesty are yours [p. 85]"*

The Torah is taken out by someone entitled the *motsi* ("the one who takes out"), who in turn hands it to the prayer leader (the *sh'liakh tsibur,* or *shatz*). The *shatz* lifts the Torah slightly three times: at each of *Sh'ma* ("Hear O Israel"), *Echad eloheinu* ("Our God is one"), and *Gadlu* ("Proclaim Adonai's greatness"). With great pomp and ceremony, the *shatz* proclaims these three biblical verses,

[Prayer leader takes the Torah and turns to face the congregation.]

שְׁמַ֖ע יִשְׂרָאֵל֙ יְיָ אֱלֹהֵ֫ינוּ יְיָ אֶחָֽד׃¹

אֶחָד֙ אֱלֹהֵ֫ינוּ גָּדוֹל אֲדוֹנֵ֫נוּ קָדוֹשׁ שְׁמֽוֹ׃²

[Prayer leader turns back to face the ark and bows while saying the following:]

גַּדְּלוּ לַיְיָ אִתִּ֑י׃ וּנְרוֹמְמָה שְׁמוֹ יַחְדָּֽו׃³

which declare God's oneness and greatness. The community repeats the first two of these verses after the *shatz.* Only the *shatz* says the *Gadlu.* After the *shatz* says the *Gadlu,* everyone sings *l'kha* ("Greatness, power, glory, victory, and majesty are yours") in unison.

Even though Torah reading takes place within the framework of the morning prayers, it is technically a separate part of the service, so the *shatz* for the morning service proper has no necessary role in the Torah liturgy (*Magen Avraham* 147:2, quoting Mordecai ben Hillel   (p. 83)

L. HOFFMAN (HISTORY)

HAVING PRAISED GOD, WE MOVE ON TO TAKE THE TORAH FROM THE ARK, ACCEPTING IT INTO THE COMMUNITY WITH AFFIRMATION OF THE GOD WHO GAVE IT. THREE STACCATO STATEMENTS PUNCTUATE THIS PART OF THE INTRODUCTION, BEGINNING WITH THE FAMILIAR SH'MA ("HEAR O ISRAEL…") AND CULMINATING IN THE INVITATION TO THE COMMUNITY TO PRAISE GOD TOGETHER.

1–2 *"Hear O Israel…"* These proclamations of God's unity and greatness appear (albeit in somewhat different form) in the eighth-century work *Massekhet Sofrim.* Despite a few additions here and there, most of what we have from the very   (p. 83)

J. HOFFMAN (TRANSLATION)

1 *"Hear O Israel"* See comments in Volume 1, *The Sh'ma and Its Blessings,* pp. 87, 91.

2 *"Our God is one"* We have a word play with the end of the prior line, "Adonai is one," which is then followed in deliberate reverse word order here, "One is our God." Others therefore translate this precisely as "One is our God." But while this reverse word order is common in Hebrew, it is awkward in English, so we resort to more common word order at the expense of losing the inversion of word order from the preceding line.

3 *"Proclaim Adonai's greatness"* Birnbaum has "exalt the Lord," but that translation misses what seems to be a deliberate repetition of the   (p. 84)

INTRODUCTION

BRETTLER (BIBLE)

[3] *"Proclaim Adonai's greatness [gadlu] with me, and let us exalt [un'rom'mah] his name together"* From Psalm 34:4, a psalm with wisdom elements. In its original setting, it is difficult to determine who the psalmist is addressing; or why, suddenly, in the midst of his own meditation, he invites unknown parties to join him in praising God. It is a perfect verse for our Siddur, however, as it continues the last line's theme of God's greatness [*gadol adonienu* —"our Lord is great"] and invites the congregational response that follows, and which begins by again asserting God's "greatness" (*g'dulah* is the noun, "greatness"; *gadol* is the adjective, "great").

—◆—

DORFF (THEOLOGY)

in the service, when we are removing the Torah from the ark in order to honor it and learn from it, we would expect the liturgy to feature biblical verses that speak about the Torah. Instead, the liturgy reminds us that God is one and unique, and that God possesses "greatness, power, glory, victory, and majesty…along with everything in heaven and on earth." It may be that the Rabbis wanted to guarantee that we worship God, the Torah's author and the source of its authority, rather than the Torah itself. (Some Sefardi liturgies, though, after these introductory lines and before the Torah reading, have the leader lift the Torah, show it to the congregation opened to the place where the reading will begin, and say the sentence that will be repeated when the Torah is lifted and dressed after the reading, namely, "This is the Torah that Moses put before the children of Israel, dictated by God and transcribed by Moses.")

[3] *"Proclaim Adonai's greatness with me"* Though the leader faced the community in declaiming the first two sentences, he or she now turns to the ark, bows (as do we all) for the first part of this sentence, "Proclaim Adonai's greatness with me," and then resumes an upright posture (as we do too) upon reaching the middle words, "and let us exalt his name together." Our body language thus communicates both our subservience to God's greatness and our role as partners with God in exalting God's name through our words and actions.

—◆—

FRANKEL (A WOMAN'S VOICE)

The mystery of divine manifestation is explored further in the next paragraph, where we encounter language familiar from the kabbalists' lexicon. As the Torah circulates in our midst we acknowledge the many faces of divine revelation, characterized by Jewish mysticism as *s'firot*, divine emanations: *g'dulah, g'vurah, tiferet, netzach, hod, malkhut.* So the elusive nature of divine revelation takes on yet another dimension: from physical symbol to disembodied name, from unity to multiplicity. What better way to characterize what happened so many centuries ago at Sinai, on God's holy mountain *(har kodsho),* when God was revealed through seventy faces in seventy tongues?

◆

Hauptman (Talmud)

authors of these prayers were trying to discredit the truth of other religions and their prophets.

3 *"Proclaim Adonai's greatness with me"* After reciting the *Sh'ma* and "Our God is one" *(echad eloheinu),* a line that yet again describes God's oneness, the prayer leader recites a verse from Psalms 34:4, inviting the congregation to "proclaim God's greatness" and "exalt his name." The verse is perfectly chosen, because at this moment the Torah is about to be circulated among the congregants. The verse appears in the Talmud in a different but related context. It is from this verse that the Talmud (Ber. 45a) derives the lesson that when three or more people dine together, they are obligated to recite the *Birkat hamazon* (Grace after Meals) together, beginning with a *zimmun,* an invitation to join in the prayer. Since *gadlu* ("proclaim") is in the plural but *itti* ("with me") is in the singular, this verse describes, at the very least, one person turning to two others and asking them to join in praise of God. And that is exactly what both the *Birkat hamazon* and the Torah reading are all about.

◆

Landes (Halakhah)

Hakohen, Germany, 1240–1298). Nonetheless, we customarily give the same *shatz* the honor of transporting the Torah from the Holy Ark to the *shulchan* (Torah-reading table).

◆

L. Hoffman (History)

beginning of the service can be found there, including what looks like an alternative form of the *Kaddish:* "May the name of the King over the kings of kings be made great *(al hakol)*" (see below). In our current rite, we say all this material before reading Torah, then read Torah, and then raise the Torah on high *(hagbahah)* and say "This is the Torah," etcetera *(Zot hatorah...).* The rabbinic prototype in *Massekhet Sofrim* seems to suggest that originally, they did *hagbahah* and said these words *before*, not *after* reading Torah — just as the Sefardi practice is to this day, possibly influenced by this reading of *Massekhet Sofrim*. But then we wonder why the *maftir*, the person who reads the *Haftarah*, does all this. The traditional reason — as a sop to compensate for awarding the *maftir* the minor honor of reading *Haftarah*, not the major one of reading Torah — is at least suspect, since there is no evidence for it. It may be, then, that all this material that we normally take to be part of removing the Torah from the ark was originally what they did when they put the Torah back in! Our text tells us that the *maftir* began with *Ashre* (Psalm 145). Indeed, if we imagine that the *maftir* had just read the *Haftarah*, and if we look at the service thereafter, we see that *Ashre* does indeed follow the full Torah liturgy as we have it. Perhaps, originally, then, the *maftir* finished the *Haftarah* and then conducted the rest of the service, since he was already at the *bimah*. He began with *Ashre*, then said "There is no God like You" (our opening lines above) and ran through most of the service that we now have as an introduction, but that Jews originally used as a conclusion to the Torah reading.

³ *"Proclaim Adonai's greatness with me"*

⁵, ¹⁰ *"Adonai's Torah…Adonai will bless his people with peace"* [p. 95] These two liturgical staples, though separated, belong conceptually together. They show us the extent to which medieval Jews saw their Torah ritual as replicating ancient models of celebrating God's revelation. A twelfth-century commentary (*Tosafot* to Meg. 32b) notes that the Hebrew for "Proclaim Adonai's greatness" contain six words, and from "Adonai's Torah" to "with peace" is forty words. 2 Samuel 6:13, which describes David's moving of the ark to Jerusalem, says that it was carried six paces, after which David stopped, sacrificed to God, and danced for joy. Also, it took forty days and nights for Torah to be revealed in the first place. Our praise of God, then, collapses time, carrying us back (via the forty words) to the forty days and nights at Sinai and (via the six words) to the movement of the ark to Jerusalem. At one and the same time, we are at Sinai with Moses, at Jerusalem with David, and here in our own sanctuary with the same Torah, celebrating in our own way.

———◆———

J. HOFFMAN (TRANSLATION)

Hebrew root *g.d.l*, first in the prior line ("[Our Lord is] great") and then here ("[Proclaim Adonai's] greatness"). The word *shem* ("name") is likewise repeated: "His name is holy" followed by "Let us exalt his name."

³ *"Exalt"* Others: "extol."

——————◆ ◆ ◆——————

E. The *Hakafah*: Taking the Torah to the Reader's Stand: "Greatness, power, glory... are yours" (*L'kha Adonai*)

[1] Greatness, power, glory, victory, and majesty are yours, Adonai, along with everything in heaven and on earth. [2] Dominion and sovereignty above all leaders are yours, Adonai. [3] Exalt Adonai our God, and bow down toward his footstool; He is holy. [4] Exalt Adonai our God, and bow down at his holy mountain, for Adonai our God is holy.

[5] May the name of the King over the kings of kings be made great, holy, praised, glorified, exalted, and extolled above all in the worlds that He created— [6] this world and the world to come— [7] according to his will and according to the will of those who fear Him and according to the will of the entire house of Israel. [8] Rock of every world, master of every creature, God of every soul, who dwells in the expanse of the high heavens and inhabits the loftiest heavens of old— [9] his holiness dwarfs the celestial beings, and his holiness dwarfs the throne of glory. [10] Similarly, your name will be sanctified through us, Adonai our God, before the sight of all the living. [11] Let us sing a new song before Him, as it is written: [12] sing to God, sing out his name. [13] Pave the way for the one who rides where the sun sets—his name being Yah—and rejoice before Him. [14] We will each see Him with our own eyes when He returns to his abode, [15] as it is written: "For they will see the return of Adonai to Zion with their own eyes." [16] And it is also said, "Adonai's glory will be revealed, and all shall see together that Adonai has spoken."

[1] לְךָ יְיָ הַגְּדֻלָּה וְהַגְּבוּרָה וְהַתִּפְאֶרֶת וְהַנֵּצַח וְהַהוֹד. כִּי כֹל בַּשָּׁמַיִם וּבָאָרֶץ [2] לְךָ יְיָ הַמַּמְלָכָה וְהַמִּתְנַשֵּׂא לְכֹל לְרֹאשׁ: [3] רוֹמְמוּ יְיָ אֱלֹהֵינוּ וְהִשְׁתַּחֲווּ לַהֲדֹם רַגְלָיו קָדוֹשׁ הוּא: [4] רוֹמְמוּ יְיָ אֱלֹהֵינוּ וְהִשְׁתַּחֲווּ לְהַר קָדְשׁוֹ כִּי קָדוֹשׁ יְיָ אֱלֹהֵינוּ:

[5] עַל הַכֹּל יִתְגַּדַּל וְיִתְקַדַּשׁ וְיִשְׁתַּבַּח וְיִתְפָּאַר וְיִתְרוֹמַם וְיִתְנַשֵּׂא. שְׁמוֹ שֶׁל־מֶלֶךְ מַלְכֵי הַמְּלָכִים הַקָּדוֹשׁ בָּרוּךְ הוּא. בָּעוֹלָמוֹת שֶׁבָּרָא. [6] הָעוֹלָם הַזֶּה וְהָעוֹלָם הַבָּא. [7] כִּרְצוֹנוֹ וְכִרְצוֹן יְרֵאָיו וְכִרְצוֹן כָּל־בֵּית יִשְׂרָאֵל. [8] צוּר הָעוֹלָמִים אֲדוֹן כָּל־הַבְּרִיּוֹת אֱלוֹהַּ כָּל־הַנְּפָשׁוֹת. הַיּוֹשֵׁב בְּמֶרְחֲבֵי מָרוֹם הַשּׁוֹכֵן בִּשְׁמֵי שְׁמֵי קֶדֶם. [9] קְדֻשָּׁתוֹ עַל־הַחַיּוֹת וּקְדֻשָּׁתוֹ עַל־כִּסֵּא הַכָּבוֹד. [10] וּבְכֵן יִתְקַדַּשׁ שִׁמְךָ בָּנוּ יְיָ אֱלֹהֵינוּ לְעֵינֵי כָּל־חָי. [11] וְנֹאמַר לְפָנָיו שִׁיר חָדָשׁ כַּכָּתוּב. [12] שִׁירוּ לֵאלֹהִים זַמְּרוּ שְׁמוֹ [13] סֹלּוּ לָרֹכֵב בָּעֲרָבוֹת בְּיָהּ שְׁמוֹ וְעִלְזוּ לְפָנָיו: [14] וְנִרְאֵהוּ עַיִן בְּעַיִן בְּשׁוּבוֹ אֶל נָוֵהוּ כַּכָּתוּב: [15] כִּי עַיִן בְּעַיִן יִרְאוּ בְּשׁוּב יְיָ צִיּוֹן: [16] וְנֶאֱמַר וְנִגְלָה כְּבוֹד

יְיָ וְרָאוּ כָל־בָּשָׂר יַחְדָּו. כִּי פִּי יְיָ
דִּבֵּר:

[17]אַב הָרַחֲמִים הוּא יְרַחֵם עַם
עֲמוּסִים וְיִזְכּוֹר בְּרִית אֵתָנִים וְיַצִּיל
נַפְשׁוֹתֵינוּ מִן־הַשָּׁעוֹת הָרָעוֹת וְיִגְעַר
בְּיֵצֶר הָרַע מִן הַנְּשׂוּאִים [18]וְיָחֹן אֹתָנוּ
לִפְלֵיטַת עוֹלָמִים וִימַלֵּא מִשְׁאֲלוֹתֵינוּ
בְּמִדָּה טוֹבָה יְשׁוּעָה וְרַחֲמִים:

[17]May the father of mercy have mercy on those He has upheld and remember the covenant with the patriarchs and save us from bad times and banish the evil inclination from those He has carried, [18]and grace us with eternal salvation and generously answer our prayers for salvation and mercy.

BRETTLER (BIBLE)

[1] *"Greatness [g'dulah], power, glory, victory, and majesty"* This unusually long list of God's attributes (1 Chron. 29:11) fits perfectly here, since the first of them, "greatness" *(g'dulah)*, reiterates the "greatness" theme of the previous two liturgical lines.

[3, 4] *"Exalt [rom'mu] Adonai our God.... Exalt [rom'mu] Adonai our God"* Two lines back, when the liturgy said, "Proclaim Adonai's greatness *[gadlu]* with me, and let us exalt *[un'rom'mah]* his name together," it invoked a common biblical pairing of words: "to be great" *(g.d.l)* and to exalt *(r.u.m)*. The liturgy first expands on the first term, "Proclaim[ing] God's greatness *[gadlu]*" by

(p. 91)

DORFF (THEOLOGY)

[1] *"Greatness, power…are yours, Adonai"* As the cantor and congregation sing these lines, the cantor carries the Torah around the congregation, beginning on his or her right as he or she turns to face the congregation. As the Torah approaches, it is common for people to touch it with the fringes on their *tallit* or with their prayer book and then to kiss the fringe or the prayer book, or, in some congregations, to kiss the Torah mantle itself. This procession with the Torah thus graphically symbolizes several important convictions of Judaism: that the Torah belongs to the people as a whole, not to the religious elite alone; that through touching it we indicate that we subscribe to it and affirm its importance for our lives; and that

through kissing it, directly or indirectly, we proclaim that we see it as a great gift.

———◆———

E. THE *HAKAFAH:* TAKING THE TORAH TO THE READER'S STAND

[1] Greatness, power, glory, victory, and majesty are yours, Adonai, along with everything in heaven and on earth. [2] Dominion and sovereignty above all leaders are yours, Adonai. [3] Exalt Adonai our God, and bow down toward his footstool; He is holy. [4] Exalt Adonai our God, and bow down at his holy mountain, for Adonai our God is holy.

[1] *"Greatness, power..."* See above, p. 81.

THE HAKAFAH: *THE COMMUNITY RESPONDS WITH COMMUNAL PRAISE AS THE TORAH IS CARRIED THROUGH THE CONGREGATION TO THE READER'S DESK, IN ORDER TO BE READ IN THE MIDST OF THE PEOPLE.*

לְךָ יְיָ הַגְּדֻלָּה וְהַגְּבוּרָה וְהַתִּפְאֶרֶת וְהַנֵּצַח וְהַהוֹד. [1]
כִּי כֹל בַּשָּׁמַיִם וּבָאָרֶץ לְךָ יְיָ הַמַּמְלָכָה וְהַמִּתְנַשֵּׂא [2]
לְכֹל לְרֹאשׁ: רוֹמְמוּ יְיָ אֱלֹהֵינוּ וְהִשְׁתַּחֲווּ לַהֲדֹם [3]
רַגְלָיו קָדוֹשׁ הוּא: רוֹמְמוּ יְיָ אֱלֹהֵינוּ וְהִשְׁתַּחֲווּ [4]
לְהַר קָדְשׁוֹ כִּי קָדוֹשׁ יְיָ אֱלֹהֵינוּ:

J. HOFFMAN (TRANSLATION)
[2] *"Sovereignty above all leaders [hamitnasei l'khol l'rosh]"* The Hebrew here is confusing. Our translation represents one possibility. Birnbaum's "Yours, O Lord, is the kingdom, and [You are] supreme over all" represents another. As above, the trope supports our translation. Either way, it is not entirely clear how the final two words (*l'khol l'rosh*) are syntactic, raising the possibility that we have all misunderstood something here.

[3] *"Bow down"* Birnbaum: "worship."

[3] *"Footstool"* Probably a metaphor for the Temple, as in Lamentations 2:1: "He did not remember his footstool in his day of wrath."

(p. 92)

⁵May the name of the King over the kings of kings be made great, holy, praised, glorified, exalted, and extolled above all in the worlds that He created— ⁶this world and the world to come— ⁷according to his will and according to the will of those who fear Him and according to the will of the entire house of Israel. ⁸Rock of every world, master of every creature, God of every soul, who dwells in the expanse of the high heavens and inhabits the loftiest heavens of old— ⁹his holiness dwarfs the celestial beings, and his holiness dwarfs the throne of glory. ¹⁰Similarly, your name will be sanctified through us, Adonai our God, before the sight of all the living. ¹¹Let us sing a new song before Him, as it is written: ¹²sing to God, sing out his name. ¹³Pave the way for the one who rides where the sun sets—his name being Yah—and rejoice before Him. ¹⁴We will each see Him with our own eyes when He returns to his abode, ¹⁵as it is written: "For they will see the return of Adonai to Zion with their own eyes." ¹⁶And it is also said, "Adonai's glory will be revealed, and all shall see together that Adonai has spoken."

¹⁷May the father of mercy have mercy on those He has upheld and remember the covenant with the

עַל הַכֹּל יִתְגַּדַּל וְיִתְקַדַּשׁ וְיִשְׁתַּבַּח⁵ וְיִתְפָּאַר וְיִתְרוֹמַם וְיִתְנַשֵּׂא. שְׁמוֹ שֶׁל־מֶלֶךְ מַלְכֵי הַמְּלָכִים הַקָּדוֹשׁ בָּרוּךְ הוּא. בָּעוֹלָמוֹת שֶׁבָּרָא. הָעוֹלָם הַזֶּה וְהָעוֹלָם הַבָּא.⁶ כִּרְצוֹנוֹ⁷ וְכִרְצוֹן יְרֵאָיו וְכִרְצוֹן כָּל־בֵּית יִשְׂרָאֵל. צוּר הָעוֹלָמִים אֲדוֹן כָּל־⁸ הַבְּרִיּוֹת אֱלוֹהַּ כָּל־הַנְּפָשׁוֹת. הַיּוֹשֵׁב בְּמֶרְחֲבֵי מָרוֹם הַשּׁוֹכֵן בִּשְׁמֵי שְׁמֵי קֶדֶם. קְדֻשָּׁתוֹ עַל־הַחַיּוֹת וּקְדֻשָּׁתוֹ⁹ עַל־כִּסֵּא הַכָּבוֹד. וּבְכֵן יִתְקַדַּשׁ¹⁰ שִׁמְךָ בָּנוּ יְיָ אֱלֹהֵינוּ לְעֵינֵי כָּל־חָי. וְנֹאמַר לְפָנָיו שִׁיר חָדָשׁ כַּכָּתוּב.¹¹ שִׁירוּ לֵאלֹהִים זַמְּרוּ שְׁמוֹ¹² סֹלּוּ¹³ לָרוֹכֵב בָּעֲרָבוֹת בְּיָהּ שְׁמוֹ וְעִלְזוּ לְפָנָיו: וְנִרְאֵהוּ עַיִן בְּעַיִן בְּשׁוּבוֹ¹⁴ אֶל נָוֵהוּ כַּכָּתוּב: כִּי עַיִן בְּעַיִן יִרְאוּ¹⁵ בְּשׁוּב יְיָ צִיּוֹן: וְנֶאֱמַר וְנִגְלָה כְּבוֹד¹⁶ יְיָ וְרָאוּ כָל־בָּשָׂר יַחְדָּו. כִּי פִּי יְיָ דִּבֵּר:

אַב הָרַחֲמִים הוּא יְרַחֵם עַם¹⁷ עֲמוּסִים וְיִזְכּוֹר בְּרִית אֵתָנִים וְיַצִּיל נַפְשׁוֹתֵינוּ מִן־הַשָּׁעוֹת הָרָעוֹת וְיִגְעַר

patriarchs and save us from bad times and banish the evil inclination from those He has carried, [18] and grace us with eternal salvation and generously answer our prayers for salvation and mercy.

בְּיֵצֶר הָרַע מִן הַנְּשׂוּאִים [18] וְיָחֹן אֹתָנוּ לִפְלֵיטַת עוֹלָמִים וִימַלֵּא מִשְׁאֲלוֹתֵינוּ בְּמִדָּה טוֹבָה יְשׁוּעָה וְרַחֲמִים:

BRETTLER (BIBLE)

citing 1 Chronicles 29:11, which attributed "greatness [g'dulah]" to God. Now, immediately afterward, we find Psalm 99:5, 9, which extends the second theme, "let us exalt [un'rom'mah] his name together."

[5] *"Above all"* Another post-biblical prayer lauding God's magnificence. The first part is constructed from predominantly rabbinic and mystical ideas, but it draws on the Bible with "inhabits the ancient highest heavens," which is a minor modification of Psalm 68:34, "who rides the ancient highest heavens."

[11] *"Let us sing a new song before Him, as it is written"* A bridge from the previous non-biblical section, which adduces biblical support for what has just been said. The idea of a "new song" is thoroughly biblical. It appears in Isaiah 42:10 and six more times in the Book of Psalms (e.g., Ps. 33:3).

[12] *"Sing to God"* Psalm 68:5. Psalm 68, one of the most difficult psalms to understand, was just cited ("who rides the ancient highest heavens"). This, and the two verses cited below, describe God as visible; the desired result of this prayer is for God to be clearly manifest.

[15] *"See the return of Adonai to Zion with their own eyes"* Isaiah 52:8, emphasizing God's visible return to Zion, a theme raised earlier ("Favor Zion with your goodness" and "Torah shall come forth from Zion"). The broader context of the verse, and the overarching theme of this entire liturgical unit, is God's kingship (Isa. 52:7, "Your God has become king"). The liturgy takes verses concerning the return to Zion after the destruction of the First Temple and applies them to the anticipated Third Temple.

[16] *"It is also said, 'Adonai's glory will be revealed'"* Isaiah 40:5, a universalistic verse, emphasizing that "*all* people" will "see" God.

[17] *"Father of mercy"* A final meditation, which again invokes God as "merciful father" (based on Psalm 103:13; see above, p. 53). Again, we find non-biblical ideas (like the "evil inclination") combined with biblical conceptions, like God's obligation to remember the "covenant." Psalm 74:20, for instance, asks God, "Look to the covenant!"

J. Hoffman (Translation)

[4] *"At his holy mountain"* Artscroll's "to" is almost certainly wrong.

[5] *"King over the kings of kings"* Translated more or less literally. Other emperors may have been the "kings of kings," so God was King over them. "King of kings of kings" would be more accurate but harder to read.

[5] *"Great, holy, praised, glorified, exalted, and extolled"* As elsewhere, the fact that many words are used in series is more important than the precise meaning of any of the individual words.

[5] *"Above all"* "Above all" modifies the entire series of verbs — a fact that is clear in the Hebrew, because the words for "above all" *(al hakol)* start the sentence in which the verbs are found.

[8] *"Every world [olamot]"* The Hebrew *olamot* expresses both spatial and temporal expanse, and thus means both "world" and "eternity." In other contexts, we usually translate this as "eternity," but here, coming after a description of the worlds that God created, the emphasis is likely on "this world" and "the next world" (the "world-to-come").

[8] *"Soul [nefesh]"* We lack a good word for *nefesh* in English because *nefesh* is both the ethereal and the physical life force. For a longer discussion, see Volume 1, *The Sh'ma and Its Blessings,* pp. 100, 102.

[8] *"The expanse of the high heavens [merchavei marom]"* Literally, "expanses of the high [place]," a particularly poetic phrase, involving both imagery and alliteration, which we try to capture in our translation of "high heavens." "The great expanse" also comes to mind, but seems too colloquial. Artscroll's "the expanses on high" has a nice ring to it. Birnbaum's "wide extended heights" captures the meaning but falls short on poetic impact.

[8] *"The loftiest heavens of old"* More literally, "the heavens of the heavens of old," but "heavens of the heavens" probably means "highest heavens." We don't want to use "high" here because we just used it above for *marom,* so, following Artscroll ("the loftiest primeval heavens") we resort to "loftiest."

[9] *"His holiness dwarfs"* Literally, "is on." The question here is whether "his holiness" is literally or figuratively "above the throne of glory." Birnbaum suggests "is above," presumably because he treats the phrase literally. We use a verb suggesting a figurative meaning. Artscroll's "is upon" doesn't seem to make sense in either case.

[10] *"Similarly [uv'khen]"* Or perhaps "nonetheless."

[10] *"Through us"* Or "among us."

[11] *"Sing"* Literally, "say."

[12] *"Sing out"* From the root *z.m.r,* translated elsewhere herein as "play instruments." (Birnbaum's "praise" perhaps reflects an understanding that the songs were to be songs of praise.) Artscroll gives us "make music for his Name," in accord with "play

instruments," but the exact connotation of the word is less important than the fact that the two words, *shiru* and *zamru*, appear in parallel phrases one after the other.

[13]*"Pave the way"* See Volume 1, *The Sh'ma and Its Blessings,* pp. 37–38.

[14]*"We will each see Him with our own eyes"* Literally, "see Him eye by eye" and often translated "eye to eye." Artscroll opts for "with a perceptive view," presumably to help the text accord with the theological presumption that we cannot ever see God eye to eye, but the original quotation from Isaiah 52:8 (immediately below) makes it clear that "each with his own eye" is the original intent.

[16]*"Also"* "Also" is absent in the Hebrew.

[16]*"All [khol basar] shall see"* Literally, "all flesh." As for "see," our translation reflects the most likely possible interpretation of the Hebrew, namely, that all shall see that God has spoken. Birnbaum opts for the other possibility, that all shall see Adonai's glory revealed.

[16]*"Has spoken"* Literally, "Adonai's mouth has spoken."

[17]*"May the father of mercy have mercy"* The root for "mercy" both times is *r.ch.m,* sometimes translated "mercy," other times "compassion" or even "love." Curiously, both Artscroll ("father of compassion, have mercy") and Birnbaum ("merciful father have compassion") switch off between "mercy" and "compassion," though not consistently.

[17]*"Those He has upheld [amusim]"* The two metaphors, "those He has upheld" and "those He has carried," below, are taken from Isaiah 46:3.

[17]*"Patriarchs [eitanim]"* In accord with Birnbaum. The Hebrew *eitanim,* literally "the strong [ones]," is probably an epithet for the patriarchs.

[17]*"Save us [nafshoteinu]"* Usually translated "literally" as "our souls." But (see above, "Soul") "soul" does not really convey the same import as *nefesh.*

[17]*"Bad times"* Literally, "the bad hours." "Hour" is often used for "time," but the appearance of the word "the" here is surprising. Probably something specific, perhaps even superstitious, was intended.

[17]*"Banish"* Literally, "scold." Birnbaum has "check" and Artscroll has "upbraid."

[18]*"Eternal salvation [pleitat olamim]"* The Hebrew *pleitah* has the original meaning of "escape." It is one of the rarer words for "salvation."

[18]*"Answer [y'malei mish'aloteinu]"* Y'malei is literally "fill," often translated as "fulfill." But "fulfill our prayers" isn't English. The object, *mish'aloteinu,* is translated by Birnbaum as "petitions" and by Artscroll as "requests." This is not the usual word for "prayer," and probably a specific type of prayer was intended, but for reasons of translation we opt for the more familiar "prayers."

[18]*"For salvation and mercy"* The words "salvation" and "mercy" hang at the end of the Hebrew sentence, seemingly ungrammatically. From context, we can guess at two

possible meanings. We opt here to make the two words modify "our prayers," which are "for salvation and mercy." Alternatively, these words may have adverbial force, describing *how* God answers our prayers: i.e., God does so "in salvation and mercy."

◆ ◆ ◆

2 | *Reading Torah*

The *Aliyot*

A. SUMMONING THE *ALIYOT:* "MAY HE HELP, SHIELD, AND SAVE" (*V'A'AZOR V'YAGEN*)

[The Torah is placed on the shulchan (the reading desk) and unrolled to the right passage. Congregants may be seated.]

[1] May He help, shield, and save all who trust in Him, and let us say: Amen. [2] Let us all ascribe greatness to our God, and give honor to the Torah. [3] Let the *kohen* approach. Come forward [name], the *kohen*. [4] Blessed is the One who gave the Torah to his people in holiness.

[5] Adonai's Torah is pure, reviving the soul.

[6] Adonai's testimony is sure, educating the simple.

[7] Adonai's laws are just, delighting the heart.

[8] Adonai's command is clear, lighting the eyes.

[9] Adonai will give strength to his people. [10] Adonai will bless his people with peace.

[11] God's way is pure, and Adonai's word is clear. [12] He protects all who seek refuge in Him. [13] All you who cling to Adonai your God are alive today.

[The Torah is placed on the shulchan (the reading desk) and unrolled to the right passage. Congregants may be seated.]

[1] וְיַעֲזֹר וְיָגֵן וְיוֹשִׁיעַ לְכָל הַחוֹסִים בּוֹ וְנֹאמַר אָמֵן: [2] הַכֹּל הָבוּ גֹדֶל לֵאלֹהֵינוּ וּתְנוּ כָבוֹד לַתּוֹרָה: [3] כֹּהֵן קְרָב. [name] יַעֲמֹד הַכֹּהֵן: בָּרוּךְ שֶׁנָּתַן תּוֹרָה לְעַמּוֹ יִשְׂרָאֵל בִּקְדֻשָּׁתוֹ:

[5] תּוֹרַת יְיָ תְּמִימָה מְשִׁיבַת נָפֶשׁ

[6] עֵדוּת יְיָ נֶאֱמָנָה מַחְכִּימַת פֶּתִי:

[7] פִּקּוּדֵי יְיָ יְשָׁרִים מְשַׂמְּחֵי לֵב

[8] מִצְוַת יְיָ בָּרָה מְאִירַת עֵינָיִם:

[9] יְיָ עֹז לְעַמּוֹ יִתֵּן [10] יְיָ יְבָרֵךְ אֶת עַמּוֹ בַשָּׁלוֹם:

[11] הָאֵל תָּמִים דַּרְכּוֹ אִמְרַת יְיָ צְרוּפָה. [12] מָגֵן הוּא לְכָל הַחוֹסִים בּוֹ: [13] וְאַתֶּם הַדְּבֵקִים בַּיְיָ אֱלֹהֵיכֶם חַיִּים כֻּלְּכֶם הַיּוֹם:

BRETTLER (BIBLE)

[1] *"May He help, shield, and save all who trust in Him"* This introductory hope is not quoted from the Bible but is biblical in conception and vocabulary. Images of God as "helper," "shield," and "savior" for those who "trust in Him" predominate in the psalms. Psalm 18:3, for instance, describes God "in whom I trust" as "my shield, my mighty savior." The psalms may have meant taking refuge in the Temple, God's house, but here it has metaphorical meaning: taking refuge in God through Torah.

[2] *"Let us all ascribe greatness to our God, and give honor to the Torah"* The first part of the line is from Deuteronomy 32:3, "I proclaim the name of *(p. 98)*

DORFF (THEOLOGY)

[3] *"Let the kohen approach. . ."* One of the two *gabbai'im*, the people who orchestrate the reading of the Torah and check to ensure that the Torah reader reads the words correctly, calls up the first person to recite the blessings surrounding the reading. Being called to the Torah in this way is *(p. 98)*

ELLENSON (MODERN LITURGIES)

[3] *"Come forward…the kohen"* As Reform Judaism has consistently opposed prayers that call for the restoration of the sacrificial cult in a rebuilt Temple, it has rejected the notion of priestly prerogatives. Most Reform prayer books have therefore dropped the practice of calling a man of *(p. 100)*

FRANKEL (A WOMAN'S VOICE)

[1] *"May He help, shield, and save"* Throughout these introductory sections leading up to our reading from the Torah scroll, we alternate continuously between referring to God in second person and third person. Immediately after pledging our loyalty to God in the *Sh'ma*, we become intimate: *l'kha Adonai*, "to You everything belongs." Then we instantly pull back, retreating from the awesome holy mountain expressly forbidden to us. Then, emboldened by our own extravagant praise of God, familiar to us from the *Kaddish* — *yitgadal v'yitkadash*

A. SUMMONING THE *ALIYOT*

[The Torah is placed on the shulchan (the reading desk) and unrolled to the right passage. Congregants may be seated.]

[1] May He help, shield, and save all who trust in Him, and let us say: Amen. [2] Let us all ascribe greatness to our God, and give honor to the Torah. [3] Let the *kohen* approach. Come forward [name], the *kohen*. [4] Blessed is the One who gave the Torah to his people in holiness.

v'yishtabakh v'yitpa'ar— we return to direct address, declaring *yitkadash shimkha*, "Your name will be sanctified." And then we beat another hasty retreat, praising God from a distance — and yet, not from a full distance, for we now claim special privilege as the people to whom God has given the Torah. In the final words recited before the first *aliyah*, the *gabbai* petitions God in the name of the congregation to protect those who safeguard the Torah. And we prove our case (and reassure ourselves at the same time) by pointing out that we have indeed kept each other alive — Torah *(p. 100)*

KUSHNER & POLEN (CHASIDISM)

[13] *"All you who cling to Adonai your God"* [Deut. 4:4] In classical Chasidic spirituality, the Hebrew verb *dalet, vet, kuf [d.v.k]* means not only to "cling to," but actually being *one with* God. This state of *d'vekut*, or *unio mystica*, is the ultimate goal, the fulfillment of religious living. It is not surprising, therefore, that Chasidic authors would pay very close attention to biblical phrases using this verbal root, as in this verse from Deuteronomy 4:4. Rabbi Menachem Mendl of Vitebsk, in his *P'ri Ha'aretz*, offers an extraordinary insight into this

(p. 101)

core yearning of human beings to be ever present within the divine.

The main idea of cleaving to God, he suggests, is that there be no interposition, no barrier whatsoever, between the self and God. Only this absence of a barrier can enable the possibility of *d'vekut*. He offers a parable in the name of the BeSHT. It is impossible to glue two pieces of silver to one another without first "scraping off" or scouring the two surfaces; otherwise, there would be nothing to which the glue might adhere. Only then can fusion occur. He cites this

L. HOFFMAN (HISTORY)

READING TORAH: THE ALIYOT. AN INTRODUCTORY PRAYER WILL SUMMON THE ALIYOT, WHO WILL COME FORWARD, ONE BY ONE, TO SAY THE BLESSINGS OVER TORAH. SPECIAL CASES OF ALIYAH (PEOPLE RECENTLY DELIVERED FROM DANGEROUS SITUATIONS, A BAR/BAT MITZVAH) RECEIVE SPECIAL ATTENTION. EVERYONE, HOWEVER, RECEIVES A MI SHEBERAKH: A PRAYER FOR THEIR OWN OR THEIR FAMILY'S WELFARE. THE UNIT ENDS WITH HAGBAHAH: HOLDING THE TORAH ON HIGH AND PROCLAIMING, "THIS IS THE TORAH.…"

[The Torah is placed on the shulchan (the reading desk) and unrolled to the right passage. Congregants may be seated.]

וְיַעֲזֹר וְיָגֵן וְיוֹשִׁיעַ לְכָל הַחוֹסִים בּוֹ וְנֹאמַר אָמֵן:[1] הַכֹּל הָבוּ גֹדֶל לֵאלֹהֵינוּ וּתְנוּ כָבוֹד לַתּוֹרָה:[2] כֹּהֵן[3] קְרָב. יַעֲמֹד[4] [name] הַכֹּהֵן: בָּרוּךְ שֶׁנָּתַן תּוֹרָה לְעַמּוֹ יִשְׂרָאֵל בִּקְדֻשָּׁתוֹ:

J. HOFFMAN (TRANSLATION)

[1] *"Save"* The word for "save" in Hebrew (*yoshi'a*) comes from the same root used for "salvation" above (*y'shu'a*), creating a clearer parallel than the English "save/salvation." It's a shame we don't have an English word "salve" anymore.

[2] *"Ascribe [havu]"* "Ascribe" in parallel with "give" (*hodu*), which follows it, is so well known that we keep it. Other possibilities would be "offer" or "render."

[3] *"Let the kohen approach"* Birnbaum doesn't translate these two words — almost certainly as just an oversight.

[4] *"In holiness"* If we had a common word "holily" we would use it.

[5] *"Soul"* See above, "Soul," and see Volume 1, *The Sh'ma and Its Blessings*, pp. 100, 102.

(p. 101)

⁵Adonai's Torah is pure, reviving the soul.

⁶Adonai's testimony is sure, educating the simple.

⁷Adonai's laws are just, delighting the heart.

⁸Adonai's command is clear, lighting the eyes.

⁹Adonai will give strength to his people. ¹⁰Adonai will bless his people with peace.

¹¹God's way is pure, and Adonai's word is clear. ¹²He protects all who seek refuge in Him. ¹³All you who cling to Adonai your God are alive today.

⁵תּוֹרַת יְיָ תְּמִימָה מְשִׁיבַת נָפֶשׁ
⁶עֵדוּת יְיָ נֶאֱמָנָה מַחְכִּימַת פֶּתִי:
⁷פִּקּוּדֵי יְיָ יְשָׁרִים מְשַׂמְּחֵי לֵב
⁸מִצְוַת יְיָ בָּרָה מְאִירַת עֵינָיִם:
⁹יְיָ עֹז לְעַמּוֹ יִתֵּן ¹⁰יְיָ יְבָרֵךְ אֶת עַמּוֹ בַשָּׁלוֹם:
¹¹הָאֵל תָּמִים דַּרְכּוֹ אִמְרַת יְיָ צְרוּפָה.
¹²מָגֵן הוּא לְכֹל הַחוֹסִים בּוֹ: ¹³וְאַתֶּם הַדְּבֵקִים בַּיְיָ אֱלֹהֵיכֶם חַיִּים כֻּלְּכֶם הַיּוֹם:

BRETTLER (BIBLE)

Adonai. Ascribe greatness to our God!" The liturgical recontextualization here, however, is remarkable. In Deuteronomy, the entire verse is about God: "our God" is the poetic parallel to "Adonai." In the new liturgical line, however, "God" is parallel to "Torah." Similarly astounding is the way in which the second part of the line, "and give honor to the Torah" reflects Psalm 115:1, where "honor" is ascribed not to Torah but to God! Torah actually replaces God here — a logical conclusion for the Rabbis, who saw Torah as the clearest manifestation of the deity.

—◆—

DORFF (THEOLOGY)

considered an honor. It is called an *aliyah*, literally, a "going up," for several reasons: physically, the platform from which the Torah is read is raised above the floor both to honor the Torah and to assist people in hearing it read (remember that these rituals were all created before the invention of microphones); socially, being given the opportunity to recite these blessings is considered an honor and is therefore a "going up" in the eyes of the community; and spiritually, reciting the blessings over the Torah brings one closer to the Torah itself, to its lessons, and thus to God.

Except during Simchat Torah, when many synagogues allow many people to be called to the Torah at once, only one person at a time is normally called to the Torah. The Conservative Movement's Committee on Jewish Law and Standards, though, has approved a ruling that would allow exceptions to that rule for family occasions, permitting, for example, a couple to be called to the Torah together on the Sabbath before their wedding (called in Yiddish an *aufruf,* a calling up) or the parents of a bar or bat mitzvah to be called up together.

The Hebrew word *aliyah* is also used to designate a section of the Torah that is read on a given Sabbath. So, for example, you might be called up for the third, fourth, fifth, sixth, or seventh *aliyah* on any given Sabbath. Traditionally, the first to be called up is a *kohen,* a descendant of Aaron, whose family served as priests in the ancient Temple, and the second to be called up is a *levi,* a descendant of the tribe of Levi, who assisted the priests in the Temple service. The Conservative Movement's Committee on Jewish Law and Standards, however, has approved calling up any Jew as the "first" and "second," regardless of ancestry, and in egalitarian synagogues that want to preserve the ancient rite, daughters as well as sons of priests or levites may be called up for the first or second *aliyah.*

The very number of such sections (called by the Hebrew plural *aliyot*) indicates the level of holiness of the day. Thus, three are called up to the Torah on weekdays, including the minor fast days and Tisha B'Av; four on the New Moon and the intermediate days of festivals; five on the festivals; six on Yom Kippur; and seven on the morning of the Sabbath. (On Shabbat afternoon, only three are called up, but that is for the practical reason that the community already read an extensive section of the Torah that morning, not because the afternoon of the Sabbath is any less holy than the morning.) This numbering makes Shabbat even holier than Yom Kippur. That is a problem, since the Torah calls Yom Kippur "the Sabbath of Sabbaths" (Lev. 23:32), and the rules of Yom Kippur are even more stringent than those of Shabbat. Nevertheless, each Sabbath is given this honor of having the largest number of people called to the Torah and the largest number of separate sections read.

On Sabbaths and festivals, after the last section of the Torah has been read and the blessing has been recited, a "half *Kaddish*" is recited (that is, only the first two paragraphs and not the three last sentences of the "full *Kaddish*"), and then yet another person is called to the Torah, the *maftir,* the one who ends the reading. (On fast days other than Yom Kippur, the third *aliyah* is the *maftir.*) That person recites the same blessings before and after the Torah reading, which on the Sabbath usually consists of a repetition of the last three or four verses of the portion that has just been read. On special Sabbaths and on festivals, the *maftir* reading is taken from another part of the Torah that is relevant to the particular day. After the *maftir* reading, the person getting that *aliyah* reads the *Haftarah,* the designated selection from the Prophets, preceded and followed by special blessings.

——◆——

Reading Torah

priestly descent to the Torah as the first *aliyah*. However, the Hamburg Temple prayer book did so, and in 1854, Geiger too stipulated that a *kohen* should be assigned the first *aliyah* and a *levi* the second. Both parties were trying to create liturgies that would not alienate traditionalists.

Interestingly, the Israeli Conservative prayer book, *Va'ani T'fillati,* unlike the American counterpart, *Siddur Sim Shalom,* omits calling a *kohen.* Both versions of *SSS* (1985, 1998) retain the priestly prerogative, but in a nod toward egalitarianism, the 1998 edition allows women as well as men of priestly descent to be called for the first *aliyah.*

———◆———

FRANKEL (A WOMAN'S VOICE)

and Israel — to this day: *v'atem had'vekim badonai eloheikhem chayim kulkhem hayom,* in effect, "all you who have stuck by God are all alive today" to tell the tale. As we now proceed to do in reading from the Torah scroll.

[3] *"Come forward...the kohen"* Historians of the *Siddur* know that its pages have occasionally served as the battleground of internal communal squabbles. Sectarian conflicts during the Second Commonwealth period, debates over relations with the Church, liberal quarrels in our time with theological doctrines such as the resurrection of the dead, restoration of animal sacrifice, and chosenness have all left their mark on the liturgy. But despite all the controversy, the prayer book has remained remarkably stable over two and a half millennia. Whether it is the fundamentally conservative nature of prayer or of the people who engage in it, the Jewish People has been reluctant to jeopardize the historical and geographical unity preserved through a commonly shared text.

In our own day, some of the most contentious debates over liturgical reform focus on the issue of hierarchy. And one of its key battlegrounds is here in the heart of the Torah service. Reformers challenge: Why continue to acknowledge ancient priestly distinctions — *kohen* and *levi* — when priesthood and Temple no longer exist? Why grant superior levels of privilege when we don't demand superior levels of sanctity? Why rank ourselves by bloodlines at a time when we are welcoming in so many new Jews by choice?

And the issue goes deeper, for until a generation ago — and in the Orthodox community to this day — women ranked even lower than the lowliest boy of thirteen. When the *gabbai* called up *kohen, levi,* or *yisrael,* it was understood that only males were intended. When names were announced, only fathers' sons were summoned. Although women congregants and mothers are now honored within most liberal congregations, the issue of hierarchy remains vexing. For what of God's gender, rendered as masculine in these *b'rakhot* as in all traditional blessings? Is it *his* Torah that we bless; are we *his* chosen people? As we struggle to untie these grammatical and sociological knots, let us remember that we do so *l'shem shamayim,* for the Torah's sake and not solely for our own.

———◆———

KUSHNER & POLEN (CHASIDISM)

verse from Isaiah 41:7, "The woodworker encourages the smith; he says of the fusion 'It is good.'" Thus, they are made one. In the same way, if there is rust or anything already on the surface of the metals to be joined, then it will be impossible to glue them permanently together. And this is the meaning of the verse in Proverbs 2:4, "If you seek it as you do silver…" In the same way, one who would cleave to God must also first prepare his or her soul so that there will be no trace of rust or any other barrier that might be in the way. Only then will the person at last be freed from grabbing onto other distractions and be able to cleave continually to God.

———◆———

J. HOFFMAN (TRANSLATION)

[6] *"Educating"* Literally, something like "making wiser." *Gates of Prayer* uses "making wise."

[7] *"Heart"* The Hebrew *lev* (literally, "heart") functions metaphorically much differently than the English "heart," in that the Hebrew suggests both emotions and intellect, while the English generally suggests emotion to the exclusion of intellect. (For a full discussion, see Volume 1, *The Sh'ma and Its Blessings,* pp. 100, 102.)

[8] *"Lighting"* The need to use a form of "light" twice, once here and once in the line above ("delighting"), necessarily creates a verbal pun in the English that is absent in the Hebrew.

[10] *"Bless"* See Volume 1, *The Sh'ma and Its Blessings,* p. 29.

——————— ◆ ◆ ◆ ———————

B. Blessings over Torah

[Torah blessings. The person receiving an aliyah (the oleh/olah) recites the first line. The congregation responds with the second, after which the oleh/olah repeats it, then says the blessing that follows. The ba'al korei (Torah reader) then reads the appropriate passage, after which the oleh/olah recites the second blessing.]

[1] Bless Adonai who is to be blessed.

[2] Blessed be Adonai who is to be blessed for ever and ever.

[3] Blessed are You, Adonai our God, ruler of the world, who chose us from all the nations and gave us his Torah. [4] Blessed are You, giver of the Torah.

[5] Blessed are You, Adonai our God, ruler of the world, who gave us the true Torah and implanted within us eternal life. Blessed are You, giver of the Torah.

[Torah blessings. The person receiving an aliyah (the oleh/olah) recites the first line. The congregation responds with the second, after which the oleh/olah repeats it, then says the blessing that follows. The ba'al korei (Torah reader) then reads the appropriate passage, after which the oleh/olah recites the second blessing.]

בָּרְכוּ אֶת־יְיָ הַמְבֹרָךְ:[1]

בָּרוּךְ יְיָ הַמְבֹרָךְ לְעוֹלָם וָעֶד:[2]

בָּרוּךְ אַתָּה יְיָ אֱלֹהֵינוּ מֶלֶךְ הָעוֹלָם[3]
אֲשֶׁר בָּחַר־בָּנוּ מִכָּל־הָעַמִּים וְנָתַן־
לָנוּ אֶת־תּוֹרָתוֹ. בָּרוּךְ אַתָּה יְיָ נוֹתֵן[4]
הַתּוֹרָה:

בָּרוּךְ אַתָּה יְיָ אֱלֹהֵינוּ מֶלֶךְ הָעוֹלָם[5]
אֲשֶׁר נָתַן־לָנוּ תּוֹרַת אֱמֶת וְחַיֵּי עוֹלָם
נָטַע בְּתוֹכֵנוּ. בָּרוּךְ אַתָּה יְיָ נוֹתֵן
הַתּוֹרָה:

BRETTLER (BIBLE)

[3] *"Who chose us from all the nations"* God's election of Israel is most clearly articulated in Deuteronomy 7:6: "For you are a people consecrated to the Adonai your God: of all the peoples on earth the Adonai your God chose you to be his treasured people." This choice conferred blessing, as Psalm 33:12 illustrates, "Happy is the nation whose God is Adonai, the people He has chosen to be his own." But chosenness also brought with it covenantal obligations, as illustrated by Amos 3:2: "You alone have I singled out of all the families of the earth. That is why I will call you to account for all your iniquities."

[3] *"And gave us his Torah"* In most biblical texts (like

(p. 106)

DORFF (THEOLOGY)

[1] *"Bless Adonai who is to be blessed"* In Sefardi liturgy, the one who is given the honor of being called to the Torah first greets the congregation that is honoring him or her with the biblical greeting *Adonai imakhem,* "May Adonai be with you" (Ruth 2:4), and the congregation responds, as that same

(p. 106)

ELLENSON (MODERN LITURGIES)

[3] *"Who chose us from all the nations"* Modern Jews have considered the notion that Jews are a "chosen people" nothing short of scandalous, fearing that the particularity implied by the idea entails antidemocratic claims of Jewish superiority. But at the same time, unwilling so quickly to

(p. 108)

HAUPTMAN (TALMUD)

[1] *"Bless Adonai who is to be blessed"* Upon being called to read from the Torah, the person who comes to the reading table recites several blessings. Although the text of these blessings does not appear in the Talmud, the Mishnah (Meg. 4:1) says that the one who opens the Torah reading recites a blessing prior to beginning the reading for the day, and the one who closes or seals the Torah reading recites a blessing upon completing the Torah reading for the day. A total of two blessings were to be recited. But the Talmud reports a

B. BLESSINGS OVER TORAH

[Torah blessings. The person receiving an aliyah (the oleh/olah) recites the first line. The congregation responds with the second, after which the oleh/olah repeats it, then says the blessing that follows. The ba'al korei (Torah reader) then reads the appropriate passage, after which the oleh/olah recites the second blessing.]

[1] Bless Adonai who is to be blessed.

[2] Blessed be Adonai who is to be blessed for ever and ever.

change in practice. Because some people would leave the synagogue early and others would arrive late, thereby missing the opportunity to hear at least one of the blessings, it became customary for each reader to recite an opening and a closing blessing (Meg. 21b). From the medieval period, we find an additional rationale given by the Franko-German school of commentators known as the Tosafot (Meg. 21b, s.v. Tana): In order not to embarrass those who did *not* know how to read from the Torah, even those who *did* know how to read were replaced by a *ba'al korei,* a

(p. 108)

KUSHNER & POLEN (CHASIDISM)

3–4 *"Blessed are You, Adonai…who…gave us his Torah. Blessed are You, giver of the Torah"* Zev Wolf of Zhitomir (*Or Hame'ir,* vol. I, 8, col. 1 bottom) notices the change in the opening Torah blessing from the past tense, "who gave," to the present tense, "giver," but literally, "who gives." He draws from this an insight into the nature of holy learning. The Torah *was given* at Mount Sinai. But in each generation, God also *is giving* it anew through the new interpretations of its teachers. The sages of each era thus draw, from the sacred texts,   *(p. 111)*

[Torah blessings. The person receiving an aliyah (the oleh/olah) recites the first line. The congregation responds with the second, after which the oleh/olah repeats it, then says the blessing that follows. The ba'al korei (Torah reader) then reads the appropriate passage, after which the oleh/olah recites the second blessing.]

¹בָּרְכוּ אֶת־יְיָ הַמְבֹרָךְ:

²בָּרוּךְ יְיָ הַמְבֹרָךְ לְעוֹלָם וָעֶד:

LANDES (HALAKHAH)

¹ *"Bless Adonai who is to be blessed"* The halakhic rules for all aspects of an *aliyah* are found in the introductory essay, pp. 29–39, above.

———◆———

L. HOFFMAN (HISTORY)

3–5 *"Who chose us from all nations…who gave us the true Torah"* Blessings before and after reading Torah are ancient, going back at least to the second century C.E. "Proof" of their having to be said is found in the *Mekhilta,* a second-century midrash (*Bo,* 16). But as with other blessings, the wording we now have was not yet fixed. Our wording comes from the Talmud (Ber. 11b). Parallel rabbinic texts contain alternatives that were once in use, including "who chose this Torah, sanctified it, and took pleasure in those who do it" *(asher bachar batorah hazot, v'kidshah v'ratsah v'oseha)* and "who commanded us to occupy ourselves with words of Torah" *(la'asok b'divrei*   *(p. 111)*

J. HOFFMAN (TRANSLATION)

3 *"From all the nations"* Or "from all other nations." The Hebrew might mean either. Our translation suggests that God looked at all the nations and chose us. The other possibility is that God chose us above all other nations.

3 *"And gave"* Or "by giving." The theological differences between "by giving" and "and gave" are great, and the Hebrew might mean either. "By giving" implies that it is precisely in the act of giving Torah that God chooses. Alternatively, God chose first, and then gave Torah to the people who were chosen.

———◆———

3 Blessed are You, Adonai our God, ruler of the world, who chose us from all the nations and gave us his Torah. 4 Blessed are You, giver of the Torah.

5 Blessed are You, Adonai our God, ruler of the world, who gave us the true Torah and implanted within us eternal life. Blessed are You, giver of the Torah.

³בָּרוּךְ אַתָּה יְיָ אֱלֹהֵינוּ מֶלֶךְ הָעוֹלָם אֲשֶׁר בָּחַר־בָּנוּ מִכָּל־הָעַמִּים וְנָתַן־לָנוּ אֶת־תּוֹרָתוֹ. ⁴בָּרוּךְ אַתָּה יְיָ נוֹתֵן הַתּוֹרָה:

⁵בָּרוּךְ אַתָּה יְיָ אֱלֹהֵינוּ מֶלֶךְ הָעוֹלָם אֲשֶׁר נָתַן־לָנוּ תּוֹרַת אֱמֶת וְחַיֵּי עוֹלָם נָטַע בְּתוֹכֵנוּ. בָּרוּךְ אַתָּה יְיָ נוֹתֵן הַתּוֹרָה:

BRETTLER (BIBLE)

Deuteronomy 4:8, "What great nation has laws and rules as perfect as all this torah") "torah" refers to the decalogue or to some section of the Pentateuch as a whole. Only in post-exilic texts, once the Torah as a whole has been canonized, does the Hebrew term *torah* mean the entire five books of Moses. In the post-exilic Nehemiah 10:30, for instance, "to follow the Torah of God" likely means to observe the complete Pentateuch.

5 *"The true Torah"* From Psalm 119:142, a late biblical meditation on the wonders of God's Torah. The synonyms and descriptions used in the psalm for "Torah" are truly astounding. This psalm, like some later literature, sees Torah as the major manifestation of God. It applies to Torah attributes that earlier literature reserves only for God. For example, Psalm 119:72 says that the Torah is "good" *(tov),* an attribute typically used elsewhere of God, as in Psalm 145:9 (the *Ashre*), "Adonai is good *[tov]* to all."

DORFF (THEOLOGY)

verse indicates, *Y'varekh'kha Adonai,* "May Adonai bless you." This beautiful custom enables the person being called to the Torah to express appreciation to the community for the honor, and the community to confirm its good wishes in return. Then, before the blessing after the Torah reading, according to some Sefardi rites, the one called to the Torah says *Emet torateinu k'doshah,* "It is true that our Torah is holy." Having just read a portion of the Torah, this sentence expresses the person's reconfirmed conviction that there is a fundamental reason to read the Torah, namely, its holiness.

In both Ashkenazi and Sefardi rites, the one called to the Torah begins in the imperative: "Bless Adonai who is to be blessed" or, better, "who is deserving of blessing."

To that, the congregation responds, "Blessed be Adonai who is to be blessed [i.e., who is deserving of blessing] for ever and ever," and the person given the *aliyah* repeats that. This interchange at each *aliyah* between the honoree and the congregation makes the blessing of God not only an expression of the person being honored, but of the entire community.

[3] *"Who...gave us his Torah"* Note the tenses of the verbs in the two blessings surrounding the reading of the Torah. God "chose" us from all the nations and "gave" the Torah — both are expressed in the past. But when it comes to the *chatimah* (the last line, or signature, of the blessing), God is described as *noten hatorah,* which is either the gerund, "giver of the Torah," or the present tense, "who gives the Torah." The same thing happens in the blessing after the Torah reading. The message is that *Not only has God given us the Torah in the past; God gives it to us anew each and every time we read it.* Speaking theologically, God's revelation is not restricted to what happened at Mount Sinai; it happens every time we read and interpret the Torah. This belief is not new: it goes back to the Talmud (Bava Batra 12a):

> *Rabbi Abdimi from Haifa said: Since the day when the Temple was destroyed, the prophetic gift was taken from the prophets and given to the sages. Is, then, a sage not also a prophet? What he meant was this: Although it [revelation] has been taken from the prophets, it has not been taken from the sages. Amemar said: A sage is even superior to a prophet, as it says, "And a prophet has a heart of wisdom" (Ps. 90:12). Who is usually compared with whom? Is not the smaller (the prophet, here) compared with the greater (sages, who "have a heart of wisdom")?*

Moreover, the midrash tells us that "matters that had not been disclosed to Moses were disclosed to Rabbi Akiba and his colleagues" (Num. Rabbah 19:6), even though Rabbi Akiba lived some 1,400 years after Moses. Furthermore, the meanings that emerge from the text for various people, or even the same person at different times, will inevitably vary because, according to the Rabbis, God intended it that way: "'Is not my word like a hammer that breaks a rock in many pieces' (Jer. 23:29)? As the hammer causes numerous sparks to flash forth, so is a Scriptural verse capable of many interpretations" (Sanhedrin 34a).

Those who are familiar with modern literary theory will recognize this immediately as an amazingly sophisticated approach to understanding how texts convey meaning. The text remains the same, but each time we read it we see new things in it. That might happen because of our own growth, our new experiences that bring a fresh understanding of the text; or it may be because of suggestions of the people with whom we are studying, be they commentators whose work we read or people who join us in the process of study. Meaning, in other words, comes through the *interaction* of a text with the people reading and interpreting it, and that interaction is new each time the reader meets the text. Thus, the Rabbis were quite astute in phrasing the blessings surrounding the reading of the Torah as they did: God not only *has given* us the Torah in the past; God gives it to us anew each time we read it.

◆——

ELLENSON (MODERN LITURGIES)

abandon this central Jewish theological concept, they have struggled to construe it in an acceptable moral way. They have redefined chosenness positively, saying that it obligates Jews to disseminate the ethical teachings of the one God before the entire world. In this view, Jews have either assumed or been assigned a mission. This universalistic understanding has permitted virtually all liberal prayer books of the past two hundred years to retain the traditional blessing (*asher bachar banu,* "who has chosen us"), with its familiar cadence and melody. It also allowed authorities like Einhorn and Wise, who believed strongly in the mission of Israel, not only to preserve the traditional Hebrew but also to translate it in clear and literal German or English.

Other authors, while not abandoning the Hebrew wording, remained uncomfortable with it. Feeling that claims of being chosen required explanation or apology, they wrote translations that muted what they perceived as the problematic dimensions of the idea, and emphasized instead its virtues. The American Reform *Union Prayer Book,* for instance, translated "Who has chosen us from among all peoples" as "Who has *called* us from among all peoples," while the British Liberal *Lev Chadash,* influenced, as we shall see, by Mordecai Kaplan, says, "You have called us to serve You."

Neither Abraham Geiger nor Mordecai Kaplan was satisfied with these minimal emendations. While Geiger believed strongly in the universal mission of Israel, he felt that the words "from among all peoples" unnecessarily denigrated others and promoted Jewish chauvinism. He therefore removed these Hebrew words from his prayer book, and in the German accompaniment, instead of "chosen" *(erkoren),* Geiger portrayed God as assigning Israel a religious calling or vocation *(berufen).*

As a strident critic of chosenness, Kaplan went even further than Geiger. In an often commented upon change that distinguishes Reconstructionist liturgy, he removed *asher bachar banu* ("who has chosen us") completely. In their stead, he wrote, *"asher kervanu l'avodato,"* which he translated as "Who hast brought us nigh to Thy service." Interestingly, current Reconstructionist liturgy *(Kol Haneshamah)* retains Kaplan's innovation but has restored the traditional Hebrew blessing as an option; but it mutes "chosen us" by rendering it "singled us out."

———◆———

HAUPTMAN (TALMUD)

trained reader, who read the entire portion for everyone. The *oleh,* the person called to the Torah, still recited the blessings before and after.

The opening line, "Bless Adonai who is to be blessed," is not a prayer in and of itself but a call to attention. The person who recites it invites the members of the congregation to join him in blessing God. The *Bar'khu* (as it is known in Hebrew), along with its one-line response ("Blessed be Adonai who is to be blessed forever and ever"), was already recited at the opening of the *Shacharit* service, right after the *P'sukei*

D'zimrah and before the *Sh'ma* (see Volume 1, *The Sh'ma and Its Blessings,* p. 29). It is clear that this responsive invitation and acceptance of the obligation to praise God was not composed for recitation at the Torah service. Its oldest use, even before it entered the daily synagogue service prior to the *Sh'ma,* seems to have been as part of the *zimmun* before the *Birkat hamazon* (M. Ber. 7:3).

The congregation responds to the invitation by the *oleh* by saying, "Blessed be Adonai, who is to be blessed for ever and ever." Having focused the congregation's attention, the *oleh* now recites the blessing specially formulated for an *aliyah* to the Torah, "Blessed are You…who chose us from all the nations and gave us his Torah. Blessed are You, giver of the Torah." This blessing expresses a standard Jewish liturgical theme: that the Jews are God's chosen people. A reference to this idea also appears, among other places, in the Friday night *Kiddush* and in the Shabbat and Festival *Amidah.* The *oleh* recites another blessing after the reading, which repeats the theme of God's giving the Torah to the Jewish People but adds that as a result, God has given them everlasting life, which means that those who keep the *mitzvot* of the Torah will enjoy life in the world-to-come upon ending their lives in this world.

While reciting these blessings, and for the duration of the *aliyah,* the *oleh* grasps one or both of the *atzei chaim,* the wooden poles around which the Torah is rolled. This suggests that although the *oleh* has delegated the trained reader to read on his or her behalf, the credit redounds to the *oleh.*

The *Bar'khu* may not be recited without a *minyan:* the presence of at least ten Jews, all older than twelve (for women) and thirteen (for men). They form a Jewish community in miniature. In addition to reading from the Torah, many other rituals too, such as reading from the Prophets (the *Haftarah*), reciting the seven wedding blessings (the *Sheva b'rakhot*), reciting the priestly blessing *(Birkat kohanim)* and saying the *Kaddish* or the *K'dushah* require a *minyan* also (M. Meg. 4:3; Ber. 21b). The determination of what requires a *minyan* is talmudic, in that the Talmud generalizes and says that for each *davar she'bik'dushah* ("every matter of holiness") a *minyan* is necessary.

The reason for requiring a minimum of ten for the Torah reading, as implied by the Talmud, is that it would be insulting to God if fewer than ten showed up to hear his Torah read in public. If God is thought of as a king, then it is not becoming to Him if his subjects do not turn out in large numbers to greet Him and praise Him. It would similarly be insulting to the bride and groom if fewer than ten guests showed up to participate in and witness their wedding ceremony.

The ten people who constitute a *minyan,* according to the Talmud, may not include women or children. Men were heads of household, which means that they were husbands to their wives, fathers to their children, and also masters to their non-Jewish slaves. These three groups — women, slaves, and minors — were all subject to and dependent on a man. It follows that they could not be counted for ritual purposes. Today, since our society sees women as occupying the same social status as men, a *minyan* is almost universally composed of ten adult Jews, men and women alike. Only nonegalitarian branches of Judaism continue to limit public ritual roles to men.

The word *aliyah* describes the act of being called to the Torah. Although the root is familiar to us from the use of *aliyah* to describe someone who "goes up" to Israel, this is not what the word means in reference to reading the Torah in the synagogue. It simply means "to be counted." The Talmud (Meg. 23a) says, *Hakol olin l'minyan shiv'ah,* that is, "Everyone may be counted in the seven people [who read from the Torah]." The Hebrew verb *olin* is the plural of *oleh*. It does not imply that the *bimah* in the ancient synagogue was raised. If anything, it was lower than the rest of the synagogue, because the prayer leader for the *Amidah* is sometimes described technically as the one who "goes down" to the place from which the service is led. *Olin,* like the singular *oleh,* simply means "to be counted"; and an *aliyah* is an opportunity to be counted.

When the Talmud says that all may be counted to read from the Torah, it adds that "all" includes minors and women. That is, women are technically eligible to read from the Torah in public. There is no problem, for instance, of a woman's voice being sexually distracting to men or of a woman's ritual impurity — two rationales that are sometimes advanced against women having an *aliyah*. However, the passage continues, the Rabbis barred women from reading from the Torah because of *k'vod hatsibur,* "the dignity of the congregation."

This phrase appears only a few times in the Talmud. In one instance, it is used to explain why a naked man may not read from the Torah in public (Meg. 24b). It is also used by Rashi, an eleventh-century commentator on the Talmud, to explain why a child who is a *kohen* may not bless a congregation of adults (Meg. 24a): it would compromise their dignity to be blessed by a child. Therefore, when this phrase is used in reference to women, it means that women, who occupy a lower status than men in a patriarchal society, shame men if they read the Torah for men. Possibly, if a woman reads it would imply that no man present could read and for that reason the community had no choice but to turn to a woman. But, even so, why would it be embarrassing for a community of illiterate men to be represented by a literate woman? The reason must be that women then were dependent on and subordinate to men. It is not comfortable for a "boss" to have his "employee" surpass him. Nowadays, however, as remarked above, egalitarian Jews hold that women enjoy equal standing with men, so that the Talmud's reasoning becomes moot. Children, on the other hand, are still dependent on their elders, so, unlike women, they have not inherited the adult Jew's right to be called to Torah.

In addition to the dignity of the congregation, the Rabbis worried also about the dignity of the Torah itself, *k'vod hatorah*. This concept underlies much of the Torah service ritual. In order to protect the honor of the Torah, the Rabbis determined that no fewer than three verses must be read for each *aliyah;* that only one reader at a time may read from the Torah; and that the more holy the day, the greater the number of persons called to read from the Torah. The Sabbath has the highest number, seven, thus indicating the biblical view and the subsequent rabbinic concretization of that view: that the Sabbath is the holiest day of the Jewish year.

KUSHNER & POLEN (CHASIDISM)

newly appropriate readings for the needs of every age. In this way, each "new" reading has actually been secret and latent within the Torah ever since it was first given at Sinai.

———◆———

L. HOFFMAN (HISTORY)

torah). The latter is still said before ordinary Torah study; the former has dropped out of use.

[4] *"Giver of the Torah" Turei Zahav,* a seventeenth-century commentary to the Shulchan Arukh, by David Halevi, notes the present tense, "giver," that is, "who gives," rather than "who gave." Why doesn't our blessing refer back to God as the One who "gave" the Torah to Israel in a singular revelation at Sinai? The answer, he proposes, is that every time we study Torah we receive new insights. As he puts it, "God always gives us the Torah, every day, for we occupy ourselves with it and God helps us find new meanings" (O. Ch. 47:5).

At stake is the doctrine of "continuous revelation." Literalists contend that once the Torah is given, nothing new can be located in it. Judaism has by and large rejected this approach. The Pharisees adopted instead the doctrine of the "oral Torah" *(Torah she'b'al peh)* which assumes that we can never do justice to the written word without an oral interpretation, said to go back equally to Sinai, even though its insights become newly available only with every passing generation. Liberal interpreters today often adopt the same principle to explain their changing perspective on tradition, but without making the claim that a new insight goes back to Sinai. Revelation never ceases, however. It continually arrives through Torah study.

———————◆ ◆ ◆———————

C. Special Cases (Deliverance from Danger, Bar/Bat Mitzvah)

[Birkat gomel: Those who have escaped a dangerous situation and who receive an aliyah say the following:]

1 Blessed are You, Adonai our God, ruler of the world, who rewards the undeserving with goodness, and who has rewarded me with goodness.

[Congregation responds:]

2 May the One who rewarded you with all goodness reward you with all goodness for ever.

[For a bar mitzvah, the father (in egalitarian congregations, the mother too) says the following. Egalitarian congregations recite this for a bat mitzvah also, replacing "this boy" with "this girl":]

3 Blessed is the One who relieved me of the punishment for this boy.

[Birkat gomel: Those who have escaped a dangerous situation and who receive an aliyah say the following:]

‎1בָּרוּךְ אַתָּה יְיָ אֱלֹהֵינוּ מֶלֶךְ הָעוֹלָם הַגּוֹמֵל לְחַיָּבִים טוֹבוֹת שֶׁגְּמָלַנִי כָּל־טוֹב:

[Congregation responds:]

‎2מִי שֶׁגְּמָלְךְ כָּל־טוֹב הוּא יִגְמָלְךְ כָּל־טוֹב סֶלָה:

[For a bar mitzvah, the father (in egalitarian congregations, the mother too) says the following. Egalitarian congregations recite this for a bat mitzvah also, replacing "this boy" with "this girl":]

‎3בָּרוּךְ שֶׁפְּטָרַנִי מֵעָנְשׁוֹ שֶׁל זֶה:

BRETTLER (BIBLE)

[3] *"Who has relieved me of the punishment"* The Bible recognizes the possibility of intergenerational punishment, especially in Exodus 34:7, where God "visits the iniquity of parents on children," but also in 2 Samuel 12. King David had arranged to have Uriah, the husband of Bathsheba, killed so that he could marry Bathsheba. As punishment, God kills the son whom Bathsheba bears to him. But the Bible nowhere suggests the novel idea that upon reaching a particular age, children become culpable for what hitherto their parents had to worry about.

———◆———

ELLENSON (MODERN LITURGIES)

[3] *"Blessed is the One who relieved me of the punishment for this boy"* This blessing is traditionally recited by the father of a bar mitzvah boy after the lad has had his *aliyah* to the Torah. The first Reform prayer book authors in Hamburg eliminated it because they opposed bar mitzvah altogether. They felt that thirteen was too young for a youth to assume adult religious responsibility. They replaced bar mitzvah with confirmation at a later age. This preference is reflected in the 1841 Hamburg Temple prayer book. Immediately after the conclusion of the second Torah blessing, the Hamburg rite calls on the prayer leader *(Vorbeter)* to summon confirmands to the Torah as follows: "Arise, pleasant *(p. 116)*

FRANKEL (A WOMAN'S VOICE)

[1] *"Who rewards the undeserving with goodness"* Why do we need to bless God publicly when we recover from illness or escape harm? Is it not enough to thank God in our hearts or in unison with the community? Certainly, this is the case when we reap good fortune, for the liturgy provides no special blessing upon choosing to give a donation out of gratitude. Why then do we need to recite a special prayer when we escape misfortune?

In adding this prayer to the Torah service, Jewish tradition has shown

C. SPECIAL CASES (DELIVERANCE FROM DANGER, BAR/BAT MITZVAH)

[Birkat gomel: Those who have escaped a dangerous situation and who receive an aliyah *say the following:]*

[1] Blessed are You, Adonai our God, ruler of the world, who rewards the undeserving with goodness, and who has rewarded me with goodness.

profound psychological insight. Nowadays, we understand that physical distress and even survival can have unexpected psychic consequences. Trauma — physical, emotional, or psychological — can isolate victims. Surviving a catastrophe, especially when loved ones don't, can produce guilt rather than gratitude. The joy of giving birth can be alloyed with depression. Recovery from illness may leave scars or disabilities in its wake.

But when we *bench gomel,* publicly acknowledging our vulnerability, we summon support from all *(p. 117)*

L. HOFFMAN (HISTORY)

[1] *"Who rewards the undeserving with goodness"* An acknowledgment of having passed safely through danger, known in Hebrew as *Birkat gomel* (beer-KAHT goh-MAYL), "blessing of reward," but still commonly referred to by the Yiddish as *goy'-m'l bensch'n* (GOY-m'l bensh'n), meaning the same thing. The Talmud (Ber. 54b) assigns the line specifically to those who have returned from a sea voyage, journeyed through the desert, recovered from illness, or been released from prison, but since then it has been generalized to

[Birkat gomel: *Those who have escaped a dangerous situation and who receive an* aliyah *say the following:*]

בָּרוּךְ אַתָּה יְיָ אֱלֹהֵינוּ מֶלֶךְ הָעוֹלָם הַגּוֹמֵל לְחַיָּבִים טוֹבוֹת שֶׁגְּמָלַנִי כָּל־טוֹב:[1]

mean passing through danger in general.

Originally, people in such straits just recited this line privately, if at all, even though the Talmud requires a *minyan* for it. By the twelfth century, we see signs of its entering the synagogue service officially. The French commentators known as Tosafot say, "It is customary to say this after reading Torah, especially for people who are so sick as to be bedridden, although not for people just with headaches or stomachaches who are not confined to bed."

Nowadays, we follow the Tosafot example, to which we have added a congregational response (v. 2 here), "May the One who rewarded you with all goodness reward you with all goodness forever." The occasions for which *Birkat gomel* is reserved now vary with local practice. For example, some women say it after successful childbirth.

[3] *"Who has relieved me of the punishment for this boy"* Most modern Jews are unaware of this traditional response by the father to his son's bar mitzvah because most synagogues no longer call for it. As our translator indicates (see Joel M. Hoffman's commentary), it sounds like a father saying of his son, "Good   *(p. 117)*

J. HOFFMAN (TRANSLATION)

[1] *"Goodness [tovot]"* Literally, "goodnesses," sometimes translated as "favors."

[2] *"For ever [selah]"* From the way it is used in Psalms, it appears that the word *selah* was a technical musical term, perhaps an instruction to those who would sing this text. But *selah* appears only at the end of certain passages, so it cannot have been anything so common as "sharp," "flat," "forte," etc.

Later, the word is held to have meant "forever."

We can reconcile these two uses if we assume that *selah* always meant "for a long time/forever" and that its musical meaning was the same as the modern-day *fermata*, which indicates that a note is to be held longer than normally.   *(p. 119)*

[Congregation responds:]

[Congregation responds:]

² May the One who rewarded you with all goodness reward you with all goodness for ever.

[For a bar mitzvah, the father (in egalitarian congregations, the mother too) says the following. Egalitarian congregations recite this for a bat mitzvah also, replacing "this boy" with "this girl":]

³ Blessed is the One who relieved me of the punishment for this boy.

²מִי שֶׁגְּמָלְךָ כָּל־טוֹב הוּא יִגְמָלְךָ
כָּל־טוֹב סֶלָה:

[For a bar mitzvah, the father (in egalitarian congregations, the mother too) says the following. Egalitarian congregations recite this for a bat mitzvah also, replacing "this boy" with "this girl":]

³בָּרוּךְ שֶׁפְּטָרַנִי מֵעָנְשׁוֹ שֶׁל זֶה:

ELLENSON (MODERN LITURGIES)

youth, in the midst of the faithful, to read from the Book of God's law. The statutes of God are upright." Deuteronomy 10:12–22, which reminds Israel of its covenantal appointment and commands Israel to fulfill its ethical task, was then read. At the conclusion of the Torah reading, he recited Jacob's blessing of his grandsons Ephraim and Manasseh (Gen. 48:16) as a blessing over the confirmands. In the twentieth century, bar mitzvah has been restored as a normative Reform ceremony, together with bat mitzvah. While most Reform prayer books include no specific blessing that would be recited immediately after the Torah blessings, parents customarily recite the *Shehecheyanu* at this time, and prayer books such as *Gates of Prayer* and *Lev Chadash* do contain special prayers for the bar or bat mitzvah during the Torah service.

Conservative liturgy has retained the traditional Hebrew here, but discomfort with its sentiments has prompted Conservative editors to supply alternative blessings in lieu of the traditional one, and to obviate the meaning of the objectionable Hebrew by composing a new English version in place of a faithful translation — a technique common to Conservative liturgy over the years. *Sim Shalom* renders the passage "Praised is the One who has brought us to this time when our child assumes the obligation of *mitzvot*" — a "translation" that has nothing to do with the Hebrew at all but expresses Conservative theology accurately. Finally, the *Shehecheyanu* is presented as a preferable parental blessing in any case, so that the traditional words, even in Hebrew, are relegated to "second-class status" and probably are not said at all.

Egalitarian sentiment has led the editors to present bat mitzvah as normative and to indicate that the mother, not just the father, should recite the blessing over the child. The 1998 edition of *SSS* explicitly instructs the *parents* (father and *mother*) of a bar or bat mitzvah to offer the blessing.

In *Va'ani T'fillati,* the Israeli authors, like their American counterparts, also provide the *Shehecheyanu* as an alternative benediction. In addition, they offer the blessing that is traditionally recited upon receiving good tidings, "Praised are You, Adonai our God, who is good and dispenses good—*hatov v'hameitiv*," for their Israeli congregants. Finally, *SVT* supplies an original composition, "Praised is the One who grants merit to my son/daughter through the *mitzvot.*"

———◆———

FRANKEL (A WOMAN'S VOICE)

those who care about our welfare. It is the community's way of ensuring that we remain our brothers' and sisters' keepers.

[3] *"Who has relieved me of the punishment for this boy"* In modern times, we have added so many new customs to conclude the bar and bat mitzvah ceremony—the synagogue's bestowal of gifts, the parents' charge and blessing, the young person's own remarks—that we may not be aware that bar mitzvah ceremonies used to end quite differently. Following his son's chanting of the Torah blessings, a Jewish father would recite a four-word *b'rakhah: Barukh shep'tarani mei'onsho shel zeh,* "Blessed is the One who has relieved me of the punishment." Although the word for "punishment" here is usually translated as "burden," it literally means "affliction." It's no wonder that modern parents in most liberal communities choose not to recite this phrase. How can we publicly describe our child as a burden—or worse, as a punishment? How can we pretend that we are honestly ready to send this unseasoned teenager off on his own? If it is indeed true that childhood is an invention of modernity, then perhaps we should acknowledge this reality not only by rejecting this declaration of our and our child's independence but also by accepting that this coming of age ceremony represents only a first step in our mutual separation, not the final one.

———◆———

L. HOFFMAN (HISTORY)

riddance." But there is hidden wisdom in the statement, which ought not to be jettisoned so quickly.

It goes back ultimately to a midrash that puzzles over the fact that even though both Jacob and Esau grew up in the same family environment, one turned to Torah and the other to idolatry. Given how little parents can control their children's future, they are instructed to breathe a sigh of relief when children become old enough to be responsible for their own affairs. Until that age, we, the parents, are responsible—quite a burden. The Rabbis thought that responsibility entailed the possibility of divine punishment, which is worse still; especially since (as our midrash makes clear, and as every parent knows) even the best parents may find their children inexplicably going wrong. As the child enters the age of responsibility, then, parents were urged to express gratitude at passing the point where they might be so punished. By the Middle Ages, when the bar mitzvah ceremony was invented, what had been midrashic advice entered the bar mitzvah rite for fathers to say.

The literal translation is "Blessed is the One who has relieved me of the punishment for this one." That is, it does not specify who the "one" is. Tradition developed two alternative interpretations of the allusion. The most widely held notion (to which I have already alluded) identified the *zeh* ("this one" on account of whom punishment arrives) as the wayward child. Since fathers are responsible for their children's education, fathers must wonder whether they are liable through their entire lifetime for their children's immoral actions. The blessing expresses their gratitude at being exempt, once the education period of a child's minority is over.

However, Mordecai Jaffe (sixteenth-century Poland) reports a surprising alternative explanation by which *zeh* ("this one") is the father! The son is relieved at being released from potential punishment occasioned on account of his father. At stake is the Torah's warning that God "visits the iniquity of parents on children and children's children, upon the third and fourth generation." Here it is the child who wonders if we have to live our whole lives worrying about punishment raining down on us for something our grandparents did — to which tradition responds that we do indeed, but only until we are thirteen years old, after which time we are punished only for our own wrongs.

Neither explanation rings true to moderns who do not believe in a simple calculus of sin and divine punishment. But by changing the rhetorical terms a bit, we can recognize that tradition is grasping at deep psychological truths here. According to the first interpretation, parents admit the limitations of parental control. They simply cannot control the destiny of their adult children. At bar/bat mitzvah time, they symbolically hand over moral autonomy to their children, admitting that the older children get, the less parents can be in charge. Seen in this light, our blessing is a statement of faith in our own children's ultimate capacity to live the good life we have taught them.

According to the second interpretation, it is our children who affirm their independence from whatever negative baggage their parents bequeath them. Visiting "the iniquity of parents on children and children's children, upon the third and fourth generation" is tantamount to saying that children suffer from family "baggage" going back generations — a fact that we can no longer doubt. Children who are beaten tend to beat their own children, for example, in an endless cycle of violence. Seen in this light, our blessing affirms an individual's ability to transcend that cycle and be free of whatever negative influences there might have been in the family history.

The tradition speaks about sin and punishment, but we can translate those terms into our own way of thinking. Parents say not "Good riddance" but "Fly free; be who you were meant to be; we will not hold you back. We cannot be responsible for you any more. But we have faith in you to be responsible for yourself." Children say, "Thank God I am free to grow unhampered by whatever negative influences I have imbibed willy-nilly, even from healthy parents." Under either interpretation, both of which are equally true as being two sides of the same psychological coin, our bar (and now bat) mitzvah affirmation ritualizes a healthy separation between parents proud to see their children grow and children with enough esteem to believe in themselves as they strike out on their own.

Even Orthodox responsa generalize this line to girls. It is not just liberal Jews, then, who may say it for daughters as well as for sons. The author of the responsum (Harav Yitzchak Nissim, *Noam* 7 [1964]) reasons that under either interpretation, girls are the same as boys. If it is the father who expresses gratitude for no longer being responsible for educating his child, that goes for girls as well as for boys. If it is the child breathing a sigh of relief that punishment from prior generations no longer need be feared, girls and boys can equally feel that way.

In egalitarian congregations, mothers join fathers in wishing their children well and expressing their faith in them as adults.

—◆—

J. HOFFMAN (TRANSLATION)

[3] *"Blessed"* A pithy, modern version of this short blessing might read simply "good riddance."

[3] *"Relieved me of"* Or "released me from."

[3] *"Boy"* The word for "boy" is absent in the Hebrew, but the use of the masculine demonstrative (*zeh,* "this") clearly indicates either a boy or a man, and context limits it to "boy." See, however, Lawrence A. Hoffman on this line.

◆ ◆ ◆

D. "May the One who blessed" (Mi sheberakh)

[Mi sheberakh: *Prayer for the well-being of the* oleh/olah. *Other versions of the prayer exist for relatives or friends of the* oleh/olah *who are sick, or for people in other circumstances where a prayer for well-being is in order.*]

[Mi sheberakh: *Prayer for the well-being of the* oleh/olah. *Other versions of the prayer exist for relatives or friends of the* oleh/olah *who are sick, or for people in other circumstances where a prayer for well-being is in order.*]

[4] May the One who blessed our ancestors, Abraham, Isaac and Jacob, also bless [name], who has come up to honor God and to honor the Torah. [5] May the holy One—blessed be He—protect and save him from all agony and anguish, and from all afflictions and disease, and bless all his efforts with success amid all of Israel, his brothers. [6] And let us say: Amen.

מִי שֶׁבֵּרַךְ אֲבוֹתֵינוּ, אַבְרָהָם יִצְחָק[4] וְיַעֲקֹב, הוּא יְבָרֵךְ אֶת [name] שֶׁעָלָה לִכְבוֹד הַמָּקוֹם וְלִכְבוֹד הַתּוֹרָה. הַקָּדוֹשׁ בָּרוּךְ הוּא יִשְׁמְרֵהוּ וְיַצִּילֵהוּ[5] מִכָּל צָרָה וְצוּקָה וּמִכָּל נֶגַע וּמַחֲלָה, וְיִשְׁלַח בְּרָכָה וְהַצְלָחָה בְּכָל מַעֲשֵׂה יָדָיו עִם כָּל יִשְׂרָאֵל אֶחָיו. וְנֹאמַר[6] אָמֵן:

D. "May the One who blessed" (*MI SHEBERAKH*)

[Mi sheberakh: Prayer for the well-being of the oleh/olah. Other versions of the prayer exist for relatives or friends of the oleh/olah who are sick, or for people in other circumstances where a prayer for well-being is in order.]

4 May the One who blessed our ancestors, Abraham, Isaac and Jacob, also bless [name], who has come up to honor God and to honor the Torah. 5 May the holy One—blessed be He—protect and save him

LANDES (HALAKHAH)

[4] *"May the One who blessed our ancestors"* During the Torah service, it is customary to pray for the sick by saying a *Mi sheberakh*, a prayer asking God to bless those who are ill. In Orthodox congregations, this prayer is often inserted after the sixth *aliyah*. Classically, it is offered separately for men and for women, but it may be offered for both at the same time, with careful adjustment of the grammar and wording.

Traditionally, the sick people's Hebrew names and their mothers'

powerlessness in the face of illness. Thus, it is not necessarily said at every Torah reading and should not be offered casually. Traditionally, this prayer is articulated covenantally for fellow Jews. Both Jews and non-Jews are the object of the prayer for the sick that is offered daily during the *Amidah* (see Volume 2, *The Amidah,* p. 117).

———◆———

[Mi sheberakh: Prayer for the well-being of the oleh/olah. Other versions of the prayer exist for relatives or friends of the oleh/olah who are sick, or for people in other circumstances where a prayer for well-being is in order.]

⁴מִי שֶׁבֵּרַךְ אֲבוֹתֵינוּ, אַבְרָהָם יִצְחָק וְיַעֲקֹב, הוּא
יְבָרֵךְ אֶת [name] שֶׁעָלָה לִכְבוֹד הַמָּקוֹם וְלִכְבוֹד
הַתּוֹרָה. ⁵הַקָּדוֹשׁ בָּרוּךְ הוּא יִשְׁמְרֵהוּ וְיַצִּילֵהוּ מִכָּל

J. HOFFMAN (TRANSLATION)

[4] *"Come up"* A technical term for coming up to read the Torah.

[5] *"Agony and anguish [tsarah v'tsukah]"* The Hebrew literally means something closer to "distress and sorrow," but the Hebrew words have been chosen because of their alliterative value — they both begin with the letter *tsadi* — an effect we try to capture in English.

[5] *"Bless all his efforts with success"* Following Birnbaum.

———◆ ◆ ◆———

Hebrew names are used, but if the mother's name is not known but the father's name is, that name may be substituted (*Y'sodei Y'shurun,* Gedaliah Felder, major North American halakhic authority, mid-twentieth century). Some congregations add the family name so that the congregation will know exactly who is ill.

The *Mi sheberakh* is not a magical incantation. It obligates the *oleh* to give *tzedakah* ("charity") and to pray personally on behalf of the person for whom the prayer is given. It summons us all to recognize our own utter from all agony and anguish, and from all afflictions and disease, and bless all his efforts with success amid all of Israel, his brothers. [6] And let us say: Amen.

צָרָה וְצוּקָה וּמִכָּל נֶגַע וּמַחֲלָה, וְיִשְׁלַח בְּרָכָה וְהַצְלָחָה בְּכָל מַעֲשֵׂה יָדָיו עִם כָּל יִשְׂרָאֵל אֶחָיו. [6]וְנֹאמַר אָמֵן:

E. Concluding Affirmation of Torah: "This is the Torah" (V'ZOT HATORAH)

[Hagbahah and g'lilah:
The Torah is raised on high while the
following is said, after which it is rolled
and dressed. Congregation rises.
In some congregations,
the Half Kaddish is recited here.]

[Hagbahah *and* g'lilah:
The Torah is raised on high while the
following is said, after which it is rolled
and dressed. Congregation rises.
In some congregations,
the Half Kaddish is recited here.]

¹This is the Torah that Moses put before the children of Israel, dictated by God and transcribed by Moses.

²It is a tree of life to those who cling to it, and its supporters are happy. ³Its ways are ways of pleasantness, and all its paths are peace. ⁴Long life is in its right hand, and in its left are riches and honor. ⁵Adonai wanted—for the sake of his righteousness—to make the Torah great and glorious.

וְזֹאת הַתּוֹרָה אֲשֶׁר־שָׂם מֹשֶׁה לִפְנֵי¹
בְּנֵי יִשְׂרָאֵל עַל־פִּי יְיָ בְּיַד־מֹשֶׁה:

עֵץ־חַיִּים הִיא לַמַּחֲזִיקִים בָּהּ²
וְתוֹמְכֶיהָ מְאֻשָּׁר: ³דְּרָכֶיהָ דַרְכֵי־
נֹעַם, וְכָל־נְתִיבוֹתֶיהָ שָׁלוֹם: ⁴אֹרֶךְ
יָמִים בִּימִינָהּ בִּשְׂמֹאלָהּ עֹשֶׁר וְכָבוֹד:
יְיָ חָפֵץ לְמַעַן צִדְקוֹ יַגְדִּיל תּוֹרָה⁵
וְיַאְדִּיר:

BRETTLER (BIBLE)

[1] *"This is the Torah...dictated by God and transcribed by Moses"* Deuteronomy 4:44 and Numbers 9:23, combined to suggest that the Torah itself claims to have been God-given as a whole, through Moses. But the verses are taken out of context. Numbers 9:23 does not refer to the Torah at all, but to Israel's path through the wilderness, which is said to have been divinely decreed and told to Moses. No single biblical verse at all conceptualizes a single Torah composed of the books Genesis through Deuteronomy. In fact, Leviticus 26:46 mentions *torot* (plural), meaning "laws" or "teachings" that God gives Moses. The Rabbis assembled this combination of biblical verses to underscore their own central theological notion of a *(p. 128)*

DORFF (THEOLOGY)

[1] *"This is the Torah"* The authority of the Torah in traditional theology depends upon the belief not only that God dictated the Torah to Moses, but that we now have that same Torah in hand — that *this* is the very Torah that Moses received from God. Orthodox belief depends upon both *(p. 128)*

ELLENSON (MODERN LITURGIES)

[1] *"This is the Torah that Moses put before the children of Israel, dictated by God and transcribed by Moses"* The congregation recites this proclamation as the Torah scroll is unrolled and raised for the congregation to see. It is composed of two biblical citations, Deuteronomy 4:44 ("This is *(p. 129)*

FRANKEL (A WOMAN'S VOICE)

[1] *"This is the Torah"* It is a common practice to point to and identify the physical body of the Torah as we end the Torah service. But why? Surely, everyone present recognizes the unrolled scroll now held aloft for what it is: *zot hatorah:* "This is the Torah!" Why do we need to proclaim this undeniable fact?

Just as we welcome the Torah into our midst by pledging our allegiance through the *Sh'ma*, so we now bring its visit to a formal close by pledging our fidelity one last time. As a community,

E. CONCLUDING AFFIRMATION OF TORAH

[Hagbahah and g'lilah: The Torah is raised on high while the following is said, after which it is rolled and dressed. Congregation rises. In some congregations, the Half Kaddish is recited here.]

[1] This is the Torah that Moses put before the children of Israel, dictated by God and transcribed by Moses.

[2] It is a tree of life to those who cling to it, and its supporters are happy. [3] Its ways are ways of

we stand together as witnesses and affirm: *This* is the very Torah that Moses brought down to us from Sinai at God's command. In so declaring, we magically transform symbol into reality, and then we hastily cloak the Torah in its garments before we awaken from the spell.

———◆———

KUSHNER & POLEN (CHASIDISM)

[1] *"This is the Torah that Moses put before the children of Israel"* [Deut. 44:4] [*Siddur Baal Shem Tov, p. 157, 1st par.*] Our sages *(Yoma 72b)* teach about this verse that if one is worthy, the Torah becomes an elixir but if one is not, then it becomes a poison. This means, says *Sefer Hazikhronot* (vol. I, 345), that if one believes Torah is sacred, it gives life, but if one does not, it becomes toxic. But why should belief have anything to do with the purely intellectual business of learning a text, albeit a sacred one? Surely knowledge is simply a   *(p. 130)*

L. HOFFMAN (HISTORY)

[1] *"This is the Torah that Moses put before the children of Israel"* Prescribed already in the eighth-century *Massekhet Sofrim.* We see at that time that women attended synagogues along with men and were treated equally, at least with regard to this part of the liturgy, since our text mandates, "It is a *mitzvah* for all the men and the women to see the writing [on the scroll] and to bow and say, 'This is the Torah....'"

———◆———

[*Hagbahah and g'lilah: The Torah is raised on high while the following is said, after which it is rolled and dressed. Congregation rises. In some congregations, the Half Kaddish is recited here.*]

וְזֹאת הַתּוֹרָה אֲשֶׁר־שָׂם מֹשֶׁה לִפְנֵי בְּנֵי יִשְׂרָאֵל[1]
עַל־פִּי יְיָ בְּיַד־מֹשֶׁה:

עֵץ־חַיִּים הִיא לַמַּחֲזִיקִים בָּהּ וְתוֹמְכֶיהָ מְאֻשָּׁר:[2]
דְּרָכֶיהָ דַרְכֵי־נֹעַם, וְכָל־נְתִיבוֹתֶיהָ שָׁלוֹם:[3] אֹרֶךְ[4]

J. HOFFMAN (TRANSLATION)

[1] *"Dictated by God and transcribed by Moses"* Literally, "by the mouth of God" and "by the hand of Moses," but Hebrew had no technical word for "dictate" or "transcribe."

[2] *"Its supporters are happy"* The Hebrew adjective *(m'ushar)* is unaccountably in the singular (literally, "Its supporters is happy"). No clear reason for this obvious grammatical error presents itself.

[5] *"His righteousness"* Who is referred to by "his?" Some hold that it refers to Israel, and others assume it refers to God. Fortunately, we can leave the English as ambiguous as the Hebrew.

———◆———

LANDES (HALAKHAH)

[1] *"This is the Torah"* One bows at *Zot hatorah* and says the words with joyful enthusiasm. Anyone outside the room should reenter for this occasion. The Torah is held aloft at this point, open for all to see. One should strive to see the actual words of the scroll at the time. (For all halakhic rules regarding *hagbahah* [raising the scroll] and *g'lilah* [binding it], see introductory essay, pp. 29–39.)

pleasantness, and all its paths are peace. [4] Long life is in its right hand, and in its left are riches and honor. [5] Adonai wanted—for the sake of his righteousness—to make the Torah great and glorious.

יָמִים בִּימִינָהּ בִּשְׂמֹאולָהּ עֹשֶׁר וְכָבוֹד:
[5] יְיָ חָפֵץ לְמַעַן צִדְקוֹ יַגְדִּיל תּוֹרָה וְיַאְדִּיר:

BRETTLER (BIBLE)

single Torah mediated by Moses and composed of the five biblical books from Genesis through Deuteronomy.

[2, 3] *"A tree of life.... Its ways are ways of pleasantness, and all its paths are peace"* A quotation in reverse order of Proverbs 3:17–18. Material is sometimes cited in reverse order in the Bible and post-biblical literature to indicate that a later source is quoting an earlier one; that may be the function of the reversal here as well. But *chokhmah*, the wisdom that Proverbs is describing, means "practical learning," not "Torah." The Rabbis, however, reinterpret *chokhmah* to mean "Torah," a development that can be found already in a pre-rabbinic, second-century B.C.E. Jewish composition, *(The Wisdom of) Ben-Sirah.*

DORFF (THEOLOGY)

those beliefs: verbal revelation (that God revealed the Torah in Hebrew words), and that we have an accurate copy of the words God gave.

Conservative, Reconstructionist, and Reform Jews, by contrast, take a historical approach to the text of the Torah, seeing it as a collection of human documents that were edited together. The evidence for that approach includes the differing, and sometimes contradictory, accounts of various events as described in the Torah; contradictions in a number of biblical laws as presented in one place in the Torah as against another; and archaeological, linguistic, and cross-cultural evidence suggesting that the Torah's laws and stories were influenced by other cultures among whose peoples the ancient Israelites lived. This approach enables liberal scholars to be completely open and honest in their research into biblical history, law, and thought; they do not have to ignore such evidence or try to explain it away. They also do not have to study the Torah "with kid gloves," as it were, refusing to apply the same techniques to its analysis that historians use for every other text.

On the other hand, the historical approach that liberal scholars use raises the important question of the authority of the biblical text. If a variety of human beings wrote the text we have in hand, why should we live our lives by it?

Approaches to that question differ, and I describe them at some length in my book *Conservative Judaism: Our Ancestors to Our Descendants* (New York: United Synagogue of Conservative Judaism, 1996), pp. 96–150. Briefly, one view maintains that God did indeed speak Hebrew words at Sinai, but people wrote them down, and what we have in hand is God's words as filtered through the scribes of the past. The Torah retains divine authority, but it is open to historical analysis. Another approach maintains that the Torah was written by human beings who were *inspired* by God. That theory, too, grounds the authority of the Torah in God's will but embraces historical study of the biblical text as a human document. Still other thinkers assert that we do not really know what happened at Sinai but that the Torah is the record of the Israelites' reactions to their encounters with God. The Torah still retains divine authority on this view, but it is interwoven with the authority that the Jewish People gave it by adopting it as their authoritative text throughout history. Historical analysis according to this view is also appropriate. Some claim that the Torah is simply a human document, and its authority completely depends on how much the contemporary community ascribes to it. Reform theorists vary in their description of revelation, but they maintain that, in any case, it is individual Jews, rather than the Jewish community in whole or in part, who must determine both the degree to which they will abide by its laws and the specific way they will do so.

In sum, then, whereas Orthodox Jews recite this line with a literalist view of revelation in mind, Conservative, Reconstructionist, and Reform Jews recite it with very different understandings of both the process of revelation and the authority of the text of the Torah. For some, this sentence in the liturgy is simply an expression of what most Jews believed in the past; for others, it is a metaphor for the continuity and divine authority of the text; and for others, it is still true, even though God's revelation given to Moses was in a nonverbal form and even though the text we have in hand bears the imprint of its human authors.

———◆———

ELLENSON (MODERN LITURGIES)

the Torah that Moses put before the children of Israel") and Numbers 9:23 ("dictated by God and transcribed by Moses"). Incidentally, the Numbers text is taken out of its biblical context. In the Bible, it actually says that the Israelites made or broke camp "as dictated by God and transcribed by Moses."

In the words of the Orthodox Artscroll *Siddur,* the combined statement "declares the cardinal tenet of faith that the Torah now in our hands is the same one that God transmitted to Moses." Non-Orthodox Jews find this dogma highly questionable. While most liberal theologians affirm that at Mount Sinai God established a covenant with Israel, they reject the belief that the entire Law was literally revealed by God to Moses there. Instead, they have held that the Torah evolved over time.

The Hamburg Temple prayer books placed this declaration in an earlier part of the Torah service and, even then, printed only the Deuteronomy part, not the Numbers phrase. *Olath Tamid,* the *Union Prayer Book,* and *Lev Chadash* eliminated both passages from their pages.

In typical fashion, Geiger preserved the Hebrew of this text for affective reasons but did not translate Numbers 9:23. Instead, he simply wrote, as the conclusion to this declaration, "It is the word of God." Wise adopted a similar approach, but he also removed the Hebrew for "transcribed by Moses" *(b'yad moshe).* His English reads, "This is the Torah which Moses laid before the children of Israel by the will of God." *Gates of Prayer* has restored the entire passage and translated it, "This is the Torah that Moses placed before the people of Israel to fulfill the word of God."

Rationalist Mordecai Kaplan could not abide this text. His 1945 Reconstructionist liturgy includes just the first words of this declaration, "This is the Torah," followed by Proverbs 3:18, "It is a tree of life." Despite Kaplan's fierce opposition to this text, *Kol Haneshamah* has restored this line as an alternative. As heirs to the Kaplan legacy, it has felt the need to explain to its Reconstructionist constituency, "Earlier Reconstructionists were concerned that it be made clear that while affirming the holiness of Torah, they did not believe that it was given to Moses at Mount Sinai. Many current Reconstructionists believe the evolutionary nature of Torah to be self-evident and have returned to the traditional line for the sake of its rich mythic imagery."

In an age where denominational lines among American Jews are highly permeable, and where sociological studies indicate that over 450,000 contemporary Reform Jews were raised in Conservative Jewish congregations, the restoration of this Hebrew declaration in the major prayer books of American Reform and Reconstructionist Judaism indicates how central this passage is for Reform and Reconstructionist congregants schooled in traditional liturgy. Furthermore, it testifies to the mantra-like power the Hebrew possesses for those familiar with it.

KUSHNER & POLEN (CHASIDISM)

matter of getting something into one's head, whereas belief concerns matters that are beyond knowledge. Knowledge of Torah should therefore have nothing to do with belief!

In tractate *Shabbat* (88b), Raba says that the right hand is an elixir, whereas the left is a toxin. Rashi explains this to mean that the right hand devotes all its effort and energy to comprehending the secret meaning of sacred text. Thus, when one learns Torah, one needs to believe with a simple faith that each and every word conceals an inner secret. And one must therefore devote all one's mental faculties toward penetrating that innermost core. Such conviction purifies the learning of Torah.

To put it in a more modern idiom, when we confront a Torah text that initially strikes us as apparently self-contradictory, incomplete, unintelligible or — God forbid — simply mistaken, we have only one of two options: "Either it is stupid, or I am." To say the former arrogantly seals us off from any further possibility of learning. To say with humility that there must be something more here that we don't understand opens the door to infinite learning. Indeed, long ago the Zohar noted that the stories in the Torah couldn't possibly be about what they seem to be about, otherwise we could write better stories (III 152a)!

In this way, the author of *Sefer Hazikhronot* concludes that if we learn Torah with the humble faith that it must contain infinite mysteries and wisdom, we are purified through our study, and Torah becomes for us an elixir.

◆ ◆ ◆

3 | Haftarah *Blessings*

A. BLESSING BEFORE

*[Blessing before reading:
on the theme of the prophets:]*

[1] Blessed are You, Adonai our God, ruler of the world, who has selected good prophets, and loved their words, spoken in truth. [2] Blessed are You, Adonai, who selects the Torah, and Moses his servant, and Israel his people, and prophets of the truth and righteousness.

*[Blessing before reading:
on the theme of the prophets:]*

בָּרוּךְ אַתָּה יְיָ אֱלֹהֵינוּ מֶלֶךְ הָעוֹלָם[1]
אֲשֶׁר בָּחַר בִּנְבִיאִים טוֹבִים וְרָצָה
בְדִבְרֵיהֶם הַנֶּאֱמָרִים בֶּאֱמֶת. בָּרוּךְ[2]
אַתָּה יְיָ הַבּוֹחֵר בַּתּוֹרָה וּבְמֹשֶׁה עַבְדוֹ
וּבְיִשְׂרָאֵל עַמּוֹ וּבִנְבִיאֵי הָאֱמֶת וָצֶדֶק:

BRETTLER (BIBLE)

[1] *"Good prophets...words, spoken in truth"* A major concern of prophecy in antiquity was verifying that the prophet accurately reflected what God has said. Legal (Deut. 13:2-6; 18:9-22), narrative (1 Kings 22), and prophetic (Jer. 28) texts all focus on that issue, which is the theme here too, in an introductory blessing that legitimates the reading of the *Haftarah* by declaring its contents true and loved by God.

[2] *"Who selects the Torah"* Critical scholarship suggests that most of the prophets spoke before the Torah was canonized, so that prophetic literature must be read independently of the Torah, which it sometimes even contradicts. In Amos *(p. 136)*

DORFF (THEOLOGY)

[2] *"Blessed are You, Adonai, who selects the Torah, and Moses his servant, and Israel his People, and prophets of the truth and righteousness"* This blessing introduces the *Haftarah,* the selections from the biblical books known as the Prophets that we read on Shabbat and on festivals. Jews divide the Bible into three parts, "The Prophets" being the second section, including not only literary prophecies of people like Isaiah, Jeremiah, and Ezekiel, who present themselves as having heard and, in some cases, actually seen God, but also historical books (Joshua, Judges, 1 and 2 Samuel, and 1and 2 Kings) that describe the history of the Jewish People from the death of Moses (c. 1250 B.C.E) *(p. 136)*

FRANKEL (A WOMAN'S VOICE)

[1] *"Who has selected good prophets"* The selections from prophetic literature known as the *Haftarot* serve to bridge the Jewish People's past and future. Chastising Israel for its moral shortcomings, the prophets also promise divine redemption. Week by week, the morality play continues: Israel sins, God's wrath erupts, Israel repents, God relents. Kingdoms rise and fall at Israel's expense; the end of history looms just over the horizon.

Framing these dramas are a set of five blessings, one before and four after the prophetic reading. Their *(p. 136)*

A. BLESSING BEFORE

[Blessing before reading: on the theme of the prophets:]

[1] Blessed are You, Adonai our God, ruler of the world, who has selected good prophets, and loved their words, spoken in truth. [2] Blessed are You, Adonai, who selects the Torah, and Moses his servant, and Israel his people, and prophets of the truth and righteousness.

HAUPTMAN (TALMUD)

[1] *"Blessed are You...who has selected good prophets"* We arrive now at the *Haftarah* benedictions. The word *Haftarah,* often mispronounced colloquially as "half-Torah," is not related to the word Torah at all. The root of *Haftarah, p.t.r,* means "to end" or "to complete." This term refers to the fact that the Torah reading is "rounded off" with a reading from the Prophets, usually with something related to the Torah portion and often with a set of verses that is upbeat or optimistic. The main exceptions are the *Haftarot* for the three weeks *(p. 137)*

LANDES (HALAKHAH)

[1] *"Who has selected good prophets"* For the halakhah of reciting the *Haftarah* and its blessings, see the introductory essay, pp. 29–39.

———◆———

[Blessing before reading: on the theme of the prophets:]

בָּרוּךְ אַתָּה יְיָ אֱלֹהֵינוּ מֶלֶךְ הָעוֹלָם אֲשֶׁר בָּחַר[1]
בִּנְבִיאִים טוֹבִים וְרָצָה בְדִבְרֵיהֶם הַנֶּאֱמָרִים בֶּאֱמֶת.
בָּרוּךְ אַתָּה יְיָ הַבּוֹחֵר בַּתּוֹרָה וּבְמֹשֶׁה עַבְדּוֹ[2]
וּבְיִשְׂרָאֵל עַמּוֹ וּבִנְבִיאֵי הָאֱמֶת וָצֶדֶק:

L. HOFFMAN (HISTORY)

HAFTARAH *BLESSINGS: THE* MAFTIR *(THE LAST READER) CHANTS THE HAFTARAH, BRACKETED BY BLESSINGS. THE FIRST BLESSING PRECEDES THE HAFTARAH; THE OTHERS FOLLOW IT.*

[1] *"Who has selected good prophets…"* The first of five blessings that begin and conclude the reading of the *Haftarah*. The fact that there are five of them, not just two, arouses suspicion. Usually, scriptural readings are bracketed only by one blessing before and one blessing after them. This introductory blessing is thematically relevant to the *Haftarah,* since it thanks God for selecting "good prophets." The first concluding blessing (p. 139) is likewise   *(p. 137)*

J. HOFFMAN (TRANSLATION)

[1] *"Loved [ratsah]"* The Hebrew, which literally means "wanted," is commonly used to express how God feels about the People Israel. Though sometimes translated as "takes pleasure in," it also means "love," a stronger term, which we choose to use here.

Spanish recognizes two words for love: *amar* represents primarily love between husband and wife, while *querer,* which literally means "to want," represents platonic love. (Unlike "like" in English, the platonic *querer* in Spanish is used between children and parents as well as between friends.) The semantic connection between "want" and "like/love" is attested in English as well: "If you like" means the same thing as "if you want." Perhaps in   *(p. 138)*

HAFTARAH BLESSINGS

BRETTLER (BIBLE)

5:25, for instance, the prophet asks rhetorically whether Israel offered sacrifices to God during the forty years of wandering in the wilderness. The assumption that sacrifice had not occurred then flatly contradicts the late priestly strata of the Torah, which suggest that it was precisely in the wilderness that the practice of daily offerings began. Rabbinic tradition, however, understands the prophets as "proto-rabbis," who interpret the Torah that was given on Sinai. For this reason, our blessing ties together the "Torah," "Moses" (the intermediary through whom the Torah was given), "Israel" (who must heed the Torah), and the "prophets" (the Torah's first legitimate interpreters).

——◆——

DORFF (THEOLOGY)

to shortly after the destruction of the First Temple in 586 B.C.E. The biblical selections that are used for the *Haftarah* include readings from both these literary prophecies and these historical books.

In the case of the literary prophecies, the Rabbis saw the prophets as having true interactions with God, albeit less reliable ones than that of Moses, whose experience gave us the Torah. "What was the distinction between Moses and the other prophets?" the Rabbis ask. "The latter looked through nine lenses...whereas Moses looked through only one.... They looked through cloudy lenses...but Moses through one that was clear" (Lev. Rabbah 1:14).

Thus, the opening blessing for the *Haftarah,* preparing us to read from the Prophets, blesses God for giving us true prophets, but takes care to mention first the most authoritative revelation: that of the Torah given to Moses.

——◆——

FRANKEL (A WOMAN'S VOICE)

themes are familiar to us from other liturgical anthologies — the Grace after Meals, the Wedding Blessings. We praise God for the prophets and their truthful words, for God's own true words, for the promise of redeeming Jerusalem and the Jewish People, and finally for the Torah itself, which we are reading on this holy day. In a way, these blessings enact what they invoke: reciting these words with true intent, we imitate God, who is described in the second blessing as the One "who does what he says, who keeps his promises" *(omer v'oseh, m'daber u'm'kayeim),* the twin phrases reinforcing the centrality of God's verbal power. We are assured that "not one of your [God's] words will return unfulfilled." So, too, we offer our words with the hope that they also will bear fruit, that God will make "our heart delight" *(yageil libenu)* and restore us to wholeness.

——◆——

136

HAUPTMAN (TALMUD)

before the holiday of Tisha B'av (the ninth day of the Hebrew month of Av, which marks the destruction of the Temple.) The *Haftarot* on those weeks anticipate the destruction by rebuking Israel for its sinful misbehavior, which occasioned the Temple's demise. Unlike the Torah, which is read from a scroll, is handwritten on parchment, and lacks vocalization and punctuation, the *Haftarah* is read in most synagogues from a printed page, with full punctuation and vocalization. It is therefore customary for the one called to read the *Haftarah* not only to recite the blessings before and after it but also to read the *Haftarah* portion itself. This is unlike the Torah reading, in that we have no specially trained reader, or *ba'al korei,* for the *Haftarah.*

The blessing before the *Haftarah* opens by saying that God selected the prophets and that they are prophets of truth. It concludes by saying that God chose the Torah, Moses, Israel, and the prophets. As noted above, these are all standard liturgical themes.

———◆———

L. HOFFMAN (HISTORY)

relevant since it guarantees that God "does what He says [and] keeps his promises" (see p. 139) — which is to say that if a prophet promises it, you can count on it. For the Rabbis, prophets predicted redemption. Our blessing tells us to believe that redemption will come because God doesn't lie.

The next three blessings, however (see pp. 139–140), are redundant at best and perhaps even irrelevant. The second ("Have compassion on Zion….") and the third ("By your power let us rejoice….") reflect standard redemptive themes (rebuilding of Zion and the coming of the messiah), so they may be, at best, extensions of the first blessing. But what do we do with the last one: "For the Torah"? Again we have a standard theme, the sanctity of the Sabbath day, as we see from its final line — the *chatimah* — which concludes, "Blessed are You…who makes the Sabbath holy." But what does that have to do with the *Haftarah?*

The late Joseph Heinemann, an outstanding pioneer in liturgical theory, suggested that all four blessings that follow the *Haftarah* were originally said as a group elsewhere and were only eventually moved here. He believed that before the end of the first century, the *Amidah* (see Volume 2, *The Amidah*) was not yet codified. Communities varied widely in what (and how many) blessings they said then. These four blessings look like such an early "proto-*Amidah*," unique in that they began with a blessing thanking God for prophets. After the *Amidah* was codified, the first of the four blessings was moved to the end of the *Haftarah* recitation as an apt concluding benediction there. But since it was "fused" in popular practice with the other three that followed it, they came along with it automatically. And there they have remained ever since.

———◆———

J. HOFFMAN (TRANSLATION)

Hebrew, as in Spanish, *rotseh,* which literally means "wants," represents a specific type of affection.

[2] *"Prophets of the truth"* Or, perhaps, "the prophets of truth." The Hebrew is ambiguous.

B. Blessings After

*[First blessing after reading:
on the theme of the prophets:]*

¹ Blessed are You, Adonai our God, ruler of the world, rock of all eternity, righteous in all generations, the faithful God, who does what He says, who keeps his promises, whose every word is true and just. ² You are faithful, Adonai our God, and your words are faithful, and not one of your words will return unfulfilled, for You are the faithful and merciful God and King. ³ Blessed are You, Adonai, the faithful God in all his words.

*[Second blessing after reading:
on the theme of rebuilding Zion:]*

⁴ Have compassion on Zion, for it is the house of our lives. ⁵ Save the humbled soul quickly in our day. ⁶ Blessed are You, Adonai, by whose power Zion rejoices in her children.

*[Third blessing after reading:
on the theme of the messiah:]*

⁷ By your power let us rejoice in Elijah the prophet, your servant, and in the kingdom of the house of David, your anointed. ⁸ Let him come quickly, that our heart delight. ⁹ Let no stranger sit on his throne, and let others no longer inherit his glory, for by your holy name You swore to him that his candle would never be extinguished. ¹⁰ Blessed are You, Adonai, Shield of David.

*[First blessing after reading:
on the theme of the prophets:]*

¹בָּרוּךְ אַתָּה יְיָ אֱלֹהֵינוּ מֶלֶךְ הָעוֹלָם צוּר כָּל־הָעוֹלָמִים צַדִּיק בְּכָל־הַדּוֹרוֹת הָאֵל הַנֶּאֱמָן הָאוֹמֵר וְעוֹשֶׂה הַמְדַבֵּר וּמְקַיֵּם שֶׁכָּל־דְּבָרָיו אֱמֶת וָצֶדֶק: ²נֶאֱמָן אַתָּה הוּא יְיָ אֱלֹהֵינוּ, וְנֶאֱמָנִים דְּבָרֶיךָ וְדָבָר אֶחָד מִדְּבָרֶיךָ אָחוֹר לֹא־יָשׁוּב רֵיקָם כִּי אֵל מֶלֶךְ נֶאֱמָן אָתָּה. ³בָּרוּךְ אַתָּה יְיָ הָאֵל הַנֶּאֱמָן בְּכָל־דְּבָרָיו:

*[Second blessing after reading:
on the theme of rebuilding Zion:]*

⁴רַחֵם עַל־צִיּוֹן כִּי הִיא בֵּית חַיֵּינוּ ⁵וְלַעֲלוּבַת נֶפֶשׁ תּוֹשִׁיעַ בִּמְהֵרָה בְיָמֵינוּ. ⁶בָּרוּךְ אַתָּה יְיָ מְשַׂמֵּחַ צִיּוֹן בְּבָנֶיהָ:

*[Third blessing after reading:
on the theme of the messiah:]*

⁷שַׂמְּחֵנוּ יְיָ אֱלֹהֵינוּ בְּאֵלִיָּהוּ הַנָּבִיא עַבְדֶּךָ וּבְמַלְכוּת בֵּית דָּוִד מְשִׁיחֶךָ ⁸בִּמְהֵרָה יָבֹא וְיָגֵל לִבֵּנוּ ⁹עַל־כִּסְאוֹ לֹא־יֵשֶׁב זָר וְלֹא יִנְחֲלוּ עוֹד אֲחֵרִים אֶת כְּבוֹדוֹ. כִּי בְשֵׁם קָדְשְׁךָ נִשְׁבַּעְתָּ לּוֹ שֶׁלֹּא יִכְבֶּה נֵרוֹ לְעוֹלָם וָעֶד. ¹⁰בָּרוּךְ אַתָּה יְיָ מָגֵן דָּוִד:

[Fourth blessing after reading: on the theme of the sanctity of the Sabbath:]

11 For the Torah, for worship, for the prophets, and for this Shabbat day that You have given us, Adonai our God, for holiness and rest, for honor and glory, for all of these, Adonai our God, we acknowledge you with thanks, and praise you. 12 May your name be praised by the mouths of all the living to the ends of time! 13 Blessed are You, Adonai, who makes the Sabbath holy.

[Fourth blessing after reading: on the theme of the sanctity of the Sabbath:]

‏11עַל־הַתּוֹרָה וְעַל־הָעֲבוֹדָה וְעַל־הַנְּבִיאִים וְעַל־יוֹם הַשַּׁבָּת הַזֶּה שֶׁנָּתַתָּ־לָּנוּ יְיָ אֱלֹהֵינוּ לִקְדֻשָּׁה וְלִמְנוּחָה לְכָבוֹד וּלְתִפְאָרֶת. עַל הַכֹּל יְיָ אֱלֹהֵינוּ אֲנַחְנוּ מוֹדִים לָךְ וּמְבָרְכִים אוֹתָךְ ‏12יִתְבָּרַךְ שִׁמְךָ בְּפִי כָל־חַי תָּמִיד לְעוֹלָם וָעֶד. ‏13בָּרוּךְ אַתָּה יְיָ מְקַדֵּשׁ הַשַּׁבָּת:

BRETTLER (BIBLE)

[1-2] *"Rock of all eternity...the faithful God.... Not one of your words will return unfulfilled"* Isaiah 26:4 and Deuteronomy 7:9, emphasizing God's reliability. The theme is especially important to the anonymous prophet of the Babylonian exile (586–538 B.C.E.), often called Deutero-Isaiah, who wrote the second half of the book of Isaiah (chapters 40-66) to console the exiles. He says, for example (48:3), "Long ago, I foretold things that happened. From my mouth they issued...and they came to pass." Isaiah 55:11 guarantees that "the word that issues from my mouth...does not return to me unfulfilled" — precisely what our blessing promises. For impact, the blessing repeats "faithful" *(ne'eman)* *(p. 145)*

DORFF (THEOLOGY)

[1] *"Blessed are You, Adonai... who does what He says"* A number of the prophets foresee a time when the People Israel will be redeemed and life's frustrations overcome. The blessing praises God for being faithful to precisely such promises and, given that fidelity, leads up to the following *(p. 146)*

ELLENSON (MODERN LITURGIES)

[1] *"Blessed are You, Adonai our God...who has selected good prophets"* While many liberal liturgies include this blessing along with those recited after recitation of the *Haftarah,* the Hamburg Temple prayer book of 1819 omitted the prophetic reading altogether, except for the morning and afternoon services of

Yom Kippur. Even these two exceptions were allowed to lapse in the 1841 edition. Consequently, all *Haftarah* blessings are missing from the Hamburg liturgy. As the Hamburg *siddurim* had a seminal influence on later Reform liturgy, several nineteenth-century Reform prayer-book authors patterned their own services here after the Hamburg model. Hence, there are no *Haftarah* blessings in works authored by Einhorn and Geiger (1870), and the 1895 edition of the *Union Prayer Book* omitted these blessings also. Even a liturgical conservative like *(p. 146)*

B. BLESSINGS AFTER

[First blessing after reading: on the theme of the prophets:]

[1] Blessed are You, Adonai our God, ruler of the world, rock of all eternity, righteous in all generations, the faithful God, who does what He says, who keeps his promises, whose every word is true and just. [2] You are faithful, Adonai our God, and your words are faithful, and not one of your words will return unfulfilled, for You are the faithful

HAUPTMAN (TALMUD)

[1] *"Blessed are You...rock of all eternity"* The blessings recited after the *Haftarah* are unusually long and of special interest. They consist of four paragraphs with themes that range far afield. The first blessing focuses on God as keeper of his word. This is a not-so-oblique reference to the fact that God, in our opinion, is obligated to fulfill all his promises, as they are recorded by the prophets, such as to bring about a glorious future for the people of Israel, return the exiles to the land of Israel, and initiate a period of peace and prosperity. *(p. 148)*

J. HOFFMAN (Translation)

[1] *"Rock of all eternity"* The word for "eternity" is the same as the word for "world" *(olam),* so our English translation misses an obvious play on words. Birnbaum suggests "creator of all the worlds," but given the phrase that follows, his interpretation seems unlikely. The two nouns, *tzur* ("rock") and *tzadik* ("righteous"), are chosen in part for their alliterative value. Together, they portray God as the reliable one within a set: a rock in the set of things that make up the spatial domain of "all worlds" and the

[First blessing after reading: on the theme of the prophets:]

¹בָּרוּךְ אַתָּה יְיָ אֱלֹהֵינוּ מֶלֶךְ הָעוֹלָם צוּר
כָּל־הָעוֹלָמִים צַדִּיק בְּכָל־הַדּוֹרוֹת הָאֵל הַנֶּאֱמָן
הָאוֹמֵר וְעוֹשֶׂה הַמְדַבֵּר וּמְקַיֵּם שֶׁכָּל־דְּבָרָיו אֱמֶת
וָצֶדֶק: ²נֶאֱמָן אַתָּה הוּא יְיָ אֱלֹהֵינוּ, וְנֶאֱמָנִים דְּבָרֶיךָ

righteous in the set of persons who make up all the generations.

[1] *"Who does what He says, who keeps his promises"* Literally, "who says and does, who speaks and sustains." These words are identical to those found in *Barukh she'amar,* the prayer that opens the *P'sukei D'zimrah* (see Volume 3, *P'sukei D'zimrah: Morning Psalms,* pp. 52, 68). There, we translated them as "who creates by speaking, who sustains by decreeing." But that prayer was about creation, so we chose a translation that properly reflects the context. Here, the same words are used to reflect on God's trustworthiness in fulfilling promises, so we translate them slightly differently. While both translations are accurate, it is unfortunate that we don't have a single translation that like the original Hebrew can be used in two different ways.

[2] *"Words are faithful"* That is, God's words come true.

[2] *"Unfulfilled"* Literally, "empty." The notion of "returning empty" is a common one, seen here but also in the *Amidah* (see Volume 2, *The Amidah,* pp. 146–147), where we translated "Do not turn us away from You empty-handed." The context there was our prayers, or words, to God; here, the context is God's promises, or words, given through the prophets. In either case, words are powerful. They effect something. They are not to be rendered null and avoid. See Lawrence A. Hoffman's note to the effect that this blessing may originally have been an alternative form of proto-*Amidah.*

[2] *"The faithful and merciful God and King"* Or, "a faithful and merciful god and king." The theological implications are great, but the Hebrew might mean either. Birnbaum translates "a faithful and merciful God and King," but with the article "a," both "God" and "King" should be in lowercase.

[4] *"House of our lives [bet chayenu]"* Birnbaum has "source," a translation that makes more sense but is unsupported by the Hebrew.

(p. 149)

and merciful God and King. ³ Blessed are You, Adonai, the faithful God in all his words.

[Second blessing after reading: on the theme of rebuilding Zion:]

⁴ Have compassion on Zion, for it is the house of our lives. ⁵ Save the humbled soul quickly in our day. ⁶ Blessed are You, Adonai, by whose power Zion rejoices in her children.

[Third blessing after reading: on the theme of the messiah:]

⁷ By your power let us rejoice in Elijah the prophet, your servant, and in the kingdom of the house of David, your anointed. ⁸ Let him come quickly, that our heart delight. ⁹ Let no stranger sit on his throne, and let others no longer inherit his glory, for by your holy name You swore to him that his candle would never be extinguished. ¹⁰ Blessed are You, Adonai, Shield of David.

[Fourth blessing after reading: on the theme of the sanctity of the Sabbath:]

¹¹ For the Torah, for worship, for the prophets, and for this Shabbat day that You have given us, Adonai our God, for holiness and rest, for honor and glory, for all of these, Adonai our God, we acknowledge you with thanks, and praise you. ¹² May your name be praised by the mouths of all the living to the ends of time! ¹³ Blessed are You, Adonai, who makes the Sabbath holy.

וְדָבָר אֶחָד מִדְּבָרֶיךָ אָחוֹר לֹא־יָשׁוּב רֵיקָם כִּי אֵל מֶלֶךְ נֶאֱמָן אָתָּה. ³ בָּרוּךְ אַתָּה יְיָ הָאֵל הַנֶּאֱמָן בְּכָל־דְּבָרָיו:

[Second blessing after reading: on the theme of rebuilding Zion:]

⁴ רַחֵם עַל־צִיּוֹן כִּי הִיא בֵּית חַיֵּינוּ ⁵ וְלַעֲלוּבַת נֶפֶשׁ תּוֹשִׁיעַ בִּמְהֵרָה בְיָמֵינוּ. ⁶ בָּרוּךְ אַתָּה יְיָ מְשַׂמֵּחַ צִיּוֹן בְּבָנֶיהָ:

[Third blessing after reading: on the theme of the messiah:]

⁷ שַׂמְּחֵנוּ יְיָ אֱלֹהֵינוּ בְּאֵלִיָּהוּ הַנָּבִיא עַבְדֶּךָ וּבְמַלְכוּת בֵּית דָּוִד מְשִׁיחֶךָ ⁸ בִּמְהֵרָה יָבֹא וְיָגֵל לִבֵּנוּ ⁹ עַל־כִּסְאוֹ לֹא־יֵשֵׁב זָר וְלֹא יִנְחֲלוּ עוֹד אֲחֵרִים אֶת כְּבוֹדוֹ. כִּי בְשֵׁם קָדְשְׁךָ נִשְׁבַּעְתָּ לּוֹ שֶׁלֹּא יִכְבֶּה נֵרוֹ לְעוֹלָם וָעֶד. ¹⁰ בָּרוּךְ אַתָּה יְיָ מָגֵן דָּוִד:

[Fourth blessing after reading: on the theme of the sanctity of the Sabbath:]

¹¹ עַל־הַתּוֹרָה וְעַל־הָעֲבוֹדָה וְעַל־הַנְּבִיאִים וְעַל־יוֹם הַשַּׁבָּת הַזֶּה שֶׁנָּתַתָּ־לָּנוּ יְיָ אֱלֹהֵינוּ לִקְדֻשָּׁה וְלִמְנוּחָה לְכָבוֹד וּלְתִפְאָרֶת. עַל הַכֹּל יְיָ אֱלֹהֵינוּ אֲנַחְנוּ מוֹדִים לָךְ וּמְבָרְכִים אוֹתָךְ ¹² יִתְבָּרַךְ שִׁמְךָ בְּפִי כָל־חַי תָּמִיד לְעוֹלָם וָעֶד. ¹³ בָּרוּךְ אַתָּה יְיָ מְקַדֵּשׁ הַשַּׁבָּת:

BRETTLER (BIBLE)

no fewer than four times. This serves as an introduction to the following paragraphs that ask God to fulfill various unfulfilled biblical prophecies.

[4] *"Have compassion on Zion"* Having established God's faithfulness, we begin a series of requests from God, all of them inherent in the prophetic writings. The initial one is the restoration of Zion (the language comes from Psalm 102:14).

[7] *"Let us rejoice in Elijah…and…your anointed"* The second request is the arrival of the messianic age, heralded by Elijah (Malachi 3:23 promises, "I will send the prophet Elijah to you before the coming of the awesome fearful day of Adonai."). By "anointed" *(mashiach),* the blessing means the messiah, a future Davidic king; in the Bible, however, *mashiach never* has this meaning. It *always* means, instead, a "real" anointed king.

[9] *"For by your holy name You swore to him that his candle would never be extinguished"* A reference to the eternal and unconditional promise of Davidic kingship. 2 Samuel 7:16 promises, "Your throne will be established forever." 1 Kings 8:25 makes the promise conditional on whether "your [David's] descendants walk before me as you have walked before me," a sentiment echoed in Psalm 132:12 ("If your sons keep my covenant, then their sons too will sit upon your throne"). But this blessing is based on the Samuel text as well as other unconditional promise texts, like Psalm 89:21–38. The image of David's lamp comes from Psalm 132:17, which, ironically, contains a conditional promise, not an unconditional one.

[10] *"Shield of David"* From 2 Samuel 22:36, repeated in Psalm 18:36, a psalm where the poet, said to be David, says of God, "You have granted me the shield of your protection."

[11] *"For the Torah"* The requests for the future are concluded on the Sabbath and festivals by a hymn of thanksgiving, as sometimes happens in the Bible also (e.g., Ps. 22). The idea that the Sabbath is for "holiness and rest" is biblical (e.g., Exod. 16:23; 20:8; 23:12). "Honor and glory" are found in the Bible only in reference to the priestly vestments (Exod. 28:2, 40), however, never the Sabbath or festivals. Adding these descriptions builds upon the sentiment of Isaiah 58:13, that the Sabbath is a "delight," and emphasizes that these days are not merely holy days of restrictions but beautiful, wondrous gifts.

[12] *"May your name be praised by the mouths of all the living"* A clear movement from the national to the universal. The Bible expects this universal recognition of God in the eschatological age. Isaiah 2:2–4, for instance, pictures "the days to come.…[when] many peoples shall go and say, 'Come let us go up to the Mount of Adonai.'" The blessing thus ends by returning implicitly to its central theme: the fulfillment of the messianic biblical prophecies.

———◆———

HAFTARAH BLESSINGS

DORFF (THEOLOGY)

blessings that call upon God to bring us the promised messianic era, ushered in by Elijah, the prophet, and ruled by an heir to the Davidic line. On that throne "let no stranger sit" — possibly a reference to false messiahs. Others should not inherit his (God's or the messiah's) glory, for it is we Jews who have kept faith with our covenant with God.

—◆—

ELLENSON (MODERN LITURGIES)

Wise removed them from his *Minhag America,* and several twentieth-century liturgies (e.g., the 1945 Sabbath Reconstructionist Prayer book of Mordecai Kaplan and the 1967 British *Service of the Heart*) have followed suit.

The omission of these blessings is striking, since the universalistic messages of the prophets have always been central for liberal Jews. We would have expected the recitation of the *Haftarah* to be equally central to the liberal Jewish service. Far from being omitted, the *Haftarah* blessings should have received an honored place in liberal Jewish worship.

It is not clear why these blessings were removed, especially since the prophetic reading itself was invariably retained. The 1845 Frankfurt Assembly of Reform Rabbis adopted a resolution that the *Haftarah* be read in the vernacular, and this position was reaffirmed by the Augsburg Rabbinic Synod of 1871. Why, then, were the blessings removed?

Several possible answers come to mind. Perhaps the aim was to shorten the length of the service through omitting these benedictions, but then we might wonder how much actual time was saved through their removal. The goal might also have been to create a more pristine form of Jewish worship based on only the most ancient prayers — a frequent concern that motivated Reform prayer-book composers. But the suspicion that the particular content of these benedictions might be somewhat later additions to the Jewish liturgical heritage was not widespread until the twentieth century. Eric Friedland, a premier historian of modern Jewish prayer books, has opined that the most likely reason these blessings were removed or abbreviated is that it was seen as "disproportionate to recite five blessings for a lesson that seldom took more than a chapter of Scripture." Whatever the reason, these blessings were restored in most American and British Reform-Liberal rites after 1940, reflecting the demographic reality that most Reform congregants of this era were of eastern European ancestry and had experienced bar mitzvah. They had fond memories of these blessings and wanted them in their service.

[4] *"Have compassion on Zion"* The 1854 Geiger prayer book removed this paragraph completely. Its Jewish nationalism was entirely at odds with Geiger's universalistic religious ethos. The *Union Prayer Book* followed suit by omitting the paragraph from its

ELLENSON (MODERN LITURGIES)

own abbreviated rendition of the *Haftarah* blessings. England's *Siddur Lev Chadash* (Liberal) has adopted this model as well. Interestingly, *Gates of Prayer* has provided two alternative sets of *Haftarah* benedictions. One set follows Geiger and omits the paragraph. The second set retains it in its entirety. In light of the positive attitude Liberal Judaism has displayed toward Zionism in past decades, the failure of prayer books such as *SLC* and *GOP* to include this paragraph in every instance cannot be said to stem from the same anti-Jewish nationalistic attitude that characterized Geiger. Contemporary American and British Reform-Liberal liturgies probably excised this paragraph because the *UPB* exerted a powerful influence on them and because they thought the blessings too long.

[5] *"Save the humbled soul quickly"* The prayer books of Israeli Reform and Conservative Judaism, *Ha'avodah Shebalev* and *Va'ani T'fillati*, feel it is inappropriate to characterize Zion as "a humbled soul" now that the State of Israel has been established. Consequently, *SVT* emends this phrase to read, "And may You cause her to rejoice and may You dwell within her forever," while *HS* states, "And save your people Israel." *Kol Haneshamah* reflects the same sensibility; it adopts the Hebrew of *HS* and renders it in English as "Be a help to Israel your people."

[6] *"By whose power Zion rejoices in her children"* Mindful of the reality of a rebuilt Jewish state, *Ha'avodah Shebalev* substitutes "Who builds Jerusalem" for the traditional *chatimah*.

[7] *"Let us rejoice in Elijah the prophet, your servant, and in the kingdom of the house of David, your anointed"* The rejection of belief in a personal messiah caused several liberal prayer books to strike this paragraph altogether. Geiger (1854), the *Union Prayer Book, Lev Chadash,* and one version of the *Haftarah* benedictions contained in *Gates of Prayer* are among these works. In the *GOP* version that does include this blessing, the translation does not affirm the belief in the coming of a personal messiah. Instead, the vision of a messianic era is promoted, as the words "Let our dream of Elijah bear fruit" indicate.

Ha'avodah Shebalev, like *GOP*, offers two versions of this paragraph. One retains the traditional benediction in its entirety. The other omits both these phrases and substitutes "Cause us, Adonai our God, to rejoice in the words of your prophets." *Kol Haneshamah* eliminates the Davidic reference, as Reconstructionist thought, in the words of Rabbi David Teutsch, editor-in-chief of the prayer book, rejects the notion "of a messianic reappearance of hereditary kingship...on both moral and theological grounds."

[8, 9] *"Let him come quickly, that our heart delight. Let no stranger sit on his throne, and let others no longer inherit his glory"* While both *Ha'avodah Shebalev* and *Kol Haneshamah* reject the traditional notion that a personal messiah descended from the house of David will reappear, they both nurture the hope that a messianic era of peace

and harmony will one day emerge. Consequently, *HS* removes these traditional petitions from one version of its *Haftarah* benedictions and places in their stead Malachi 3:24: "May God turn the hearts of the parents to their children, and the hearts of the children to the parents." *KH* too adopts this change and adds a slightly altered version of Isaiah 56:7, "And may your house be called a house of prayer for all peoples."

[10] *"Shield of David" Ha'avodah Shebalev* (Israeli Reform) concludes this blessing with the traditional *chatimah* taken from the previous blessing, "Who makes Zion joyful through her children," while *Kol Haneshamah* (Reconstructionist) concludes, "Who brings an everlasting peace."

———◆———

HAUPTMAN (TALMUD)

[4–7] *"Have compassion on Zion.... let us rejoice...in the kingdom of the house of David"* The second paragraph asks, or rather instructs, God to have compassion on Zion — the *aluvat nefesh,* "the miserable one" — and to save her. Its concluding words are identical to the fifth of the seven wedding blessings, which also asks for reuniting Zion, the grieving mother, with her children. The third paragraph asks for the restoration of the kingship of the house of David, a request made on many other occasions as well, such as in the *Birkat hamazon* (Grace after Meals). These links to other "series of blessings" prayers indicate that it is a common liturgical phenomenon that when asking for one thing, we then ask for a whole set of related things. Weddings trigger that kind of liturgical response. Grace after Meals does the same, and so does the occasion of concluding the Sabbath morning readings from Torah and the Prophets. In all three instances, we request favor upon the Land of Israel, the restoration of the kingship of David, and so forth. What we have is a standard litany of requests to redeem Zion by bringing back her children, rid the Jews of foreign rulers, and restore the kingship of the house of David. This set of paragraphs is, in a sense, a very condensed form of the weekday *Amidah,* which also lays out before God a long list of national aspirations. No opportunity is missed to remind God of what He promised and what the Jewish People still lacks and deeply desires.

[11] *"For the Torah, for worship"* The concluding lengthy paragraph thanks God for everything, including the Torah, the Prophets, the Temple service, and the Sabbath as a day of rest and sanctity. Ending a series of petitions with thanks, as if the requests had already been granted, is yet another standard feature of Jewish prayer.

———◆———

J. HOFFMAN (TRANSLATION)

⁶*"By whose power Zion rejoices [m'samei'ach tsiyon]"* Birnbaum has (the more common) "makes Zion rejoice." But immediately below, the same verb *s.m.ch* is used with "us" as the object —*samcheinu,* that is, God will *m'samei'ach* us, so to speak. Since we translate that as "by your power let us rejoice," we use the same construction here, so as to maintain the parallelism.

⁷*"Elijah the prophet"* The intent seems to be that we will rejoice in the arrival of Elijah the prophet.

⁹*"Throne"* Literally, "chair."

⁹*"Let others no longer inherit his glory"* Birnbaum, "possess." Given the phrase "no longer" *(od),* the sense here is that others have inherited/possessed David's glory before, but that we hope that they will cease to do so. "Possessing his glory" is in apposition to "sitting on his throne," so we must see this as a prayer against rulers of Jerusalem other than David and his line.

◆ ◆ ◆

4 | *Prayers for the Community*

A. FOR THOSE OF ANTIQUITY: "MAY SALVATION ARISE" (*Y'KUM PURKAN*)

[Y'kum purkan *No. 1:*
For the scholars who lived in times past:]

¹ May salvation arise from heaven: grace, kindness, and compassion, long life, abundance, and help from heaven, healthy bodies, perfect light, progeny who live and endure and who never abandon or treat lightly the wisdom of Torah— ² may all these be granted to our masters and teachers, the holy fellowships in the Land of Israel and in Babylonia; ³ also to the heads of the *Kallah*, the exilarchs, the heads of the academies, and the *Dayyanei D'bava*; and to their students and their students' students, and to all engaged in Torah. ⁴ May the master of the universe bless them, extend their lives, make their days numerous, and lengthen their years. ⁵ May they be saved from all distress and evil illness. ⁶ May our master in heaven sustain them in all seasons and times, ⁷ and let us say: Amen.

[Y'kum purkan *No. 1:*
For the scholars who lived in times past:]

יְקוּם פֻּרְקָן מִן־שְׁמַיָּא חִנָּא וְחִסְדָּא
וְרַחֲמֵי וְחַיֵּי אֲרִיכֵי וּמְזוֹנֵי רְוִיחֵי
וְסִיַּעְתָּא דִשְׁמַיָּא וּבַרְיוּת גּוּפָא
וּנְהוֹרָא מְעַלְיָא. זַרְעָא חַיָּא וְקַיָּמָא
זַרְעָא דִּי לָא־יִפְסֵק וְדִי לָא־יִבְטֵל
מִפִּתְגָמֵי אוֹרַיְתָא. ²לְמָרָנָן וְרַבָּנָן
חֲבוּרָתָא קַדִּישָׁתָא דִּי בְּאַרְעָא
דְיִשְׂרָאֵל וְדִי בְּבָבֶל. ³לְרֵישֵׁי כַלֵּי
וּלְרֵישֵׁי גַלְוָתָא וּלְרֵישֵׁי מְתִיבָתָא
וּלְדַיָּנֵי דִי בָבָא. לְכָל־תַּלְמִידֵיהוֹן,
וּלְכָל־תַּלְמִידֵי תַלְמִידֵיהוֹן וּלְכָל
מָאן־דְּעָסְקִין בְּאוֹרַיְתָא: ⁴מַלְכָּא
דְעָלְמָא יְבָרֵךְ יָתְהוֹן. יַפִּישׁ חַיֵּיהוֹן
וְיַסְגֵּא יוֹמֵיהוֹן וְיִתֵּן אַרְכָה לִשְׁנֵיהוֹן.
⁵וְיִתְפָּרְקוּן וְיִשְׁתֵּיזְבוּן מִן כָּל־עָקָא,
וּמִן כָּל־מַרְעִין בִּישִׁין. ⁶מָרָן דִּי
בִשְׁמַיָּא יְהֵא בְּסַעְדְּהוֹן כָּל זְמַן וְעִדָּן.
⁷וְנֹאמַר אָמֵן:

151

BRETTLER (BIBLE)

[1] *"May salvation arise"* A prayer for those who study Torah. The idea of an institution given over to the study of Torah is post-biblical, though some late biblical texts see study as incumbent on the individual. Psalm 1:1–2 promises happiness to "The man [singular] who has not followed the counsel of the wicked, or taken the path of sinners, or joined the company of the insolent; rather, the Torah of Adonai is his delight, and he studies that Torah day and night."

————◆————

ELLENSON (MODERN LITURGIES)

[1] *"May salvation arise"* These specific paragraphs have been removed from every single Reform prayer book in Germany, America, and Israel during the last two centuries, as they call, among other things, for blessing upon the leaders of a Babylonian community that has long since disappeared. At the same time, the idea of asking God for blessing upon Jewish communal leadership and for the welfare of the lands in which Jews live has been deemed compelling. Therefore, liberal liturgies have either recast these paragraphs in original ways or supplied new prayers in the vernacular that call for peace and harmony for all humankind, and support for good government.

Such prayers are not confined to the Reform Movement. Prayer books of all denominations display a variety of prayers in Hebrew, German, and English for the government. Prayers for the State of Israel also appear almost universally in Jewish liturgies.

[2, 3] *"Our masters and teachers, the holy fellowships in the Land of Israel and in Babylonia; also to the heads of the Kallah, the exilarchs, the heads of the academies, and the Dayyanei D'bava"* German Orthodox prayer books preserved these lines in Hebrew but

A. FOR THOSE OF ANTIQUITY

[Y'kum purkan No. 1: For the scholars who lived in times past:]

[1] May salvation arise from heaven: grace, kindness, and compassion, long life, abundance, and help from heaven, healthy bodies, perfect light, progeny who live and endure and who never abandon or treat lightly the wisdom of Torah— [2] may all these be granted to our masters and teachers, the holy fellowships in the

rarely translated them. Conservative liturgies retained the prayer as a whole but omitted these lines in particular, since prayers on behalf of the exilarch and the Geonim, authorities who long ago headed the rabbinical academies of Babylonia, have seemed irrelevant.

————◆————

LANDES (HALAKHAH)

1, 1 *"May salvation arise from heaven....
May the One who blessed our ancestors"*
[p. 155] These prayers are halakhically
difficult because technically, they
constitute *tachanunim* ("requests for
mercy"), which we do not say on
Shabbat or holidays except in the
Amidah, since they involve a certain
"breaking of the heart" (*Imrei Noam,*
Ber. 486). The Gra (*Ma'aseh Rav* 138)
nonetheless mandates saying them,
because at their core is a prayer for
blessings upon scholars and supporters
of the community, and these deserve to

L. HOFFMAN (HISTORY)

*PRAYERS FOR THE COMMUNITY: WE PRAY
IN TURN FOR THE SCHOLARS WHO LIVED
IN TIMES PAST, FOR THE COMMUNITY
TODAY, FOR THE GOVERNMENT, FOR A
MONTH OF BLESSING (IF THE NEW MOON
ARRIVES DURING THE COMING WEEK),
AND FOR OUR MARTYRS.*

1 *"May salvation arise"* [*Y'kum purkan
No. 1*] Two prayers follow, one after the
other, beginning with the same words.
The first one is remarkable in that it
requests blessing for people and for
institutions long gone. It is not clear
who the "holy fellowships"
were. We may have a
nontechnical but flowery
term for the Torah
academies in general. But
this may be a reference to
special groups, perhaps
(among others) the ascetic
community known as "the
mourners of Zion" who
prayed incessantly for Zion's
redemption. The heads of
the *Kallah* were scholars
charged with twice-annual
conferences that drew rabbis from all
over back to the Babylonian academies
for their version of continuing
education. The exilarch was, in a sense,
the Jewish "king" who represented
Babylonian Jewry to the host
government. The heads of the
academies were the Geonim, the chief
rabbis of the time (especially in
Babylonia), who headed up academies
that trained rabbis and then sent them
off to minister to congregations
worldwide. We are not sure who the
Dayyanei D'bava were, but they may

[Y'kum purkan No. 1: For the scholars who lived in times past:]

יְקוּם פֻּרְקָן מִן־שְׁמַיָּא חִנָּא וְחִסְדָּא וְרַחֲמֵי וְחַיֵּי
אֲרִיכֵי וּמְזוֹנֵי רְוִיחֵי וְסִיַּעְתָּא דִשְׁמַיָּא וּבַרְיוּת גּוּפָא
וּנְהוֹרָא מְעַלְיָא. זַרְעָא חַיָּא וְקַיָּמָא זַרְעָא דִּי
לָא־יִפְסַק וְדִי לָא־יִבְטֵל מִפִּתְגָּמֵי אוֹרַיְתָא. ²לְמָרָנָן
וְרַבָּנָן חֲבוּרָתָא קַדִּישָׁתָא דִּי בְּאַרְעָא דְיִשְׂרָאֵל

be said when the largest percentage of
the community is present, namely, on
Shabbat and Yom Tov. It follows from
his reasoning that one would not say
these prayers when there is no *minyan*
(see also *R'ma* 284:7 and *Mishnah
B'rurah* 101:119).

—◆—

(p. 154)

Land of Israel and in Babylonia; [3] also to the heads of the *Kallah,* the exilarchs, the heads of the academies, and the *Dayyanei D'bava;* and to their students and their students' students, and to all engaged in Torah. [4] May the master of the universe bless them, extend their lives, make their days numerous, and lengthen their years. [5] May they be saved from all distress and evil illness. [6] May our master in heaven sustain them in all seasons and times, [7] and let us say: Amen.

וְדִי בְּבָבֶל. [3] לְרֵישֵׁי כַלֵּי וּלְרֵישֵׁי גַלְוָתָא וּלְרֵישֵׁי מְתִיבָתָא וּלְדַיָּנֵי דִי בָבָא. לְכָל־תַּלְמִידֵיהוֹן, וּלְכָל־תַּלְמִידֵי תַלְמִידֵיהוֹן וּלְכָל מָאן־דְּעָסְקִין בְּאוֹרָיְתָא: [4] מַלְכָּא דְעָלְמָא יְבָרֵךְ יָתְהוֹן. יַפִּישׁ חַיֵּיהוֹן וְיַסְגֵּא יוֹמֵיהוֹן וְיִתֵּן אַרְכָה לִשְׁנֵיהוֹן. [5] וְיִתְפָּרְקוּן וְיִשְׁתֵּיזְבוּן מִן כָּל־עָקָא, וּמִן כָּל־מַרְעִין בִּישִׁין. [6] מָרָן דִּי בִשְׁמַיָּא יְהֵא בְּסַעְדְּהוֹן כָּל זְמַן וְעִדָּן. [7] וְנֹאמַר אָמֵן:

L. HOFFMAN (HISTORY)

have been second-in-command to the Geonim in the Babylonian academies. All these officials disappeared when geonic society ended. It is hard to know exactly, but we should probably date the prayer to the late geonic era and assume that it was composed outside of both Babylonia and the Land of Israel, since members of either center generally prayed for themselves alone, whereas this prayer prays for the welfare of the sages and academies in both places.

[1] *"Perfect light"* From the Targum (ancient Aramaic translation) to Job 33:28, which refers to the perfect light of the hereafter. In context, Job, who has suffered unjustly, has been visited by "comforters" trying to find meaning in his plight. When Job denies any meaning whatsoever, Elihu, a younger man who was afraid to speak up, finally takes the plunge, saying that Job must be wrong because God is greater than any mortal. God punishes people on this earth rather than punish them in the hereafter. He holds that in the end, God redeems the contrite sinner so that "he will enjoy light" — the perfect light of the hereafter. The whole point of the book of Job is that Elihu and his comforting friends are wrong, and Job is right. But rabbinic theology thought otherwise.

♦ ♦ ♦

154

B. FOR THE COMMUNITY TODAY

I. "MAY SALVATION ARISE" (Y'KUM PURKAN)

[Y'kum Purkan No. 2:
for the congregation present:]

[1] May salvation arise from heaven: grace, kindness, and compassion, long life, abundance, and help from heaven, healthy bodies, perfect light, progeny who live and endure and who never abandon or treat lightly the wisdom of Torah— [2] may all these be granted to this holy congregation, old and young, to their children and their wives. [3] May the master of the universe bless them, extend their lives, make their days numerous, and lengthen their years. [4] May they be saved from all distress and evil illness. [5] May our master in heaven sustain them in all seasons and times, [6] and let us say: Amen.

II. "MAY THE ONE WHO BLESSED" (MI SHEBERAKH)

[Communal Mi sheberakh:
a second prayer for the congregation:]

[1] May the One who blessed our ancestors Abraham, Isaac, and Jacob bless this entire holy congregation along with every holy congregation, them and their wives and sons and daughters and all that they own, [2] and those who dedicate synagogues for worship, and those who enter them to pray, and those who provide candles for light, wine for *Kiddush* and for *Havdalah,* and food for guests and charity for the poor, and all who faithfully occupy themselves with the needs of the public. [3] May the Holy One, blessed be He, pay their reward, and banish all their disease, and heal their entire body, and forgive all their sins, and grant them blessing and success in all the works of their hands with all of Israel, their brothers, [4] and let us say: Amen.

[Y'kum Purkan No. 2:
for the congregation present:]

יְקוּם פֻּרְקָן מִן־שְׁמַיָּא חִנָּא וְחִסְדָּא וְרַחֲמֵי וְחַיֵּי אֲרִיכֵי וּמְזוֹנֵי רְוִיחֵי, וְסִיַּעְתָּא דִשְׁמַיָּא וּבַרְיוּת גּוּפָא וּנְהוֹרָא מְעַלְיָא. זַרְעָא חַיָּא וְקַיָּמָא. זַרְעָא דִּי לָא־יִפְסַק, וְדִי לָא יִבְטַל מִפִּתְגָּמֵי אוֹרַיְתָא. [2] לְכָל־קְהָלָא קַדִּישָׁא הָדֵן רַבְרְבַיָּא עִם זְעֵרַיָּא טַפְלָא וּנְשַׁיָּא. [3] מַלְכָּא דְעָלְמָא יְבָרֵךְ יָתְכוֹן יַפִּישׁ חַיֵּיכוֹן וְיַסְגֵּא יוֹמֵיכוֹן וְיִתֵּן אַרְכָה לִשְׁנֵיכוֹן. [4] וְתִתְפָּרְקוּן וְתִשְׁתֵּיזְבוּן מִן כָּל־עָקָא וּמִן כָּל־מַרְעִין בִּישִׁין. [5] מָרָן דִּי בִשְׁמַיָּא יְהֵא בְסַעְדְּכוֹן כָּל־זְמַן וְעִדָּן. [6] וְנֹאמַר אָמֵן:

[Communal Mi sheberakh:
a second prayer for the congregation:]

[1] מִי שֶׁבֵּרַךְ אֲבוֹתֵינוּ אַבְרָהָם יִצְחָק וְיַעֲקֹב הוּא יְבָרֵךְ אֶת כָּל־הַקָּהָל הַקָּדוֹשׁ הַזֶּה עִם כָּל־קְהִלּוֹת הַקֹּדֶשׁ, הֵם וּנְשֵׁיהֶם וּבְנֵיהֶם וּבְנוֹתֵיהֶם וְכָל אֲשֶׁר לָהֶם. [2] וּמִי שֶׁמְּיַחֲדִים בָּתֵּי כְנֵסִיּוֹת לִתְפִלָּה. וּמִי שֶׁבָּאִים בְּתוֹכָם לְהִתְפַּלֵּל. וּמִי שֶׁנּוֹתְנִים נֵר לַמָּאוֹר וְיַיִן לְקִדּוּשׁ וּלְהַבְדָּלָה וּפַת לָאוֹרְחִים וּצְדָקָה לַעֲנִיִּים. וְכָל־מִי שֶׁעוֹסְקִים בְּצָרְכֵי צִבּוּר בֶּאֱמוּנָה. [3] הַקָּדוֹשׁ בָּרוּךְ הוּא יְשַׁלֵּם שְׂכָרָם וְיָסִיר מֵהֶם כָּל־מַחֲלָה וְיִרְפָּא לְכָל־גּוּפָם וְיִסְלַח לְכָל־עֲוֹנָם וְיִשְׁלַח בְּרָכָה וְהַצְלָחָה בְּכָל־מַעֲשֵׂה יְדֵיהֶם עִם כָּל־יִשְׂרָאֵל אֲחֵיהֶם. [4] וְנֹאמַר אָמֵן:

155

BRETTLER (BIBLE)

[1] *"May salvation arise"* This blessing includes some typical biblical elements, like divine compassion, a long life, and children. The request for "perfect light" or "vision" —*n'hora ma'alya could be either*— though never found in the Bible, is based on the idea that light resides with God (Dan. 2:22). The prayer for Torah-abiding children is never found in the Bible.

[2] *"To this holy congregation"* The congregation is defined here as including children and women. It parallels Deuteronomy 31:12, where those who must hear the reading of the Torah once every seven years are defined as "men, women, children, and the strangers in your *(p. 159)*

ELLENSON (MODERN LITURGIES)

[2] *"All who faithfully occupy themselves with the needs of the public"* As a sign of the importance of the birth of the modern Jewish State, Reconstructionist and Conservative prayer books attach the additional phrase "And with the rebuilding of the Land of Israel" to those communal leaders upon whom God's blessing is invoked.

———◆———

FRANKEL (A WOMAN'S VOICE)

[1] *"May salvation arise [Y'kum purkan]"* So much of our liturgy is devoted to the "big picture" — the Jewish People, the earth and all its inhabitants, the ruined and redeemed Jerusalem — that we seldom have an opportunity to pray for our local concerns. If any part of the service affords this opportunity, it is the Torah service. This is the time when we ask for healing, one name at a time; express our individual gratitude for escaping harm; celebrate one child's entry into the adult community. It is as if the Torah, by its physical *(p. 159)*

B. FOR THE COMMUNITY TODAY

[Y'kum Purkan *No. 2: for the congregation present:*]

[1] May salvation arise from heaven: grace, kindness, and compassion, long life, abundance, and help from heaven, healthy bodies, perfect light, progeny who live and endure and who never abandon or treat lightly the wisdom of Torah— [2] may all these be granted to this holy congregation, old and young, to their children

HAUPTMAN (TALMUD)

[1] *"May salvation arise from heaven"* We come now to three connected paragraphs, the first two in Aramaic, beginning with *Y'kum purkan*, "May salvation arise from heaven." Because of its opening line, the second paragraph appears to be a verbatim repetition of the first. But it is not. The first paragraph asks for a long series of blessings to be bestowed on the teachers and students of the Torah academies in Israel and in Babylonia — an appropriate request immediately after concluding the week's Torah *(p. 159)*

L. HOFFMAN (HISTORY)

[1] *"May salvation arise"* [Y'kum purkan No. 2]

[1] *"May the One who blessed"* [Mi sheberakh] The second Y'kum purkan differs substantially from the first in that it prays for the welfare of the community that has gathered. It is followed by a Hebrew version of roughly the same thing, which appears first in an eleventh-century French work from the school of Rashi, *Machzor Vitry*. The Hebrew prayer teaches us something about the centrality of synagogue life in the

[Y'kum Purkan No. 2: for the congregation present:]

יְקוּם פֻּרְקָן מִן־שְׁמַיָּא חִנָּא וְחִסְדָּא וְרַחֲמֵי וְחַיֵּי¹
אֲרִיכֵי וּמְזוֹנֵי רְוִיחֵי, וְסִיַּעְתָּא דִשְׁמַיָּא וּבַרְיוּת
גּוּפָא וּנְהוֹרָא מְעַלְיָא. זַרְעָא חַיָּא וְקַיָּמָא. זַרְעָא
דִּי לָא־יִפְסַק, וְדִי לָא יִבְטַל מִפִּתְגָּמֵי אוֹרַיְתָא.
לְכָל־קְהָלָא קַדִּישָׁא הָדֵן רַבְרְבַיָּא עִם זְעֵירַיָּא²

Middle Ages. Prayers are offered not just in general for the congregation but in particular for "those who dedicate synagogues for worship...those who provide candles for light, wine for *Kiddush* and for *Havdalah*, and food for guests and charity for the poor, and all who occupy themselves with the needs of the public." The original text goes further still by stipulating "those who admit guests to their home." Medieval European Jews saw the synagogue as the center of their communal world — a combination not only of study, prayer, and gathering but also of the social

service network that reached out to Jews in need or Jews passing through town who needed a place to stay or food to eat.

This is not the only "communal" *Mi sheberakh* that Jews have known. At times, we have added others. Perhaps the most striking is found in a mid-nineteenth-century *chazzan*'s handbook from the Spanish Portuguese synagogue in New York. In 1840, Jews in Damascus were arrested and charged with the blood libel. At stake was a chronic competition between Jewish and Christian bankers in Turkey's tottering Ottoman empire. Christians in the ascendancy were trying to rid themselves of their economic rivals forever. Fortunately for *(p. 160)*

J. HOFFMAN (TRANSLATION)

[1] *"Ancestors [avot]"* "Ancestors" or "fathers" is the usual translation, but in light of the names that follow, perhaps "patriarchs" would be better. *Avot* may be a technical term here. (Some Reform versions add the word *imahot*— "mothers" or "matriarchs" — and then list the matriarchs here as well.)

[2] *"Dedicate synagogues [m'yachadim batei k'nisiyot]"* Following Birnbaum. Literally, the verb *m'yachadim* means "make one." Perhaps this was an oblique reference to saying the *Sh'ma* and declaring God's name one?

[2] *"Candles"* Birnbaum: "lamps." *(p. 161)*

and their wives. ³May the master of the universe bless them, extend their lives, make their days numerous, and lengthen their years. ⁴May they be saved from all distress and evil illness. ⁵May our master in heaven sustain them in all seasons and times, ⁶and let us say: Amen.

[Communal Mi sheberakh:
a second prayer for the congregation:]

¹May the One who blessed our ancestors Abraham, Isaac, and Jacob bless this entire holy congregation along with every holy congregation, them and their wives and sons and daughters and all that they own, ²and those who dedicate synagogues for worship, and those who enter them to pray, and those who provide candles for light, wine for *Kiddush* and for *Havdalah,* and food for guests and charity for the poor, and all who faithfully occupy themselves with the needs of the public. ³May the Holy One, blessed be He, pay their reward, and banish all their disease, and heal their entire body, and forgive all their sins, and grant them blessing and success in all the works of their hands with all of Israel, their brothers, ⁴and let us say: Amen.

טַפְלָא וּנְשַׁיָּא. ³מַלְכָּא דְעָלְמָא יְבָרֵךְ יָתְכוֹן יַפִּישׁ חַיֵּיכוֹן וְיַסְגֵּא יוֹמֵיכוֹן וְיִתֵּן אַרְכָה לִשְׁנֵיכוֹן. ⁴וְתִתְפָּרְקוּן וְתִשְׁתֵּיזְבוּן מִן כָּל־עָקָא וּמִן כָּל־מַרְעִין בִּישִׁין. ⁵מָרָן דִּי בִשְׁמַיָּא יְהֵא בְסַעְדְּכוֹן כָּל־זְמַן וְעִדָּן. ⁶וְנֹאמַר אָמֵן:

[Communal Mi sheberakh:
a second prayer for the congregation:]

¹מִי שֶׁבֵּרַךְ אֲבוֹתֵינוּ אַבְרָהָם יִצְחָק וְיַעֲקֹב הוּא יְבָרֵךְ אֶת כָּל־הַקָּהָל הַקָּדוֹשׁ הַזֶּה עִם כָּל־קְהִלּוֹת הַקֹּדֶשׁ, הֵם וּנְשֵׁיהֶם וּבְנֵיהֶם וּבְנוֹתֵיהֶם וְכָל־אֲשֶׁר לָהֶם. ²וּמִי שֶׁמְּיַחֲדִים בָּתֵּי כְנֵסִיּוֹת לִתְפִלָּה. וּמִי שֶׁבָּאִים בְּתוֹכָם לְהִתְפַּלֵּל. וּמִי שֶׁנּוֹתְנִים נֵר לַמָּאוֹר וַיַּיִן לְקִדּוּשׁ וּלְהַבְדָּלָה וּפַת לְאוֹרְחִים וּצְדָקָה לַעֲנִיִּים. וְכָל־מִי שֶׁעוֹסְקִים בְּצָרְכֵי צִבּוּר בֶּאֱמוּנָה. ³הַקָּדוֹשׁ בָּרוּךְ הוּא יְשַׁלֵּם שְׂכָרָם וְיָסִיר מֵהֶם כָּל־מַחֲלָה וְיִרְפָּא לְכָל־גּוּפָם וְיִסְלַח לְכָל־עֲוֹנָם וְיִשְׁלַח בְּרָכָה וְהַצְלָחָה בְּכָל־מַעֲשֵׂה יְדֵיהֶם עִם כָּל־יִשְׂרָאֵל אֲחֵיהֶם. ⁴וְנֹאמַר אָמֵן:

BRETTLER (BIBLE)

communities," but it contrasts sharply with Exodus 19:14–15, where the covenantal community is composed of men only.

[1] *"May the One who blessed"* As in the previous paragraph, the congregation is defined very inclusively, though our prayer highlights especially those who have served the synagogue. The Bible knows no synagogues. Previous generations of scholars suggested that Ezekiel 11:16, which refers to a *mikdash m'at,* "a diminished sanctuary," implies that the synagogue arose during the Babylonian exile (sixth century B.C.E.). We now know that it developed only several centuries later, and that the reference in Ezekiel suggests a divine presence, not an institutionalized place of worship among the exiles.

———◆———

FRANKEL (A WOMAN'S VOICE)

presence, personalizes the service for us. Here is our chance to have a private audience with the crown.

There are two prayers that begin the same way here. Significantly, they are in Aramaic, the language of the scholar class in Babylonia during the period that we call geonic — roughly the eighth to the eleventh centuries, the era when they were probably composed. If we extrapolate from the original historical circumstances that prompted their composition to our own time, we can say that this is where we focus on communal needs, praying for the welfare of our leaders and scholars, and then for our own "holy congregation" *(kahala kadisha hadayn).* The second *Y'kum purkan* petitions God specifically on behalf of a local synagogue community and is followed by a Hebrew prayer that does the same thing. After requesting that all members of the community may enjoy long life; material well-being; and studious, healthy children, the prayer singles out for special blessing those individuals who give of their means and time to support Jewish communal institutions and needy individuals by sustaining synagogues, providing wine and candles for *Kiddush* and *Havdalah,* feeding the hungry. It is a list that Jewish federations would have no problem honoring today.

———◆———

HAUPTMAN (TALMUD)

portion. The second paragraph repeats the entire series of petitions found in the first, word for word, but then goes on to ask for them to be bestowed on a different set of people: the entire congregation, the great and the small, the children and the women. Another subtle difference is that the first paragraph is formulated in the third person, requesting benefits for all teachers and students, and the second paragraph is formulated in the second person, addressing only those present and asking that they be blessed.

159

[1] *"Progeny who live and endure and who never abandon or treat lightly the wisdom of Torah"* One rather noticeable omission from the lists of petitions in Jewish prayer is a request for children. Even though many fertility figurines have been unearthed in ancient Israel, presumably used by women in an attempt to conceive, and despite the fact that infertility is one of the defining characteristics of many major female characters in the Bible, statutory Jewish prayer is silent on the subject of children. One possible explanation is that Jewish prayer, for the most part, is collective in its goals and requests. Aside from petitioning God for wisdom, forgiveness, and healing for individuals, the *Amidah* asks for things for the entire Jewish people, such as the ingathering of the exiles. The absence of a request for children may also be a negative response to the pagan fertility rituals so common in the ancient Near East. Or perhaps a prayer for children is so personal that there is no place for it in the Siddur. Ironically, the Rabbis acknowledge that they derive many rules of statutory prayer from Hannah (Ber. 31a), the biblical woman who beseeched God for a child, but they fail to include the essence of her request in the standard petitions of the liturgy.

Here, however, in this Aramaic prayer, we do find at least a short plea for children. It comes in a single line. After asking for favor in the eyes of God, and for mercy, long life, ample sustenance, physical health, and divine light (perhaps a reference to spiritual well-being), we ask for children who will live and be well and who will devote themselves to the study of the Torah. This is the only formal request for children in the entire Siddur.

[1] *"May the One who blessed our ancestors... bless this entire holy congregation"* The third paragraph, this one in Hebrew, repeats part of the second by again asking God to bless the "entire holy congregation." However, it then breaks new ground by singling out for praise those who support and maintain synagogues — those who establish them, pray in them, make donations for their upkeep, and give food to the wayfarer and gifts to the poor (who, it seems, came to the synagogue to ask for help). Note that when asking for blessings for the entire congregation, it says "them and their wives and sons and daughters." This wording suggests that a community in the past was composed of men only. Women and children came under the heading of the members of a man's household.

———◆———

L. HOFFMAN (HISTORY)

the Jews involved, both France and England had colonial designs on Turkey and its Middle East colonies, so when Adolph Cremieux and Sir Moses Montefiore, two outstanding dignitaries representing French and British Jewry, respectively, consulted with their governments, they were dispatched as official representatives to lodge a protest with the Ottoman authorities in Turkey. They ended the persecution in Damascus, although not before several Jews were tortured and some even killed.

Back in the United States, Sefardi Jews had watched the affair with horror, especially since, as Sefardim, they identified with the victims. When England and France seemed miraculously to save the Jews from all-out mass murder, the *chazzan* of New York's leading Sefardi synagogue composed a *Mi sheberakh* seeking God's blessing on the British and French governments and peoples for their noble action.

The latest widespread composition, appearing mostly in Sefardi prayer books from the modern State of Israel, is a prayer for the Israeli defense forces:

> *"May the One who blessed...bless the soldiers of the* Hagganah, *the army that defends Israel; those who stand guard over the our land and the cities of our God, from the border of Lebanon to Egypt and from the Mediterranean to the* aravah *[the western border]; on land, sea, and air. May God defeat their enemies before them. May the Holy One of Blessing guard and save our forces from all trouble and distress and from all wounds and illness. May God strengthen them in spirit and body and send blessing and success in all they do. May God destroy their enemies under them, and crown them with the diadem of deliverance and victory, that through them there be fulfilled the biblical verse (Deut. 20:4), "It is Adonai your God who marches with you to do battle for you against your enemy to bring you victory"* (Siddur Imre Fi Hashalem K'minhag Sefarad V'edot Hamizrach [Jerusalem, 1961]).

———◆———

J. HOFFMAN (TRANSLATION)

[3] *"Works of their hands [ma'aseh y'deihem]"* A literal, and slightly unnatural, translation, but one that captures the flavor of the Hebrew.

[3] *"Brothers"* Others: "brethren," but that word seems archaic.

———————◆ ◆ ◆———————

C. For the Government: "The One who grants salvation" (HONOTEN T'SHUAH)

[Prayer for the government—in this case, the American government; Jews in other countries adjust the prayer to reflect their own officials:]

¹The One who grants salvation to kings and dominion to princes, his kingdom is an eternal kingdom. ²The One who delivers David his servant from an evil sword, who opens a way in the sea, a path in the mighty water, ³He will bless, keep, protect, help, exalt, magnify, and raise up the president and his vice-president, and all the public servants of this land.

⁴In his mercy may the King over the kings of kings give them life and guard them, and save them from sorrow, anguish, and harm. ⁵In his mercy may the King over the kings of kings grant them and all their advisors wisdom to do well by us and by all of Israel. ⁶In their days and in our days Judah will be saved, Israel will dwell securely, and a redeemer will come to Zion. ⁷May this be God's will. ⁸Let us say: Amen.

[Prayer for the government—in this case, the American government; Jews in other countries adjust the prayer to reflect their own officials:]

הַנּוֹתֵן תְּשׁוּעָה לַמְּלָכִים וּמֶמְשָׁלָה לַנְּסִיכִים, מַלְכוּתוֹ מַלְכוּת כָּל עוֹלָמִים; ²הַפּוֹצֶה אֶת דָּוִד עַבְדּוֹ מֵחֶרֶב רָעָה, הַנּוֹתֵן בַּיָּם דָּרֶךְ, וּבְמַיִם עַזִּים נְתִיבָה, ³הוּא יְבָרֵךְ וְיִשְׁמוֹר וְיִנְצוֹר וְיַעֲזוֹר וִירוֹמֵם וִיגַדֵּל וִינַשֵּׂא לְמַעְלָה אֶת הַנָּשִׂיא וְאֶת מִשְׁנֵהוּ וְאֶת כָּל שָׂרֵי הָאָרֶץ הַזֹּאת.

⁴מֶלֶךְ מַלְכֵי הַמְּלָכִים בְּרַחֲמָיו יְחַיֵּם וְיִשְׁמְרֵם, וּמִכָּל צָרָה וְיָגוֹן וָנֶזֶק יַצִּילֵם. ⁵מֶלֶךְ מַלְכֵי הַמְּלָכִים בְּרַחֲמָיו יִתֵּן בְּלִבָּם וּבְלֵב כָּל יוֹעֲצֵיהֶם וְשָׂרֵיהֶם לַעֲשׂוֹת טוֹבָה עִמָּנוּ וְעִם כָּל יִשְׂרָאֵל. ⁶בִּימֵיהֶם וּבְיָמֵינוּ תִּוָּשַׁע יְהוּדָה, וְיִשְׂרָאֵל יִשְׁכּוֹן לָבֶטַח, וּבָא לְצִיּוֹן גּוֹאֵל. ⁷וְכֵן יְהִי רָצוֹן, ⁸וְנֹאמַר אָמֵן.

163

BRETTLER (BIBLE)

[1] *"The One who grants salvation to kings"* This blessing for the government derives from Jeremiah 29:7, where the prophet tells the exiles that "they should seek the welfare of the city to which I have exiled you and pray to Adonai on its behalf, for in its prosperity, you shall prosper." Though no prayers for foreign governments have been preserved from the biblical period, the biblical attitude toward foreign nations where the exiles resided is generally positive. (Psalm 137:8–9 is an exception: "Fair Babylon, you predator, a blessing on him who repays you in kind what you have inflicted on us; a blessing on him who seizes your babies and dashes them against the rocks.")

[1–2] *"His kingdom is an eternal kingdom. The One who delivers David his servant"* A careful reading of our prayer shows it to be a plea for messianic redemption by God. This line, for instance, emphasizes God as the ultimate ruler, and then introduces David. Though David is not explicitly mentioned later, the reference here sets a messianic tone for the prayer as a whole. The following citation from Isaiah 43:6, "who opens a way in the sea," makes the messianism explicit since in the biblical context, it emphasizes God's future redemption of Israel, building upon the traditions concerning God as liberator from Egypt (see Exodus 14–15, where God splits the sea for the fleeing Israelites).

[4] *"The King over the kings of kings"* This phrase, repeated twice in quick succession, picks up the earlier reference (see above) "his kingdom is an eternal kingdom," emphasizing again that it is really God who rules.

[5] *"And all their advisors"* Perhaps recalling the tremendous power of royal officials like Haman to influence the king to hurt the Jews.

[6] *"In their days and in our days Judah will be saved, Israel will dwell securely"* From Jeremiah 23:6; again, in context, messianic. Verses 5–6 there read, "'See,

C. FOR THE GOVERNMENT

[Prayer for the government—in this case, the American government; Jews in other countries adjust the prayer to reflect their own officials:]

[1] The One who grants salvation to kings and dominion to princes, his kingdom is an eternal kingdom. **[2]** The One who delivers David his servant from an evil sword, who opens a way in the sea, a path in the mighty water, **[3]** He will bless, keep, protect, help, exalt, magnify, and

a time is coming,' declares Adonai, 'when I will raise up a true branch of David's line. He shall reign as king and shall prosper, and he shall do what is just and right in the land. In his days, Judah shall be saved and Israel will dwell securely. And this is the name by which he shall be called: "Adonai is our vindicator."'"

[6] *"And a redeemer will come to Zion"* From Isaiah 59:20. Given the fact that this citation immediately follows the one from Jeremiah 23:6, there is little doubt that the "redeemer" in question

(p. 166)

LANDES (HALAKHAH)

[1] *"The One who grants salvation"* Many communities have added a prayer for the State of Israel, composed by Chief Rabbi Isaac Herzog and Israeli Nobel Laureate S. Y. Agnon. A controversial section of the prayer is the reference to Israel as *reshit ts'michat g'ulatenu* (loosely translated, "the beginning of the dawn of our redemption"), which some people find dangerously messianic. People familiar with the composition of the prayer tell us that the intended reference is to the redemptive possibility of the State of

[Prayer for the government—in this case, the American government; Jews in other countries adjust the prayer to reflect their own officials:]

הַנּוֹתֵן תְּשׁוּעָה לַמְּלָכִים וּמֶמְשָׁלָה לַנְּסִיכִים, [1] מַלְכוּתוֹ מַלְכוּת כָּל עוֹלָמִים; הַפּוֹצֶה אֶת דָּוִד [2] עַבְדּוֹ מֵחֶרֶב רָעָה, הַנּוֹתֵן בַּיָּם דֶּרֶךְ, וּבְמַיִם עַזִּים נְתִיבָה, הוּא יְבָרֵךְ וְיִשְׁמֹר וְיִנְצֹר וְיַעֲזֹר וִירוֹמֵם [3]

Israel, not the certainty that it has already entered a state of redemption (conversation with Shlomo Yosef Zevin, premier writer on halakhic issues, Jerusalem).

Another prayer often offered here, especially in Israel, is a *Mi sheberakh* for the soldiers of the Israel Defense Force. This moving prayer, composed by Chief Rabbi of the I. D. F., Shlomo Goren, is probably better situated among the *Mi sheberakh* sections during the Torah service itself.

———◆———

L. HOFFMAN (HISTORY)

[1] *"The One who grants salvation"* "Rabbi, is there a prayer for the czar?" asks a character in a celebrated line in *Fiddler on the Roof*—as if to imply that the very idea is laughable. But there is such a prayer. Jews prayed for the czar all the time in prerevolutionary Russia.

Jews have been praying for the government for centuries. In theory, the idea goes back to Jeremiah 29:7, in which Jewish exiles were advised to "seek the welfare" of whatever city they found themselves in. The Rabbis adapted this teaching to their own situation under Rome. On the one hand, they were realistic about Roman rule, advising, "Do not get friendly with the   *(p. 166)*

J. HOFFMAN (TRANSLATION)

[1] *"Grants salvation"* The Hebrew verb *hanoten* is clearly in the present tense, though the past might make more sense here and below. As for "salvation," the Hebrew *t'shu'ah* is certainly "salvation" or "deliverance" elsewhere. Birnbaum's "victory" makes more sense in context, but there is little support for it in the Hebrew.

[1] *"His kingdom"* The awkward English syntax follows the Hebrew, though in Hebrew it is less so.

[2] *"An evil sword"* Birnbaum: "the evil sword."

[3] *"Public servants"* Literally, "servants," but in context, the proper English term is "public servants."

(p. 168)

raise up the president and his vice-president, and all the public servants of this land.

⁴ In his mercy may the King over the kings of kings give them life and guard them, and save them from sorrow, anguish, and harm. ⁵ In his mercy may the King over the kings of kings grant them and all their advisors wisdom to do well by us and by all of Israel. ⁶ In their days and in our days Judah will be saved, Israel will dwell securely, and a redeemer will come to Zion. ⁷ May this be God's will. ⁸ Let us say: Amen.

וִיגַדֵּל וִינַשֵּׂא לְמַעְלָה אֶת הַנָּשִׂיא וְאֶת מִשְׁנֵהוּ וְאֶת כָּל שָׂרֵי הָאָרֶץ הַזֹּאת.

⁴ מֶלֶךְ מַלְכֵי הַמְּלָכִים בְּרַחֲמָיו יְחַיֶּם וְיִשְׁמְרֵם, וּמִכָּל צָרָה וְיָגוֹן וָנֶזֶק יַצִּילֵם. ⁵ מֶלֶךְ מַלְכֵי הַמְּלָכִים בְּרַחֲמָיו יִתֵּן בְּלִבָּם וּבְלֵב כָּל יוֹעֲצֵיהֶם וְשָׂרֵיהֶם לַעֲשׂוֹת טוֹבָה עִמָּנוּ וְעִם כָּל יִשְׂרָאֵל. ⁶ בִּימֵיהֶם וּבְיָמֵינוּ תִּוָּשַׁע יְהוּדָה, וְיִשְׂרָאֵל יִשְׁכּוֹן לָבֶטַח, וּבָא לְצִיּוֹן גּוֹאֵל. ⁷ וְכֵן יְהִי רָצוֹן, ⁸ וְנֹאמַר אָמֵן.

BRETTLER (BIBLE)

is David, who was mentioned at the beginning of the prayer. The "prayer for the government" is thus framed as a prayer for the realization of the kingship of God through the dawning of the messianic age and the arrival of the messiah. Though covert (the word "messiah" never appears in the prayer), the message is clear: Current governments are important and should be blessed, but they are only a prelude to the future.

L. HOFFMAN (HISTORY)

government" (M. Avot 1:10), which "appears friendly when it is their own best interests, but does not stand by you when you are in need" (M. Avot 2:3). On the other hand, they anticipated the famous European social contract theory by 1,500 years. Seventeenth-century philosophers like Thomas Hobbes and John Locke argued that government came about because (as Hobbes put it) the alternative was a state of nature in which life is "nasty, brutish, and short." Only a ruler can prevent people from tearing each other apart; therefore, as long as the government is reasonably benign, it is better than the jungle-like state of each person for him- or herself. Already by the second century, "R. Hanina, the deputy high priest said, 'Pray for the welfare of the government, since, were it not for the fear of it, people would swallow each other up alive'" (M. Avot 3:2).

Inserting an actual prayer into the liturgy came much later, however. David Abudarham (fourteenth-century Spain) tells us, "Customarily, we say a blessing for the king, asking God to help him and strengthen him against his enemies." The prayers probably varied from place to place at first, however. Rabbi Barry Schwartz has shown that our standard version may come from pre-expulsion Spain (prior to 1492), but the first reference to it is somewhat later, from 1565 or 1566, in Turkey. Spanish emigres from 1492 had moved primarily to the Ottoman empire, the rising Turkish power in the eastern Mediterranean. They were welcomed by the government, which saw them as a valuable economic asset. Our prayer appears in a manuscript with the name of Selim II written in, along with his title "Sultan." By then, the prayer had been used for some time, obviously, since "Selim the Sultan" was written into the space designed for his or for other names of rulers under whom Jews found themselves. But we do not know just how far back the prayer goes.

Turkey had trade connections beyond the Mediterranean, however. Holland, for instance, broke free of the Spanish empire in 1569, aided and abetted by Turkish threats of war against Spain. A prominent Turkish family of the time was the Mendes clan, of whom Dona Gracia Mendes and her nephew Joseph Nasi were prominent. Joseph had supported Selim in his dynastic quarrels with a rival, and when Selim succeeded to the throne, Joseph and his aunt were able to establish an international trading firm with connections in Holland.

The prayer for the government apparently traveled to Holland, then, where Jews had good reason to say it. The newly liberated Protestant state had thrown off Spanish Catholic power, putting an end to the Inquisition within its borders and allowing Marranos to declare their Judaism. A large Jewish community quickly developed (made famous by Rembrandt, who found the Jews to be interesting subjects for his painting). For a long time, the first *printed* edition of a Siddur with this prayer was said to come from Holland in 1658.

In fact, however, an earlier version is now known. It was printed in Venice in 1622, with a Spanish translation and instructions (also in Spanish) as to how to say the prayer ("The cantor will recite this blessing, which is for the preservation of the government").

The prayer is cited by Manassah ben Israel, a leader of Dutch Jewry who lobbied to have Jews return legally to England. In 1665 and again in 1656, he petitioned for an overturn of the edict of expulsion that went back to 1290, using the fact that Jews pray for the government as part of his argument.

[6] *"A redeemer will come to Zion"* The prayer for the government ends with messianic hope. A 1665 English translation of the prayer omits the messianic aspiration, probably because by then the Puritan government of Oliver Cromwell had been replaced by the monarchy under Charles II. Messianism had been rife under Cromwell, but Charles wanted nothing to do with the idea of a worldwide kingdom of David that would replace his own.

By contrast, at exactly the same time — 1665 — the false messiah Sabbatai Zevi announced himself publicly, claiming to be the long-awaited Davidic redeemer. His followers developed their own liturgy, including an alteration in the prayer for the government. They prayed for Sabbatai, whom they saw as the rightful ruler of the world.

——◆——

J. HOFFMAN (TRANSLATION)

[4] *"King over the kings of kings"* See above, "King over the kings of kings."

[5] *"Wisdom [lev]"* Literally, "heart." See above, "Meditation of my heart."

[6] *"In their [the government's] days and in our days"* This is a literal translation of the Hebrew, but it seems ridiculously redundant. If we understand "our days" (an expression that frequently appears in the liturgy) to mean "the days in which we live" (i.e., "now"), then "our days" and "their days" both mean "now." How could "their days" not be the same as "our days," and why are both terms used here? One possibility is that we have misunderstood the meaning of "our days" and that it is an expression akin to "according to our reckoning," "as far as we are concerned," or perhaps "according to our destiny." If "our days" really does mean "according to our destiny," then this phrase would mean "according to our destiny and their destiny." This might also explain why "in our days" occurs so frequently with "quickly." Rather than repetition for emphasis, "quickly in our days" might mean "quickly, as is our destiny."

———— ◆ ◆ ◆ ————

D. For a Month of Blessing: Blessing of the New Moon (Birkat Hachodesh)

[Prayer recited on Shabbat M'vorakhim (The Sabbath of Blessing), the Sabbath preceding the new moon:]

[1] May it be your will, Adonai our God and our ancestors' God, to make this new month one of goodness and blessing for us, [2] and give us long lives, lives of peace, lives of goodness, lives of blessing, lives of prosperity, lives of health, lives full of awe of God and awe of sin, [3] lives devoid of shame and disgrace, lives of wealth and honor, lives with love of Torah and awe of God, lives that fulfill our hearts' desires for goodness. [4] Amen.

[5] May the One who did miracles for our ancestors and redeemed them from slavery to freedom also redeem us soon by gathering the exiles from the four corners of the earth. [6] All of Israel are connected. [7] And let us say: Amen.

[8] May the first day of [insert month] on [insert day(s) of the week] fall on us and on all of Israel for goodness. [9] May the holy One—blessed be He—make it one of life and peace, of happiness and joy, of salvation and comfort for us and for all of Israel. [10] And let us say: Amen.

[Prayer recited on Shabbat M'vorakhim (The Sabbath of Blessing), the Sabbath preceding the new moon:]

[1] יְהִי רָצוֹן מִלְּפָנֶיךָ יְיָ אֱלֹהֵינוּ וֵאלֹהֵי אֲבוֹתֵינוּ שֶׁתְּחַדֵּשׁ עָלֵינוּ אֶת־הַחֹדֶשׁ הַזֶּה לְטוֹבָה וְלִבְרָכָה. [2] וְתִתֶּן־לָנוּ חַיִּים אֲרֻכִּים חַיִּים שֶׁל־שָׁלוֹם. חַיִּים שֶׁל־טוֹבָה. חַיִּים שֶׁל־בְּרָכָה. חַיִּים שֶׁל־פַּרְנָסָה. חַיִּים שֶׁל־חִלּוּץ עֲצָמוֹת. חַיִּים שֶׁיֵּשׁ בָּהֶם יִרְאַת שָׁמַיִם וְיִרְאַת חֵטְא. [3] חַיִּים שֶׁאֵין בָּהֶם בּוּשָׁה וּכְלִמָּה. חַיִּים שֶׁל־עֹשֶׁר וְכָבוֹד. חַיִּים שֶׁתְּהֵא בָנוּ אַהֲבַת תּוֹרָה וְיִרְאַת שָׁמַיִם. חַיִּים שֶׁיִּמָּלְאוּ מִשְׁאֲלוֹת לִבֵּנוּ לְטוֹבָה. [4] אָמֵן סֶלָה:

[5] מִי שֶׁעָשָׂה נִסִּים לַאֲבוֹתֵינוּ וְגָאַל אוֹתָם מֵעַבְדוּת לְחֵרוּת. הוּא יִגְאַל אוֹתָנוּ בְּקָרוֹב וִיקַבֵּץ נִדָּחֵינוּ מֵאַרְבַּע כַּנְפוֹת הָאָרֶץ. [6] חֲבֵרִים כָּל־יִשְׂרָאֵל. [7] וְנֹאמַר אָמֵן:

[8] רֹאשׁ חֹדֶשׁ [insert month] יִהְיֶה בְּיוֹם [insert day(s) of the week] הַבָּא עָלֵינוּ וְעַל־כָּל־יִשְׂרָאֵל לְטוֹבָה: [9] יְחַדְּשֵׁהוּ הַקָּדוֹשׁ בָּרוּךְ הוּא עָלֵינוּ וְעַל כָּל־עַמּוֹ בֵּית יִשְׂרָאֵל. לְחַיִּים וּלְשָׁלוֹם. לְשָׂשׂוֹן וּלְשִׂמְחָה. לִישׁוּעָה וּלְנֶחָמָה. [10] וְנֹאמַר אָמֵן:

BRETTLER (BIBLE)

[1] *"May it be your will"* A prayer for the approaching new month. The new moon was a significant festival in the biblical period. Many texts pair it with the Sabbath (e.g., 2 Kings 4:23; Isa. 1:13; Amos 8:5). A special offering was sacrificed on this day (Num. 28:11–15), work was avoided (Amos 8:5), and trumpets were sounded as a reminder to God of Israel's existence (Num. 10:10).

[5] *"May the One who did miracles"* Often in Deutero-Isaiah (Isaiah 40 ff.— see above, "Rock of all eternity....."), the Exodus from Egypt is invoked as a typological event that will be repeated as the Jews return from Babylon to Israel (e.g., Isa. 52:11–12).

(p. 172)

DORFF (THEOLOGY)

[1] *"May it be your will...to make this new month"* This prayer for the new month serves both practical and theological ends. Practically speaking, in days when people did not have ready access to a Jewish calendar, it notified them of the days during the coming week when Rosh Chodesh, the

(p. 173)

ELLENSON (MODERN LITURGIES)

[3] *"Lives of wealth ['osher — with an 'ayin] and honor"* Ha'avodah Shebalev substitutes yosher, "uprightness," for "abundance," while Kol Haneshamah inserts osher (with an aleph), "happiness."

(p. 173)

FRANKEL (A WOMAN'S VOICE)

[1] *"Make this new month one of goodness and blessing"* The Siddur embodies in its structure the dual calendars of Jewish time: the annual solar cycle of pilgrimage festivals, High Holy Days, and minor fasts and festivals; and the recurrent periodic rhythms of Shabbat and new moons. Like several other prayers in the Torah service, these New Moon blessings are personal and petitionary. In the first paragraph, we ask for a good life for ourselves, for both material and spiritual happiness, for the gifts of a good name and a (p. 174)

D. FOR A MONTH OF BLESSING

[Prayer recited on Shabbat M'vorakhim (The Sabbath of Blessing), the Sabbath preceding the new moon:]

[1] May it be your will, Adonai our God and our ancestors' God, to make this new month one of goodness and blessing for us, [2] and give us long lives, lives of peace, lives of goodness, lives of blessing, lives of prosperity, lives of health, lives full of awe of God and awe of sin, [3] lives devoid of

HAUPTMAN (TALMUD)

[2] *"Long lives, lives of peace"* Except for the Shabbat before Rosh Hashanah, the Shabbat before a new moon features a prayer for the month to come. It would appear that the prayer, which early on mentions the approach of a new month, was written expressly for this occasion. But that is not so. This prayer was composed for daily recitation by Rav, a third-century Rabbi of the Babylonian Talmud. The Talmud tells us (Ber. 16b) that several Rabbis completed the statutory prayers by adding personal prayers of (p. 174)

LANDES (HALAKHAH)

[1] *"Make this new month"* The Hebrew calendar, unlike the secular one, is lunar: the length of a month equals the number of days between new moons and is therefore flexible. Long ago, people knew when a new month began only by proclamation: not knowing when the first day of a month (Rosh Chodesh) fell meant not knowing when to observe the holidays occurring during that month. The proclamation was inserted during the Torah service, as this was when the largest community was present. Today we use a fixed,

[Prayer recited on Shabbat M'vorakhim (The Sabbath of Blessing), the Sabbath preceding the new moon:]

יְהִי רָצוֹן מִלְּפָנֶיךָ יְיָ אֱלֹהֵינוּ וֵאלֹהֵי אֲבוֹתֵינוּ [1]
שֶׁתְּחַדֵּשׁ עָלֵינוּ אֶת־הַחֹדֶשׁ הַזֶּה לְטוֹבָה וְלִבְרָכָה.
וְתִתֶּן־לָנוּ חַיִּים אֲרֻכִּים חַיִּים שֶׁל־שָׁלוֹם. חַיִּים [2]
שֶׁל־טוֹבָה. חַיִּים שֶׁל־בְּרָכָה. חַיִּים שֶׁל־פַּרְנָסָה.
חַיִּים שֶׁל־חִלּוּץ עֲצָמוֹת. חַיִּים שֶׁיֵּשׁ בָּהֶם יִרְאַת
שָׁמַיִם וְיִרְאַת חֵטְא. חַיִּים שֶׁאֵין בָּהֶם בּוּשָׁה [3]

astronomically based calendar, but the announcement of the new month still stands.

The first paragraph is based on a talmudic prayer cited in the name of Rav (Ber. 16b). It centers on the theme of praying for personal renewal by virtue of the moon's renewal. It is thought by some to be a later addition to the liturgy. Many authorities (e.g., the Gra) therefore do not recite it. The general custom, however, is to say it with great fervor. Halakhist and theologian Eliezer Berkowitz (Berlin, Chicago, Jerusalem) referred *(p. 175)*

L. HOFFMAN (HISTORY)

[1] *"Make this new month one of goodness and blessing"* Recited on the Sabbath prior to the new moon (Rosh Chodesh) known as *Shabbat m'vor'akhim* ("the Sabbath of blessing"). Rosh Hashanah is commonly recognized as a time of new beginning. But Rosh Hashanah is just the first "new moon," and in Judaism, every new moon, or month, heralds renewal. Our prayer anticipates that time of renewal by asking us to get ready for it.

In antiquity, every new moon was celebrated as a women's holiday from work. The day before the new moon later became known as *Yom Kippur Katan* ("a little Day of Atonement") in which we might *(p. 175)*

J. HOFFMAN (TRANSLATION)

[1] *"Make [t'chadesh] this new month [hachodesh hazeh]"* Literally, t'chadesh is "renew upon us," the word for "renew" coming from the same root, *ch.d.sh,* that gives us the word for "month" *(chodesh).* Hebrew often matches verbs and objects (as in "to dream a dream" or "to shoe [put on] a shoe,") so probably this introduction is something like "to month the new month," an expression that obviously needs modifying in English. "This new month" is, literally, just "this month."

[2] *"Long lives"* Or, "a long life."

[2] *"Peace"* Or, perhaps, "peacefulness."

(p. 176)

shame and disgrace, lives of wealth and honor, lives with love of Torah and awe of God, lives that fulfill our hearts' desires for goodness. [4]Amen.

[5]May the One who did miracles for our ancestors and redeemed them from slavery to freedom also redeem us soon by gathering the exiles from the four corners of the earth. [6]All of Israel are connected. [7]And let us say: Amen.

[8]May the first day of [insert month] on [insert day(s) of the week] fall on us and on all of Israel for goodness. [9]May the holy One—blessed be He—make it one of life and peace, of happiness and joy, of salvation and comfort for us and for all of Israel. [10]And let us say: Amen.

וּכְלִמָּה. חַיִּים שֶׁל־עֹשֶׁר וְכָבוֹד. חַיִּים שֶׁתְּהֵא בָנוּ אַהֲבַת תּוֹרָה וְיִרְאַת שָׁמַיִם. חַיִּים שֶׁיִּמָּלְאוּ מִשְׁאֲלוֹת לִבֵּנוּ לְטוֹבָה. [4]אָמֵן סֶלָה:

[5]מִי שֶׁעָשָׂה נִסִּים לַאֲבוֹתֵינוּ וְגָאַל אוֹתָם מֵעַבְדוּת לְחֵרוּת. הוּא יִגְאַל אוֹתָנוּ בְּקָרוֹב וִיקַבֵּץ נִדָּחֵינוּ מֵאַרְבַּע כַּנְפוֹת הָאָרֶץ. [6]חֲבֵרִים כָּל־יִשְׂרָאֵל. [7]וְנֹאמַר אָמֵן:

[8]רֹאשׁ חֹדֶשׁ [insert month] יִהְיֶה בְּיוֹם הַבָּא עָלֵינוּ [insert day(s) of the week] וְעַל־כָּל־יִשְׂרָאֵל לְטוֹבָה: [9]יְחַדְּשֵׁהוּ הַקָּדוֹשׁ בָּרוּךְ הוּא עָלֵינוּ וְעַל כָּל־עַמּוֹ בֵּית יִשְׂרָאֵל. לְחַיִּים וּלְשָׁלוֹם. לְשָׂשׂוֹן וּלְשִׂמְחָה. לִישׁוּעָה וּלְנֶחָמָה. [10]וְנֹאמַר אָמֵן:

BRETTLER (BIBLE)

The Exodus has since become the paradigmatic event of divine salvation, so it is invoked here.

[9]*"Of life and peace, of happiness and joy, of salvation and comfort"* The blessings are listed as pairs — a common biblical device, related perhaps to the biblical fondness for parallelism, generally. Most poetic lines are divided into two parts, where many words in the second part mirror those in the first, often as synonyms. These synonyms are often also used in nonpoetic contexts as word pairs bound by "and." The first two pairs found here, "life and peace" and "happiness and joy," are biblical (Mal. 2:5; Isa. 22:13). The final pair is not directly attested, though the verbs related to the nouns "salvation" and "comfort" are used together in Judges 2:18.

DORFF (THEOLOGY)

beginning day(s) of the new month, would fall. People needed to know the proper days because, for instance, the Grace after Meals *(Birkat Hamazon)* is different on the new moon. The announcement also alerted people to the special days, if any, of the coming month and the preparations needed for them. During the entire month of Elul, for instance, Psalm 27 is recited each morning and evening in preparation for the High Holy Days, and some recite other confessional prayers as well. (Everyone, incidentally, would know about the coming of Tishre, the month beginning with Rosh Hashanah, so this prayer is not said on the Sabbath preceding Rosh Hashanah). Finally, in some Jewish communities in some eras, women observed special rites on Rosh Chodesh, so this announcement would tell them of the proper days for those rites as well.

Theologically, though, this prayer marks Rosh Chodesh as a miniature Rosh Hashanah. If our lease on life is up for renewal at the end of each year, causing us to pray to God to forgive our sins and insure us a good new year, each month we become similarly aware of the tentative character of our hold on life and its blessings. Therefore, the prayer asks God first for life, then for the blessings that individuals normally want and need, and then for the communal blessing of redemption. The solemnity of Rosh Hashanah to an extent accompanies the recitation of this prayer as well, for it is recited antiphonally while the congregation stands, with someone holding a Torah scroll, and it is often sung in a quasi–High Holy Day mode.

Note, too, that the prayer asks God for both material and spiritual gifts. We ask God for health and prosperity but also for a life filled with moral resolve, with honor, with love of Torah, and with respect for God.

———◆———

ELLENSON (MODERN LITURGIES)

[9]*"May the holy One — blessed be He — make it one of life and of peace...for us and for all of Israel"* Liberal prayer books sometimes include the prayer for the new month, but, disturbed by its particularity, they have taken steps to include the welfare of all peoples in it. This universalistic sensibility led Geiger to omit "the House of Israel" altogether and to speak of "one Father in Heaven, one brotherhood on earth." The *Union Prayer Book* followed his example and stated, "Help us to spend this month in love of Thee and in the service of man." *Kol Haneshamah* simply substitutes "all who dwell on earth —*kol yoshvei teivel*" for "all his people the House of Israel."

———◆———

PRAYERS FOR THE COMMUNITY

FRANKEL (A WOMAN'S VOICE)

worthy character. The second half of the prayer invokes blessing upon the entire Jewish People. In the middle of the prayer, functioning like a hinge between local and national concerns, we announce the name and first day of the new month.

For Jewish women in particular, the beginning of a new month represents a special occasion. Women's menses mirror the cyclical waxing and waning of the moon. According to the ancient Midrash, because the Israelite women refused to give Aaron their jewelry to make the golden calf, God rewarded them with Rosh Chodesh, the first day of the new month, as their special holiday. And so, for centuries, Rosh Chodesh has been observed as a women's holiday: a time off from housework and a time for women to gather together as a community. In our own time, Jewish women have renewed and expanded this custom by forming Rosh Chodesh groups that meet at the start of each month, observing a sacred time for celebration, study, and sisterhood.

◆

HAUPTMAN (TALMUD)

their own. Among the examples given is this prayer of Rav. If we delete the line that mentions the new month, we will have a faithful rendition of Rav's words in the Talmud. Among other things, he asks for a long life, a life of prosperity, fear of Heaven and of sin, freedom from humiliation, a life of dignity, love of Torah, and fulfillment of all one's wishes for good. When a reference to the new moon was interpolated at some point in time into the opening line, this daily meditation was successfully and aptly converted into a prayer for the new month.

[3] *"Lives devoid of shame and disgrace"* One remarkable feature of Rav's prayer is the reference to a life free of shame. This is not the only place in the Siddur where such a request is made. In the blessing that precedes the morning recitation of the *Sh'ma* (*Ahavah rabah ahavtanu*, "You have loved us most lovingly" — see Volume 1, *The Sh'ma and Its Blessings*, p. 67) the same expression appears: "unite our hearts to love and revere your name, that we will never be shamed." We do not know what Rav and the author of *Ahavah rabah* were anxious about. It is possible they feared becoming dependent on others for a handout. That interpretation is suggested by the fact that the theme of being shamed is found again as part of the *Birkat hamazon* (the Grace after Meals).

In today's world, the request to be spared shame and humiliation is easily understood. All too often, in professional and personal settings, one's dignity is compromised with much resulting emotional pain. Were the Rabbis making reference to similar circumstances in their own lives? Perhaps it was hard to be a Jew in a gentile environment. Perhaps Jews were subject to humiliation just because they were Jews. Even if the historical reference remains obscure, the various requests that Rav makes of God resonate with us today.

174

⁶*"All of Israel are connected"* Only the first paragraph of the prayer for the new month is attributable to Rav (See "Long lives…lives of peace," above). The remaining paragraphs were composed in differing times and places and were eventually tacked together to make a composite prayer that requests a variety of blessings in the month ahead. Here, we find a brief statement asking God to redeem us by returning us to the Land of Israel, accompanied by the powerful observation that "All Israel is connected," or, more literally, all Jews are *chaverim,* that is, "friends." Our translation, which emphasizes the stronger sense of inherent connectedness, suggests the sense of an ideal state of our being joined together in our Land at the end of time.

—◆—

LANDES (HALAKHAH)

me to Judah Halevi's medieval philosophical masterpiece, *The Kuzari.* Halevi justified public worship by saying that private prayers are apt to be self-centered. They may ask for the worshiper's personal well-being but inadvertently oppose the communal best interests. When we pray publicly, however, the other worshipers present remind us to have in mind only that which is for the good of all. Berkowitz held that our prayer here is public, not private, so we have in mind only the public good. That is why the final phrase, "a life in which you will fulfill the wishes of our hearts," adds immediately afterward, "for good."

⁵*"May the One who did miracles"* The reader holds the Torah while reciting this.

⁸*"May the first day of…."* At this point, the exact time of the appearance of the new moon in Jerusalem is announced in language that the community understands (*Sha'arei Ephraim* 10:37). The reader announces the name of the month and the day(s) on which Rosh Chodesh falls. These are repeated by the congregation. When the month has a two-day Rosh Chodesh, the announcement is, for example, *Yom rishon v'yom sheni* ("Sunday and Monday"). If Rosh Chodesh falls on the next Shabbat, we say, *Yom Shabbat kodesh* ("the holy Sabbath day"). When it falls on the next Saturday and on Sunday, we say, *Yom Shabbat kodesh umacharato yom rishon* ("the holy Sabbath day and the next day, Sunday").

—◆—

L. HOFFMAN (HISTORY)

confess our sins and start the new moon afresh. Jews in the Land of Israel before the Crusades actually had a *Kiddush* (an opening mealtime prayer) for Rosh Chodesh, just as we have a *Kiddush* for Sabbaths and major holidays. It was that important to them.

—◆—

175

J. HOFFMAN (TRANSLATION)

[2] *"Prosperity [parnasah]"* It is not clear whether the idea here is "wealthy" or simply "not poor." *Parnasah* can mean simply "making a living."

[2] *"Health"* Literally, "strong bones." Birnbaum has "physical health."

[2] *"Full of"* Literally, "that have in them."

[2] *"God"* Literally, "heaven." "Awe of heaven" was an expression meaning piety, that word being what Birnbaum uses here.

[3] *"Devoid of"* Literally, "that do not have in them." This list thus appears in contradistinction to the one before it.

[3] *"Lives that fulfill"* The Hebrew literally reads, "lives that will be full of."

[4] *"Amen"* In the Hebrew, *selah.* See above, *"Selah."*

[6] *"Connected"* Literally, "friends." But "friends" seems inadequate in context.

[9] *"Peace"* Again, or "peacefulness."

◆ ◆ ◆

E. For Our Martyrs: "In his great mercy, may the father of mercy" (Av harachamim)

[Hazkarat Nishmot Hak'doshim: commemoration of the martyrs:]

[Hazkarat Nishmot Hak'doshim: *commemoration of the martyrs:*]

[1] In his great mercy, may the father of mercy who dwells on high in mercy attend to the righteous, the upright and the honest, the holy communities that gave their lives in the name of God's holiness.

[2] Beloved friends in life, even in death they were not parted. [3] Swifter than eagles, stronger than lions, they did their Master's will, their Rock's desire. [4] Our God will remember them favorably among the other righteous of the world, and will avenge his servants' spilled blood, as it is written in the Torah of Moses, the man of God, [5] "Nations of the world, make his people joyful, for He avenges the blood of his servants, renders vengeance to his foes, and forgives his land, his people." [6] And by your servants the prophets it is written, [7] "I will cleanse their blood which I have not yet cleaned. [8] Adonai dwells in Zion." [9] And in the holy writing it is also said, [10] "Why should the nations say, [11] 'Where is their God?' [12] Before our eyes let the vengeance of your servants' spilled blood be known among the nations." [13] And it is also said, [14] "The one who demands blood remembers them; He does not forget the cry of the humble." [15] And it is said, [16] "He judges the nations, filling it with bodies, crushing heads across the land. [17] He will drink from the stream by the path, and therefore raise heads."

[1]אַב הָרַחֲמִים שׁוֹכֵן מְרוֹמִים. בְּרַחֲמָיו הָעֲצוּמִים. הוּא יִפְקֹד בְּרַחֲמִים. הַחֲסִידִים וְהַיְשָׁרִים וְהַתְּמִימִים. קְהִלּוֹת הַקֹּדֶשׁ שֶׁמָּסְרוּ נַפְשָׁם עַל קְדֻשַּׁת הַשֵּׁם.

[2]הַנֶּאֱהָבִים וְהַנְּעִימִים בְּחַיֵּיהֶם וּבְמוֹתָם לֹא נִפְרָדוּ. [3]מִנְּשָׁרִים קַלּוּ מֵאֲרָיוֹת גָּבֵרוּ. לַעֲשׂוֹת רְצוֹן קוֹנָם וְחֵפֶץ צוּרָם: [4]יִזְכְּרֵם אֱלֹהֵינוּ לְטוֹבָה. עִם שְׁאָר צַדִּיקֵי עוֹלָם. וְיִנְקֹם נִקְמַת דַּם עֲבָדָיו הַשָּׁפוּךְ: כַּכָּתוּב בְּתוֹרַת מֹשֶׁה אִישׁ הָאֱלֹהִים. [5]הַרְנִינוּ גוֹיִם עַמּוֹ כִּי דַם עֲבָדָיו יִקּוֹם. וְנָקָם יָשִׁיב לְצָרָיו וְכִפֶּר אַדְמָתוֹ עַמּוֹ. [6]וְעַל יְדֵי עֲבָדֶיךָ הַנְּבִיאִים כָּתוּב לֵאמֹר. [7]וְנִקֵּיתִי דָמָם לֹא נִקֵּיתִי. [8]וַיְיָ שֹׁכֵן בְּצִיּוֹן: [9]וּבְכִתְבֵי הַקֹּדֶשׁ נֶאֱמַר. [10]לָמָּה יֹאמְרוּ הַגּוֹיִם [11]אַיֵּה אֱלֹהֵיהֶם. [12]יִוָּדַע בַּגּוֹיִם לְעֵינֵינוּ. נִקְמַת דַּם עֲבָדֶיךָ הַשָּׁפוּךְ: [13]וְאוֹמֵר. [14]כִּי דוֹרֵשׁ דָּמִים אוֹתָם זָכָר. לֹא שָׁכַח צַעֲקַת עֲנָוִים: [15]וְאוֹמֵר. [16]יָדִין בַּגּוֹיִם מָלֵא גְוִיּוֹת מָחַץ רֹאשׁ עַל אֶרֶץ רַבָּה: [17]מִנַּחַל בַּדֶּרֶךְ יִשְׁתֶּה עַל כֵּן יָרִים רֹאשׁ.

BRETTLER (BIBLE)

[1] *"Father of mercy"* The main theme of this composition is post-biblical. Martyrdom, which prompted it, arose because of religious intolerance, while the polytheistic ancient near-eastern societies that were home to biblical society were fundamentally tolerant. The only exception is from the very end of the biblical period (second century B.C.E.), when Antiochus IV Epiphanes persecuted the Jews, prompting the writing of the Book of Daniel, which portrays loyalty to God despite persecution. The ultimate defeat of Antiochus is now commemorated by Chanukah. The reason for his strong antipathy to the Jewish religion remains

(p. 180)

ELLENSON (MODERN LITURGIES)

[1] *"In his great mercy, may the father of mercy who dwells on high"* Countless nineteenth-century prayer-book authors regarded this prayer as offensive for a modern age marked by tolerance and enlightenment. Hamburg, Geiger, Wise, and Einhorn all struck this martyrology from their prayer books. Even traditionalists such as Isak Noa Mannheimer (1763–1865) of Vienna and Michael Sachs (1808–1864) of Berlin, whose prayer book revisions were minimal, found it troublesome. Mannheimer followed the model of his Reform colleagues and removed it from his 1843 *T'fillot Yisrael,* while Sachs left it untranslated in his 1855 *Das Gebetbuch der Israeliten.* Leopold Stein of Frankfurt, whose 1860

Seder Ha'avodah had a seminal influence upon Conservative liturgy in the United States, preserved the prayer but altered its wording. Rather than asking God to take vengeance upon the nations, Stein concluded, "And the nations will fear the Name of the Lord, and all the rulers of the earth will stand in awe before His glory." *Sim Shalom* adopts something of this model by omitting the last lines (Ps. 110:6–7): "And it is said, 'He judges the nations, filling it with bodies, crushing heads across the land.'"

———◆———

E. FOR OUR MARTYRS

[Hazkarat Nishmot Hak'doshim: *commemoration of the martyrs:*]

[1] In his great mercy, may the father of mercy who dwells on high in mercy attend to the righteous, the upright and the honest, the holy communities that gave their lives in the name of God's holiness.

[2] Beloved friends in life, even in death they were not parted. [3] Swifter than eagles, stronger than

LANDES (HALAKHAH)

[1] *"In his great mercy, may the father of mercy"* This too is a *tachanun,* involving special heartbreak because of its theme of Jewish persecution. It actually is omitted on certain occasions: when a wedding celebrant or celebrants of a *brit milah* are present, and on the Sabbath when we bless the new moon, except for the new moon of the sad month of Av (Gra, *Ma'aseh Rav* 138). Some communities say it only on the Sabbaths that fall between Pesach and Shavuot, the traditional public mourning period called the *S'firah* (lit.,

[Hazkarat Nishmot Hak'doshim: *commemoration of the martyrs:*]

אַב הָרַחֲמִים שׁוֹכֵן מְרוֹמִים. בְּרַחֲמָיו הָעֲצוּמִים.[1] הוּא יִפְקֹד בְּרַחֲמִים. הַחֲסִידִים וְהַיְשָׁרִים וְהַתְּמִימִים. קְהִלּוֹת הַקֹּדֶשׁ שֶׁמָּסְרוּ נַפְשָׁם עַל קְדֻשַּׁת הַשֵּׁם. הַנֶּאֱהָבִים וְהַנְּעִימִים בְּחַיֵּיהֶם וּבְמוֹתָם לֹא נִפְרָדוּ.[2] מִנְּשָׁרִים קַלּוּ מֵאֲרָיוֹת גָּבֵרוּ. לַעֲשׂוֹת רְצוֹן קוֹנָם[3]

"the counting," since we count the days between the two holidays). These varied customs of saying or not saying it produced the famous story about Rabbi Isser Zalman Meltzer (1870–1953), a Rosh Yeshivah (head of the yeshivah) in Russia, who was imprisoned by the Bolsheviks for teaching Torah. He emigrated to Israel as a fervent Orthodox Zionist and became head of a yeshivah in Jerusalem and, later, dean of all yeshivah heads in Israel. Rabbi Menachem Sacks of Jerusalem and Chicago, an intimate of Rabbi Meltzer, told me this story.   (p. 181)

L. HOFFMAN (HISTORY)

[1] *"The holy communities that gave their lives"* This prayer is known technically as *Hazkarat n'shamot* ("Memorial for the souls") or *Hazkarat nishmot hak'doshim* ("Memorial for the souls of the holy"). It refers specifically to the martyrs killed in the Rhineland in the first Crusade (1096). "The holy," then, are those martyrs who were said to have died *al kiddush hashem,* "for the sanctity of God." Many prayers extolling these martyred souls were composed, some of them (according to Rabbi Yoel Kahn) so filled with anger and so theologically radical that they never made it to our prayer books. They often likened the dead to Isaac, who was almost killed on an altar. But   (p. 181)

J. HOFFMAN (TRANSLATION)

[1] *"Great mercy"* Birnbaum: "infinite mercy."

[1] *"In mercy"* The Hebrew, like the English, contains the word *rachamim* three times. See above ("May the father of mercy have mercy") for a discussion on the nuances of that word.

[1] *"Attend to"* Birnbaum: "remember."

[1] *"In the name of God's holiness [al k'dushat hashem]"* Literally, "for the sanctification of God," a common idiom used to represent dying for God, and clearly used technically here, as this prayer emerged from the experience of Jewish martyrdom at the hands of the Crusaders (see Lawrence A. Hoffman).

[2] *"Beloved friends in life"* This whole line, from "beloved" to   (p. 181)

lions, they did their Master's will, their Rock's desire. [4] Our God will remember them favorably among the other righteous of the world, and will avenge his servants' spilled blood, as it is written in the Torah of Moses, the man of God, [5] "Nations of the world, make his people joyful, for He avenges the blood of his servants, renders vengeance to his foes, and forgives his land, his people." [6] And by your servants the prophets it is written, [7] "I will cleanse their blood which I have not yet cleaned. [8] Adonai dwells in Zion." [9] And in the holy writing it is also said, [10] "Why should the nations say, [11] 'Where is their God?' [12] Before our eyes let the vengeance of your servants' spilled blood be known among the nations." [13] And it is also said, [14] "The one who demands blood remembers them; He does not forget the cry of the humble." [15] And it is said, [16] "He judges the nations, filling it with bodies, crushing heads across the land. [17] He will drink from the stream by the path, and therefore raise heads."

וְחָפֵץ צוּרָם: [4] יִזְכְּרֵם אֱלֹהֵינוּ לְטוֹבָה. עִם שְׁאָר צַדִּיקֵי עוֹלָם. וְיִנְקוֹם נִקְמַת דַּם עֲבָדָיו הַשָּׁפוּךְ: כַּכָּתוּב בְּתוֹרַת מֹשֶׁה אִישׁ הָאֱלֹהִים. [5] הַרְנִינוּ גוֹיִם עַמּוֹ כִּי דַם עֲבָדָיו יִקּוֹם. וְנָקָם יָשִׁיב לְצָרָיו וְכִפֶּר אַדְמָתוֹ עַמּוֹ. [6] וְעַל יְדֵי עֲבָדֶיךָ הַנְּבִיאִים כָּתוּב לֵאמֹר. [7] וְנִקֵּיתִי דָּמָם לֹא נִקֵּיתִי. [8] וַיְיָ שֹׁכֵן בְּצִיּוֹן: [9] וּבְכִתְבֵי הַקֹּדֶשׁ נֶאֱמַר. [10] לָמָּה יֹאמְרוּ הַגּוֹיִם [11] אַיֵּה אֱלֹהֵיהֶם. [12] יִוָּדַע בַּגּוֹיִם לְעֵינֵינוּ. נִקְמַת דַּם עֲבָדֶיךָ הַשָּׁפוּךְ: [13] וְאוֹמֵר. [14] כִּי דֹרֵשׁ דָּמִים אוֹתָם זָכָר. לֹא שָׁכַח צַעֲקַת עֲנָוִים: [15] וְאוֹמֵר. [16] יָדִין בַּגּוֹיִם מָלֵא גְוִיּוֹת מָחַץ רֹאשׁ עַל אֶרֶץ רַבָּה: [17] מִנַּחַל בַּדֶּרֶךְ יִשְׁתֶּה עַל כֵּן יָרִים רֹאשׁ.

BRETTLER (BIBLE)

unclear. Elsewhere in the Bible, Israelites are killed as a result of acts of political rebellion, not because of unusual religious beliefs.

[4] *"As it is written"* Three quotations concerning divine vengeance follow, one from each of the canonical divisions: the Torah (Deut. 32:43), Prophets (Joel 4:21), and Writings (Ps. 79:10); it is as if the entire Bible is being invoked.

[13] *"And it is also said"* The structure of the previous section, with three "vengeance" verses, one from each of the canonical divisions of the Bible, suggests that the following verses (Pss. 9:13; 110:6–7) were not an original part of the prayer. They extend the previous verses by adding the new themes of "the cry of the humble" and God's excessive victory over the nations.

◆——

LANDES (HALAKHAH)

While visiting a small community in Poland on Shabbat, he witnessed worshipers vigorously arguing about whether or not *Av harachamin* should be recited that day. Eventually, they asked the great rabbi what his custom was. He replied, "That is the custom!" That is, the proper custom is to argue over whether or not to say it.

◆——

L. HOFFMAN (HISTORY)

these martyrs were better than Isaac because they actually did give up their lives for God, whereas Isaac was saved at the last minute.

Our prayer, though filled with pent-up anger and asking God to "avenge his servants' spilled blood," nonetheless made it into our weekly Shabbat service. It is said also as part of the *Yizkor* service of Yom Kippur, Sukkot, Passover, and Shavuot.

◆——

J. HOFFMAN (TRANSLATION)

"lions," is a direct quote from 2 Samuel 1:23. It described David and Jonathan, who were beloved friends in life and even in death were not parted one from the other. It is taken out of context here, but it points to the Bible's prime example of closeness as friends.

[4] *"The man of God"* It would be the wrong register, but the colloquial "God's main man" is a tempting translation.

[5] *"Nations of the world"* Literally, just "nations," but "Nations, make his people joyful" is almost impossible to read, and "Nations of the world" seems better than the archaic "O nations."

⁷ *"Cleanse their blood"* This is almost certainly an idiom. Birnbaum suggests "avenge their blood," which makes sense in context but otherwise seems unsupported. Another likely possibility is "declare their blood innocent."

¹⁴ *"The one who demands blood [doresh damim]" Or "avenges."* *Doresh* is not the usual word for "avenge," as used elsewhere in this paragraph, but it is a citation from Psalm 9:13. The *Jewish Publication Society Bible* translates it as "He who requites bloodshed." The *New Revised Standard Bible* has "avenges."

¹⁶ *"Filling it [malei g'viyot]"* It is not clear what the "it" is. Birnbaum suggests "the battlefield." The phrase is embedded in a citation from Psalms 110:6. *JPS* translates it as "[He works judgment upon the nations] heaping up corpses," thus avoiding the need for a direct object for malei altogether. The *NRSV* says, "He will execute judgment upon the nations, filling them with corpses." The "it" here stands for the nations among whom the corpses will be piled.

◆ ◆ ◆

5 | *Concluding Prayers*

Returning the Torah to the Ark

A. REJOICING IN TORAH: "HAPPY IS THE ONE" (*ASHRE*)

[1] Happy are they who dwell in your house; they will ever praise You (Ps. 84:5).

[2] Happy is the people like this. [3] Happy is the people whose God is Adonai (Ps. 144:15).

[4] David's Psalm:

[5] I will exalt You, my God the king, and praise your name for ever and ever.

[6] Every day I will praise You, and extol your name for ever and ever.

[7] Great is Adonai and highly praised. Endless is his greatness.

[8] Generation upon generation will praise your deeds, and tell of your mighty acts.

[9] I will speak of your wondrous acts, and your glorious majesty in its splendor.

[10] People tell of your awe-inspiring might, and I proclaim your greatness.

[11] People spread your very great renown, and sing of your righteousness.

[12] Gracious and merciful is Adonai, endlessly patient and most kind.

[13] Adonai is good to all, showering all his creatures with mercy.

[1] אַשְׁרֵי יוֹשְׁבֵי בֵיתֶךָ. עוֹד יְהַלְלוּךָ סֶּלָה:

[2] אַשְׁרֵי הָעָם שֶׁכָּכָה לּוֹ. [3] אַשְׁרֵי הָעָם שֶׁיְיָ אֱלֹהָיו:

[4] תְּהִלָּה לְדָוִד.

[5] אֲרוֹמִמְךָ אֱלוֹהַי הַמֶּלֶךְ. וַאֲבָרְכָה שִׁמְךָ לְעוֹלָם וָעֶד:

[6] בְּכָל־יוֹם אֲבָרְכֶךָּ. וַאֲהַלְלָה שִׁמְךָ לְעוֹלָם וָעֶד:

[7] גָּדוֹל יְיָ וּמְהֻלָּל מְאֹד. וְלִגְדֻלָּתוֹ אֵין חֵקֶר:

[8] דּוֹר לְדוֹר יְשַׁבַּח מַעֲשֶׂיךָ. וּגְבוּרֹתֶיךָ יַגִּידוּ:

[9] הֲדַר כְּבוֹד הוֹדֶךָ. וְדִבְרֵי נִפְלְאֹתֶיךָ אָשִׂיחָה:

[10] וֶעֱזוּז נוֹרְאֹתֶיךָ יֹאמֵרוּ. וּגְדֻלָּתְךָ אֲסַפְּרֶנָּה:

[11] זֵכֶר רַב־טוּבְךָ יַבִּיעוּ. וְצִדְקָתְךָ יְרַנֵּנוּ:

[12] חַנּוּן וְרַחוּם יְיָ. אֶרֶךְ אַפַּיִם וּגְדָל־חָסֶד:

[13] טוֹב־יְיָ לַכֹּל. וְרַחֲמָיו עַל־כָּל־מַעֲשָׂיו: **183**

¹⁴יוֹדֽוּךָ יְיָ כָּל־מַעֲשֶׂיךָ. וַחֲסִידֶיךָ
יְבָרְכֽוּכָה:

¹⁵כְּבוֹד מַלְכוּתְךָ יֹאמֵֽרוּ. וּגְבוּרָתְךָ
יְדַבֵּֽרוּ:

¹⁶לְהוֹדִֽיעַ לִבְנֵי הָאָדָם גְּבוּרֹתָיו.
וּכְבוֹד הֲדַר מַלְכוּתוֹ:

¹⁷מַלְכוּתְךָ מַלְכוּת כָּל־עֹלָמִים.
וּמֶֽמְשַׁלְתְּךָ בְּכָל־דּוֹר וָדֹר:

¹⁸סוֹמֵךְ יְיָ לְכָל־הַנֹּפְלִים. וְזוֹקֵף
לְכָל־הַכְּפוּפִים:

¹⁹עֵינֵי כֹל אֵלֶֽיךָ יְשַׂבֵּֽרוּ. וְאַתָּה
נוֹתֵן־לָהֶם אֶת־אָכְלָם בְּעִתּוֹ:

²⁰פּוֹתֵֽחַ אֶת־יָדֶךָ. וּמַשְׂבִּֽיעַ לְכָל־חַי
רָצוֹן:

²¹צַדִּיק יְיָ בְּכָל־דְּרָכָיו. וְחָסִיד
בְּכָל־מַעֲשָׂיו:

²²קָרוֹב יְיָ לְכָל־קֹרְאָיו. לְכֹל אֲשֶׁר
יִקְרָאֻֽהוּ בֶאֱמֶת:

²³רְצוֹן־יְרֵאָיו יַעֲשֶׂה. וְאֶת־שַׁוְעָתָם
יִשְׁמַע וְיוֹשִׁיעֵם:

²⁴שׁוֹמֵר יְיָ אֶת־כָּל־אֹהֲבָיו. וְאֵת
כָּל־הָרְשָׁעִים יַשְׁמִיד:

²⁵תְּהִלַּת יְיָ יְדַבֶּר־פִּי. וִיבָרֵךְ כָּל־בָּשָׂר
שֵׁם קָדְשׁוֹ לְעוֹלָם וָעֶד:

²⁶וַאֲנַֽחְנוּ נְבָרֵךְ יָהּ מֵעַתָּה וְעַד־עוֹלָם
הַלְלוּיָהּ:

¹⁴All your creatures will thank You, Adonai, and your faithful will praise You.

¹⁵They will tell of the glory of your kingdom, and speak of your might.

¹⁶Announce his greatness to humankind, and the majestic glory of his kingdom.

¹⁷Your kingdom is a kingdom for all times, and your reign for every generation.

¹⁸Adonai supports all who fall, and uprights all who are bent over.

¹⁹The eyes of all look to You, and You give them timely food.

²⁰You open your hand, and satisfy every living being.

²¹Adonai is righteous in all his ways, and gracious in all his acts.

²²Adonai is near to all who call upon Him, to all who call upon Him in truth.

²³He does the will of those who revere Him, and hears their cry and saves them.

²⁴Adonai guards all who love Him, and destroys all who are wicked.

²⁵Let my mouth speak Adonai's praise, and all creatures praise his holy name for ever and ever.

²⁶Let us praise Adonai from now and ever more. Halleluyah (Ps. 115:18).

BRETTLER (BIBLE)

[4-5] *"David's Psalm: I will exalt You"* Psalm 145, but preceded by Pss. 84:5 and 144:15. Linguistic evidence suggests that Psalm 145 is post-exilic, later than most of the other Psalms. In the Bible, Psalms 145 to 150 compose a unit. Psalm 145 ends with the self-exhortation: "Let my mouth speak Adonai's praise, and all creatures praise his holy name for ever and ever"; the five following psalms do precisely that, each one opening with "Halleluyah" ("Praise God").

This psalm is an alphabetic acrostic, where each verse follows the order of the Hebrew alphabet. In the Hebrew, the *nun* verse is missing, although a [secondary?] *nun* verse [possibly added later?]

(p. 189)

DORFF (THEOLOGY)

[1] *"Happy are they who dwell in your house"* Anyone who recites these opening verses together with Psalm 145 three times each day is, according to the Talmud, to be assured a place in the world-to-come (Ber. 4b). The psalm is therefore recited not only here, but twice more: in the preparatory section of the morning (*Shacharit*) service (the *P'sukei D'zimrah* —see Volume 3), and as the opening for the afternoon (*Minchah*) service: a total of three times daily.

Why is this psalm so special as to require recitation three times a day? The reason given in the Talmud is that this psalm is an alphabetic acrostic and that it celebrates the providential sustenance of God: "You *(p. 191)*

FRANKEL (A WOMAN'S VOICE)

[1] *"Happy are they who dwell in your house"* What does it mean to live in God's house? Where is it? How big is it? What is its architecture, its floor plan, its style? How many people can it accommodate? Who cleans it, and who repairs it? What goes on between its walls? Is it safe from fire and theft?

Clearly, the image of God's house is only a metaphor. But metaphors tell us much about the larger context of meaning in which they have been chosen to function. In this familiar

(p. 191)

A. REJOICING IN TORAH (*ASHRE*)

[1] Happy are they who dwell in your house; they will ever praise You (Ps. 84:5).

[2] Happy is the people like this. [3] Happy is the people whose God is Adonai (Ps. 144:15).

[4] David's Psalm:

[5] I will exalt You, my God the king, and praise your name for ever and ever.

HAUPTMAN (TALMUD)

[1] *"Happy are they who dwell in your house"* When the Gemara asks from where in the Bible do we learn about preparation for prayer, R. Joshua b. Levi answers (Ber. 32b) that it is from the verse, "Happy are they who dwell in your house" (Ps. 84:5). The Hebrew word for "dwell" is *yeshvu*, which also means "to sit." R. Joshua reads the verse midrashically to imply that those who take the time to sit in the synagogue prior to prayer are *me'usharim*, "happy" or "blessed." From another verse, the Gemara then derives the *(p. 192)*

KUSHNER & POLEN (CHASIDISM)

[18] *"Adonai supports all who fall"* Psalm 145:14. We have a tradition in the name of Rabbi Mordecai Yosef Liener of Izbica commenting on the meaning of "supporting those who fall." He teaches that not only does God support those who fall *(somekh noflim)*, but so must lovers also. Izbica notes that according to Jewish law, all you need to get married is a coin. But then why does everyone use a wedding ring instead? This may be explained by considering the shape of a ring. It is round, just like the Hebrew letter *samekh,* (p. 193)

¹אַשְׁרֵי יוֹשְׁבֵי בֵיתֶךָ. עוֹד יְהַלְלוּךָ סֶּלָה:

²אַשְׁרֵי הָעָם שֶׁכָּכָה לּוֹ. ³אַשְׁרֵי הָעָם שֶׁיְיָ אֱלֹהָיו:

⁴תְּהִלָּה לְדָוִד.

⁵אֲרוֹמִמְךָ אֱלוֹהַי הַמֶּלֶךְ. וַאֲבָרְכָה שִׁמְךָ לְעוֹלָם וָעֶד:

LANDES (HALAKHAH)

[1–2] *"Happy are they...Happy is the people"* It is possible that these two introductory verses highlight the alphabetical structure of Psalm 145 by reiterating for us the first letter, *alef,* since *ashre* (the first word of both verses) begins with that letter. Each *alef* is vocalized with a *patach* (the "ah" sound), formed by opening one's mouth. That sound is considered reminiscent of a form of "stuttering," as when we grope for a word and cannot find it, so say only, "Ah, ah, ah...." The sense of stuttering to find the (p. 194)

L. HOFFMAN (HISTORY)

CONCLUDING PRAYERS: PARALLELING THE INTRODUCTION, THIS CONCLUSION DRAWS THE SACRED DRAMA TO AN END. PART A IMPLICITLY REJOICES IN TORAH, WITH THE FAMILIAR ASHRE, PSALM 145, WHICH ASSURES US HOW HAPPY WE ARE TO KNOW GOD AS OUR COVENANTAL PARTNER. (SEE ALSO THE ESSAY ON ASHRE IN VOLUME 3, P'SUKEI D'ZIMRAH, PP. 31–37.)

[1–3] *"Happy [ashre] are they...Happy [ashre] is the people...Happy [ashre] is the people"* This introduction to Psalm 145, consisting of two additional verses from Psalms (84:5 and 144:15), is a play on words. By medieval days, Psalm 145 was being said three times daily. The Talmud (p. 194)

J. HOFFMAN (TRANSLATION)

[4] *"David's Psalm [T'hillah l'david]"* Often translated, "a Psalm by David," but saying "David's Psalm" is preferable, because like the title in Hebrew, it leaves the exact connection between David and the psalm ambiguous. On the other hand, "a Psalm by David" makes it clear that this is but one of many, a fact clearly indicated by the Hebrew.

The whole of Psalm 145 is an alphabetic acrostic, each letter of the alphabet being used in order to start a line. We have no hope of capturing this in English. In addition to its acrostic nature, this Psalm has particularly lyrical Hebrew, whereas our English translation contains only hints of this beauty. (p. 195)

⁶Every day I will praise You, and extol your name for ever and ever.

⁷Great is Adonai and highly praised. Endless is his greatness.

⁸Generation upon generation will praise your deeds, and tell of your mighty acts.

⁹I will speak of your wondrous acts, and your glorious majesty in its splendor.

¹⁰People tell of your awe-inspiring might, and I proclaim your greatness.

¹¹People spread your very great renown, and sing of your righteousness.

¹²Gracious and merciful is Adonai, endlessly patient and most kind.

¹³Adonai is good to all, showering all his creatures with mercy.

¹⁴All your creatures will thank You, Adonai, and your faithful will praise You.

¹⁵They will tell of the glory of your kingdom, and speak of your might.

¹⁶Announce his greatness to humankind, and the majestic glory of his kingdom.

¹⁷Your kingdom is a kingdom for all times, and your reign for every generation.

¹⁸Adonai supports all who fall, and uprights all who are bent over.

בְּכָל־יוֹם אֲבָרְכֶךָּ. וַאֲהַלְלָה שִׁמְךָ ⁶
לְעוֹלָם וָעֶד:

גָּדוֹל יְיָ וּמְהֻלָּל מְאֹד. וְלִגְדֻלָּתוֹ אֵין ⁷
חֵקֶר:

דּוֹר לְדוֹר יְשַׁבַּח מַעֲשֶׂיךָ. וּגְבוּרֹתֶיךָ ⁸
יַגִּידוּ:

הֲדַר כְּבוֹד הוֹדֶךָ. וְדִבְרֵי נִפְלְאֹתֶיךָ ⁹
אָשִׂיחָה:

וֶעֱזוּז נוֹרְאֹתֶיךָ יֹאמֵרוּ. וּגְדֻלָּתְךָ ¹⁰
אֲסַפְּרֶנָּה:

זֵכֶר רַב־טוּבְךָ יַבִּיעוּ. וְצִדְקָתְךָ ¹¹
יְרַנֵּנוּ:

חַנּוּן וְרַחוּם יְיָ. אֶרֶךְ אַפַּיִם ¹²
וּגְדָל־חָסֶד:

טוֹב־יְיָ לַכֹּל. וְרַחֲמָיו עַל־כָּל־ ¹³
מַעֲשָׂיו:

יוֹדוּךָ יְיָ כָּל־מַעֲשֶׂיךָ. וַחֲסִידֶיךָ ¹⁴
יְבָרְכוּכָה:

כְּבוֹד מַלְכוּתְךָ יֹאמֵרוּ. וּגְבוּרָתְךָ ¹⁵
יְדַבֵּרוּ:

לְהוֹדִיעַ לִבְנֵי הָאָדָם גְּבוּרֹתָיו. ¹⁶
וּכְבוֹד הֲדַר מַלְכוּתוֹ:

מַלְכוּתְךָ מַלְכוּת כָּל־עֹלָמִים. ¹⁷
וּמֶמְשַׁלְתְּךָ בְּכָל־דּוֹר וָדֹר:

סוֹמֵךְ יְיָ לְכָל־הַנֹּפְלִים. וְזוֹקֵף ¹⁸
לְכָל־הַכְּפוּפִים:

¹⁹The eyes of all look to You, and You give them timely food.

²⁰You open your hand, and satisfy every living being.

²¹Adonai is righteous in all his ways, and gracious in all his acts.

²²Adonai is near to all who call upon Him, to all who call upon Him in truth.

²³He does the will of those who revere Him, and hears their cry and saves them.

²⁴Adonai guards all who love Him, and destroys all who are wicked.

²⁵Let my mouth speak Adonai's praise, and all creatures praise his holy name for ever and ever.

²⁶Let us praise Adonai from now and ever more. Halleluyah (Ps. 115:18).

¹⁹עֵינֵי כֹל אֵלֶיךָ יְשַׂבֵּרוּ. וְאַתָּה נוֹתֵן־לָהֶם אֶת־אָכְלָם בְּעִתּוֹ:

²⁰פּוֹתֵחַ אֶת־יָדֶךָ. וּמַשְׂבִּיעַ לְכָל־חַי רָצוֹן:

²¹צַדִּיק יְיָ בְּכָל־דְּרָכָיו. וְחָסִיד בְּכָל־מַעֲשָׂיו:

²²קָרוֹב יְיָ לְכָל־קֹרְאָיו. לְכֹל אֲשֶׁר יִקְרָאֻהוּ בֶאֱמֶת:

²³רְצוֹן־יְרֵאָיו יַעֲשֶׂה. וְאֶת־שַׁוְעָתָם יִשְׁמַע וְיוֹשִׁיעֵם:

²⁴שׁוֹמֵר יְיָ אֶת־כָּל־אֹהֲבָיו. וְאֵת כָּל־הָרְשָׁעִים יַשְׁמִיד:

²⁵תְּהִלַּת יְיָ יְדַבֶּר פִּי. וִיבָרֵךְ כָּל־בָּשָׂר שֵׁם קָדְשׁוֹ לְעוֹלָם וָעֶד:

²⁶וַאֲנַחְנוּ נְבָרֵךְ יָהּ מֵעַתָּה וְעַד־עוֹלָם הַלְלוּיָהּ:

BRETTLER (BIBLE)

is found in the Dead Sea Scrolls and in the Septuagint, the ancient Greek Bible translation. The Bible knows many instances of acrostics, all following alphabetic order, but later Jewish liturgical poetry, like poems in old Babylonian Akkadian tradition, has acrostics that spell out the author's name. The purpose of writing alphabetic acrostic poetry is unclear. It may be a mnemonic aid to memory (by those who recited it or by scribes who wrote it), or perhaps it expresses a notion of completeness, in the case of this psalm, the complete greatness of God.

⁵*"My God the king"* An expression of God's kingship, but in this case, a psalm that describes the type of king God is: great, mighty, powerful, good, compassionate, righteous, and near. The centrality of kingship is evident from the fourfold repetition of *malkhut* ("kingdom") in lines 5, 11, 12, and 13.

⁷ *"Great is Adonai"* God is here spoken of in the third person, in distinction to the surrounding verses, which employ the second person "You." This variation, which continues throughout the psalm, expresses a type of schizophrenic indecision by the psalmist, who sometimes talks to and sometimes about God, balancing the need to be distant from such a great, domineering deity (third person) while praying to Him (second person).

^{10–11} *"People tell of your awe-inspiring might.... People spread your very great renown...righteousness"* Two successive verses with parallel structure, rather unusual in biblical poetry, where parallelism often occurs within a poetic line but rarely is extended from one line to another. On closer scrutiny, we see that the second verse is really a modification of the first: God is not only mighty and great, but righteous as well, a notion that leads naturally to the next two verses, which highlight God's mercy and goodness.

¹² *"Gracious and merciful is Adonai"* A selective quotation and reworking of God's attributes found, among other places, in Exodus 34:6–7; however, the section of the Exodus text (v. 7) that mentions intergenerational punishment ("He visits the iniquities of the fathers upon children and children's children, upon the third and fourth generation") is omitted here (as in Jon. 4:2), because here the emphasis is on a purely good God.

¹⁴ *"All [kol] your creatures"* "All" or "every" *(kol),* another theme of this psalm, is introduced early (v. 2, "Every day") and is used close to twenty times, to emphasize that all must praise the God of all.

¹⁴ *"And your faithful [chasidim] "* Meaning anyone who follows God; alternatively, *chasidim* may already have been a name given to a particular group of specially pietistic Jews, as in medieval Germany or today.

¹⁷ *"Your kingdom is a kingdom for all times"* A combination of the psalm's two themes: God's kingdom and his eternality.

¹⁸ *"Adonai supports all who fall"* As before, the theme of God's greatness is immediately followed by descriptions of his mercy and kindness.

^{22–24} *"Adonai is near to all who call upon Him.... He does the will of those who revere Him...Adonai guards all who love Him, and destroys all who are wicked."* The theology of these verses is remarkably straightforward: call out to God in truth, and you will be saved, since God heeds the righteous and destroys the wicked. A similar theology may be seen in Psalm 1, which praises the righteous, noting that they will flourish, while comparing the wicked to chaff. The initial chapters of Daniel similarly illustrate how the righteous triumph, even under the most extreme circumstances.

There are, however, other retribution theologies in the Bible. Job depicts a very different world than the one described here, and several psalms as well suggest that God sometimes forgets or ignores the righteous sufferer. Psalm 13, for instance asks:

How long, O Lord? Will You forget me forever?
How long will You hide your face from me?
How long must I bear pain in my soul
And have sorrow in my heart all day long?

[25] *"Let my mouth speak Adonai's praise, and all creatures praise his holy name for ever and ever"* After describing a powerful and good God, the psalm arrives at the only possible conclusion: God must be praised by all *(kol)* forever. The conclusion reiterates the psalm's central themes, ending as it began, with a call for "praise" "for ever and ever." This structure, where the end returns to the beginning, is called an *inclusio*, or "envelope," structure and is very common in Bible. The Tower of Babel story, for instance, begins (Gen. 11:1), "All the earth *[kol ha'arets]* had one language…" and ends (11:9), "Adonai confounded the speech of all the earth…and scattered them over the face of all the earth *[kol ha'arets]*."

However, despite the return to the same language, the psalm is not static; it opened with the psalmist alone praising God for ever, but closes with a call for "all creatures" to do so.

—◆—

DORFF (THEOLOGY)

open your hand, and satisfy every living being" (Ps. 145:16). The alphabetic order would ensure that it would be easy to remember; the central verse expresses our hope that God at least provide for our basic needs, without which we could hardly have the luxury to anticipate that our spiritual needs be met as well — as expressed two verses later: "Adonai is near to all who call upon Him, to all who call upon Him in truth."

—◆—

FRANKEL (A WOMAN'S VOICE)

psalm, God's house exists on several scales, like *matrushka* dolls nested within each other.

Imagine then that we are ancient pilgrims living when this psalm was composed and sung. The first house we enter is probably God's house, the Temple in Jerusalem. It was here that the Levites would sing this psalm of David, accompanied by musical instruments and dance. Then we peer outside the windows of this house to take in "the majestic glory of his [God's] kingdom," a sweeping landscape of wonders, awe-inspiring might, and glory. And then, we find our way into the kitchen where the poor, the downtrodden, and the hungry gather, grateful for God's open hand. It is in this intimate chamber that we encounter "Adonai [who] is near to all who call upon Him."

—◆—

HAUPTMAN (TALMUD)

obligation to tarry at the conclusion of prayer as well, before returning to mundane pursuits. Knowing that Jews are obliged to pray three times daily *(Shacharit, Minchah, and Ma'ariv),* it considers, perhaps in jest, what will happen if pious people really follow this advice. They would have to spend at least an hour praying three times a day as well as a preparatory hour and a concluding hour each time: nine hours a day in total! How, then, will they study? How will they work? The answer the Gemara gives is that since such people would all be pious, these issues will work themselves out.

It is no coincidence that the very verse cited by R. Joshua b. Levi, "Happy are they who dwell in your house" *(Ashre yoshvei veitekha),* was chosen to introduce the beginning of Psalm 145. Since every single time that Psalm 145 *(T'hillah l'david)* appears in the prayer book it is preceded by these two *ashre* verses *(Ashre yoshvei veitekha* [84:5] and *Ashre ha'am shekakhah lo* [144:15]), most people think that they are part of the psalm itself. But that is not so. The first of these two verses, which speaks of dwelling in God's house, is taken by the Rabbis to refer to a synagogue. A synagogue is sacred space. Entering it is assumed to evoke some acknowledgment by the person entering. This verse provides the opportunity for such an observation.

[4] *"David's Psalm [T'hillah l'david]"* "Said Rabbi Elazar b. Abina: Anyone who recites *T'hillah l'david* (Psalm 145) three times every day is guaranteed to enter into the world-to-come. Why? It cannot be simply because it is an alphabet acrostic [although it is that], because [if we wanted to find the best possible acrostic], we would have cited another acrostic [Psalm 119] that is a better one because it repeats the alphabet eight times over. Rather, it must be because this psalm includes the line 'You open your hand, and satisfy every living being'" (Ber. 4b).

It is all too easy to think that the reason for seeing a psalm as ideal for praising God is that it praises God many times over using the alphabet arbitrarily to make sure that we heap up lines of praise. The implication of such a view would be that somehow, we are eventually able to give God praise that is comprehensive. Rabbi Elazar b. Abina implicitly denies the possibility of all-comprehensive praise of God. Psalm 145 is singled out instead because of a particular aspect of God that deserves being singled out for praise: God's merciful care of all living things, to make sure that the basic needs of every single creature are met. It is not so much that God is all-powerful as it is that God uses his power to benefit all. That is why we say Psalm 145 three times daily: God is concerned about and actively involved in the world that He created — a vital tenet of rabbinic thinking.

[13] *"Showering all his creatures with mercy"* The midrash to this verse (Bereshit Rabbah 33) tells the following story: In the days of R. Tanchuma, there was a drought. The people came to him and asked him to declare a fast, which he did. But still the rain did not come. So he called everyone together and began to preach: "My children, if you have compassion for each other, God will have compassion for you." As they were distributing funds to the poor, they noticed that one man was giving money to a woman he had divorced (which, to people at that time, suggested that the two were

involved in a sexual relationship). They reported this to R. Tanchuma, who sent for the man and asked him, "What have you been doing?" "Giving money to my former wife," replied the man, "because she was in great need and I took pity on her." Upon hearing this, R. Tanchuma turned his face to heaven and said, "Lord of the universe, just as this man, who no longer had any obligation to support this woman, behaved compassionately toward her, You, the all-compassionate One, should certainly take pity on us, your children, the descendants of Abraham, Isaac, and Jacob!"

The beauty of this anecdote is that it assumes that divine behavior is contingent upon human conduct. It is not enough that we direct our hearts to God and pray and declare fasts. He will not turn to us until we first turn to others. Worship of God is necessary but insufficient. In addition to acts of piety, Judaism requires acts of loving-kindness. Ironically, here, the person who is suspected of sinning turns out to be the most pious of all, the one who brings the rain. The subsidiary message seems to be that one should do what is right even if at the risk of having others assume impure motives when there are only pure ones.

[18] *"Adonai supports all who fall and uprights all who are bent over"* "Said Rabbah bar Chin'nah Saba in the name of Rav: One who prays should bend his knees and bow down when saying *barukh* [i.e., during the opening words of the *Amidah*] but stand straight when saying God's name. The reason for straightening up when uttering God's name is that the verse says, 'Adonai supports all who fall and uprights all who are bent over" (Ber. 12a). This rather playful interpretation of the verse tells us that although we bow down before God out of a sense of awe and thanksgiving and supplication, still, when saying his name, we must straighten up, which means we must sense our own importance as his creatures. We see here a complicated blend of subjection to someone greater than oneself and independent regard for oneself. If God created us and assigned us a job to do in this world, we should see ourselves as having been invested with importance. At the same time, we must never forget that we are dependent on God. This ongoing tension is characteristic of the religious person's outlook on life.

KUSHNER & POLEN (CHASIDISM)

the first letter of the phrase *somekh noflim,* "Adonai supports all who fall...." This reminds lovers that they must uphold one another when they stumble or fall. They say, "With this ring," if you fall I will *samakh* you, I will support and uphold you. You are not giving a ring, you are giving a *samekh*. Indeed, when couples exchange rings, they pledge themselves to be present to support and uphold one another. And surely *that* is God's presence.

LANDES (HALAKHAH)

right words to praise God leads dramatically to the full articulation of praise that Psalm 145 contains.

[20] *"You open your hand, and satisfy every living being"* Because this is the core verse of the psalm, a reason for its being chosen in the first place, according to the Talmud, it must be said with the *kavvanah* (the thought in one's mind) that God's providence extends over all living beings in order to sustain them. I believe it is fitting to add the personal intention of imitating God's ways in this respect, for the Talmud tells us, "As God clothes the naked…so must you clothe the naked. As God visited the sick, so must you visit the sick…" (Sot. 14a). Similarly, therefore, as God sustains those who are hungry, so must we.

———◆———

L. HOFFMAN (HISTORY)

had already remarked, "Those who says Psalm 145 daily are sure to receive a share in the world-to-come" (Ber. 4b). Eventually, in fact, the words "three times daily" were added to our talmudic text, reflecting the success of making Psalm 150 a thrice-daily staple. Whether purposefully or not, the "happy" prospect of receiving a share in the world-to-come, reinforced by a threefold recitation of the prayer that is supposed to guarantee that share, is alluded to in this introduction to the psalm, which contains the word "happy" three times. Classical Jewish literature usually refers to the psalm by its first words, "David's Psalm," but the introduction is so inextricably linked to the psalm liturgically that even the Talmud calls it *Ashre*, and it is almost universally called *Ashre* today.

The addition of the two introductory verses was linked to another talmudic teaching (Ber. 32b) to the effect that before one begins to pray, one should "linger for an hour in the synagogue," the idea being that before the main statutory prayers (especially the *Amidah*), one should prepare oneself spiritually. The Talmud cites Ps. 84:5 as proof for that lesson. "Happy are they who dwell in your house; they will ever praise You" — that is, before we "praise You" in the *Amidah,* it is necessary to "dwell in your house," meaning "in the synagogue" for a while. Whether this lesson had anything to do with the choice of Ps. 84:5 as an introductory verse here is not clear, but the medieval authorities believed it did, since one of the three recitations of *Ashre* precedes the morning *Amidah* (see Volume 3, *P'sukei D'zimrah,* p. 115). Some of them added other introductory psalm verses also, all of them with the word *ashre* in them, in an attempt to drag out the preparation time as long as possible. It may be that Ashkenazi custom retained the practice of having only our two verses in order to retain the word play denoting "three."

Other medieval authorities could not believe that the Talmud really meant to promise the world-to-come to people who said this psalm daily but did not merit reward in other ways as well. Rabbi Samuel ben Meir, known as the Rashbam (1085–1174), explained, "Saying this prayer does not guarantee the world-to-come if your deeds are evil. The Talmud means to say that people who habitually take ethical stock of their affairs will naturally be careful in reciting this psalm as well. Knowing that they are God-fearing and that they turn away from evil, they may be certain that they merit the world-to-come."

[20] *"You open your hand, and satisfy every living being"* According to the Talmud, this is the most important line in the psalm because it celebrates God's gracious care for all creatures. Medieval Jews concentrated special attention on the line when they arrived at it.

———◆———

J. HOFFMAN (TRANSLATION)

[6] *"Extol [ahal'lah]"* Translated immediately above as "praise," but here it follows *avar'kheka,* which we translate as "praise." In order to retain the two verbs with different meaning, we choose "extol" here.

[9] *"I will speak of your wondrous acts"* The Hebrew might also mean, "I will speak words of your wonders."

[14] *"All your creatures will thank"* In keeping with our translation elsewhere, "acknowledge You with thanks" might be more accurate, but the two parts of this line exhibit similar structure in the Hebrew, which we have tried to mimic in the English translation.

[16] *"Announce [l'hodi'a] his greatness"* The Hebrew is the infinitive "to announce" (*L'hodi'a*), but that choice was governed by the need for a word beginning with a *lamed,* so as to preserve the acrostic. The infinitive makes more sense in Hebrew than it would in English.

[16] *"The majestic glory [k'vod hadar]"* In Hebrew, too, this is a reversal of "glorious majesty" (*hadar k'vod*) a few lines up.

[20] *"Satisfy every living being"* It is not clear how the last word of this line (*ratson,* literally "favor") relates to the rest of the line. Here we assume that it is part of a verbal idiom meaning "to satisfy." Another possibility is that it is an adverb, as in Birnbaum's "satisfy every living thing with favor."

———— ◆ ◆ ◆ ————

B. Israel's Praise of God

i. "Let them praise" (Y'hal'lu)

[Congregation rises as prayer leader
lifts Torah and says:]

1 Let them praise Adonai's name, for his name alone is exalted.

ii. "His majesty is above"
(Hodo al erets)

2 His majesty is above earth and heaven. 3 He is the strength of his nation, the praise of his faithful, of the children of Israel, the people near to Him. 4 Halleluyah!

[Congregation rises as prayer leader
lifts Torah and says:]

יְהַלְלוּ אֶת־שֵׁם יְיָ כִּי־נִשְׂגָּב שְׁמוֹ
לְבַדּוֹ.

²הוֹדוֹ עַל־אֶרֶץ וְשָׁמָיִם: ³וַיָּרֶם קֶרֶן
לְעַמּוֹ תְּהִלָּה לְכָל־חֲסִידָיו לִבְנֵי
יִשְׂרָאֵל עַם קְרֹבוֹ ⁴הַלְלוּיָהּ.

BRETTLER (BIBLE)

[1] *"Let them praise Adonai's name"* The first part of Psalm 148:13. The return of the Torah mirrors the removing of it from the ark by emphasizing the name of God (see "Proclaim Adonai's greatness…exalt his name," above). Here too there is a remarkable identification of God with the Torah (see "There is no god like You," above).

[2] *"His majesty is above earth and heaven"* The continuation of Psalm 148:13, along with the following v. 14, emphasizing God's power. This is connected to the presence of the ark of covenant (see "With the moving of the ark," above), and is highlighted in Psalm 29, which follows.

———◆———

DORFF (THEOLOGY)

[2] *"His majesty is above earth and heaven"* The prayers selected for returning the Torah to the ark act as bookends to the prayers that we uttered when we removed the Torah from the ark to read it. Both then and now, the themes are the sovereignty of God, the author of the Torah (whatever your theory of revelation), and the blessing that God's Torah constitutes for us.

———◆———

FRANKEL (A WOMAN'S VOICE)

[1] *"Let them praise Adonai's name"* What does it mean to us as a community to receive the Torah in our midst? And how does it feel to have it withdraw back into the ark? In a very real sense, the Torah is as close as Jews come to representing God physically; we honor its body and garments with more reverence than we accord any human dignitary. So, when we prepare to return the Torah to the ark, we experience both sadness and fear. Our protector is departing!

B. ISRAEL'S PRAISE OF GOD

[Congregation rises as prayer leader lifts Torah and says:]

[1] Let them praise Adonai's name, for his name alone is exalted.

[2] His majesty is above earth and heaven. [3] He is the strength of his nation, the praise of his faithful, of the children of Israel, the people near to Him. [4] Halleluyah!

All we are left with is a name, *the* Name that remains unnamable. As we carry around the Torah in its final processional, we declare *Y'hall'lu et shem adonai,* "Let them praise Adonai's name." We reassure ourselves, as we relinquish our guardian, that even our enemies must acknowledge God's sovereignty. And so we continue, quoting Psalm 148: *Vayarem keren l'amo!* "God has raised up [our] people's strength!" It's bravado on our part, keeping up our spirits. Is it any wonder

(p. 200)

[Congregation rises as prayer leader lifts Torah and says:]

יְהַלְלוּ אֶת־שֵׁם יְיָ כִּי־נִשְׂגָּב שְׁמוֹ לְבַדּוֹ. [1]

הוֹדוֹ עַל־אֶרֶץ וְשָׁמָיִם: [2] וַיָּרֶם קֶרֶן לְעַמּוֹ תְּהִלָּה [3] לְכָל־חֲסִידָיו לִבְנֵי יִשְׂרָאֵל עַם קְרֹבוֹ הַלְלוּיָהּ. [4]

J. HOFFMAN (TRANSLATION)

[2] *"Above"* Literally, "on." See also "Adonai's voice peals across," below.

[3] *"Strength"* A dubious translation, trying to understand the idiom "to lift up a horn." Perhaps a particular sort of strength is intended, either military or sexual. We have, for instance, the literal imagery of "raising up David's horn" for the sake of his progeny. (See Volume 2, *The Amidah*, p. 143.)

◆ ◆ ◆

CONCLUDING PRAYERS

FRANKEL (A WOMAN'S VOICE)

that we follow this declaration with psalms to God's boundless might and special protectiveness of the Jewish People?

———◆———

C. The Universe's Praise of God (Psalm 29): "David's Psalm" (Mizmor l'david)

⁵מִזְמוֹר לְדָוִד.

⁵ **D**avid's Psalm:

⁶ To Adonai, you heavenly beings, to Adonai ascribe honor and might! ⁷ Ascribe the honor of his name to Adonai. ⁸ Bow down before Adonai in holy beauty. ⁹ Adonai's voice peals across the water—the thunder of the God of honor—across great water. ¹⁰ Adonai's voice is mighty. ¹¹ Adonai's voice is glorious. ¹² Adonai's voice can break cedar trees, and Adonai can smash the cedar trees of Lebanon and make them dance like a calf, Lebanon and Sirion like a wild ox. ¹³ Adonai's voice can carve out flames of fire. ¹⁴ Adonai's voice can make the desert tremble. ¹⁵ Adonai can make the Kadesh desert tremble. ¹⁶ Adonai's voice can pierce oak trees, and strip forests. ¹⁷ In his palace everything says "honor." ¹⁸ Adonai reigned during the flood, and Adonai will reign supreme forever. ¹⁹ Adonai will give strength to his people. ²⁰ Adonai will bless his people with peace.

⁶הָבוּ לַיְיָ בְּנֵי אֵלִים הָבוּ לַיְיָ כָּבוֹד וָעֹז: ⁷הָבוּ לַיְיָ כְּבוֹד שְׁמוֹ. ⁸הִשְׁתַּחֲווּ לַיְיָ בְּהַדְרַת־קֹדֶשׁ. ⁹קוֹל יְיָ עַל־הַמָּיִם. אֵל־הַכָּבוֹד הִרְעִים יְיָ עַל־מַיִם רַבִּים. ¹⁰קוֹל־יְיָ בַּכֹּחַ. ¹¹קוֹל יְיָ בֶּהָדָר: ¹²קוֹל יְיָ שֹׁבֵר אֲרָזִים. וַיְשַׁבֵּר יְיָ אֶת־אַרְזֵי הַלְּבָנוֹן: וַיַּרְקִידֵם כְּמוֹ־עֵגֶל. לְבָנוֹן וְשִׂרְיוֹן כְּמוֹ בֶן־רְאֵמִים. ¹³קוֹל־יְיָ חֹצֵב לַהֲבוֹת אֵשׁ. ¹⁴קוֹל יְיָ יָחִיל מִדְבָּר. ¹⁵יָחִיל יְיָ מִדְבַּר קָדֵשׁ. ¹⁶קוֹל יְיָ יְחוֹלֵל אַיָּלוֹת. וַיֶּחֱשֹׂף יְעָרוֹת. ¹⁷וּבְהֵיכָלוֹ כֻּלּוֹ אֹמֵר כָּבוֹד: ¹⁸יְיָ לַמַּבּוּל יָשָׁב. וַיֵּשֶׁב יְיָ מֶלֶךְ לְעוֹלָם: ¹⁹יְיָ עֹז לְעַמּוֹ יִתֵּן. ²⁰יְיָ יְבָרֵךְ אֶת־עַמּוֹ בַשָּׁלוֹם.

BRETTLER (BIBLE)

[5] *"David's Psalm [Ps. 29]"* Many scholars consider this to be one of the oldest biblical psalms, reflecting an Israelite version of a Canaanite psalm to the storm god; this explains, for example, why the thunderstorm is placed in Lebanon and Sirion. The psalm's theme of divine power fits well the idea of "the ark of the covenant of Adonai of hosts enthroned on the cherubim" (1 Sam. 4:4), namely, that the ark is connected to God, the warrior, who controls the divine "hosts," or warriors. The temple imagery that suffuses this psalm makes it appropriate liturgically, though the temple of the psalm is the heavenly temple, in which the divine beings, *b'nei elim* (literally "sons of God"), praise their master.

[9] *"Adonai's voice peals across the water"* The first of several expressions of God's might, alluding to an ancient myth (reflected in prebiblical Canaanite literature) that as part of creation, God vanquished the Ocean and River.

———◆———

FRANKEL (A WOMAN'S VOICE)

[6] *"To Adonai ascribe honor and might"* This psalm begins by exhorting us to "ascribe the honor of his name to Adonai." Then a series of dramatic natural images — thunder, tempest, lightning, and earthquake — makes us aware of how very puny our voices must seem by comparison. Are they not swallowed up by the voice that shatters mountains and rattles the desert? Why then do we waste our breath? Does God really need our praise? Does God even hear our words?

In reciting this psalm, we are doing much more than *describing* God's

C. THE UNIVERSE'S PRAISE OF GOD: "DAVID'S PSALM"

[5] David's Psalm:

[6] To Adonai, you heavenly beings, to Adonai ascribe honor and might! [7] Ascribe the honor of his name to Adonai. [8] Bow down before Adonai in holy beauty. [9] Adonai's voice peals across the water—the thunder of the God of honor—across great water. [10] Adonai's voice is mighty.

grandeur. Through these words, we *become* God's breath, God's voice, the embodiment of God's *kavod* ("honor"). In praising God's strength *(oz)*, we pray that God will grant us the same: *Adonai oz l'amo yitayn,* "Adonai will give strength to his people" — a kind of divine quid pro quo.

———◆———

LANDES (HALAKHAH)

[5] *"David's Psalm"* Read on Shabbat because it (Psalm 29, *mizmor l'david*) is actively joyous. On other occasions, we say Psalm 24, "A psalm of David" (*l'david mizmor*).

———◆———

⁵מִזְמוֹר לְדָוִד.

⁶הָבוּ לַיָי בְּנֵי אֵלִים הָבוּ לַיָי כָּבוֹד וָעֹז: ⁷הָבוּ לַיָי כְּבוֹד שְׁמוֹ. ⁸הִשְׁתַּחֲווּ לַיָי בְּהַדְרַת־קֹדֶשׁ. ⁹קוֹל יְיָ עַל־הַמָּיִם. אֵל־הַכָּבוֹד הִרְעִים יְיָ עַל־מַיִם רַבִּים.

J. HOFFMAN (TRANSLATION)

[5] *"David's Psalm [Ps. 29]"* Often translated, "a Psalm by David," but the title in Hebrew leaves the exact connection between David and the psalm ambiguous: is it "of David" or "by David"? Our English translation retains the ambiguity. On the other hand, "a Psalm by David" makes it clear that this is but one psalm of many, and that is a fact clearly indicated by the Hebrew but not by our English.

As with most psalms, Psalm 29 praises God with poetic language and loose meter. While our translation contains hints of the poetic language, we make no attempt to capture the meter.

[6] *"Heavenly beings"* Literally, "children of the gods."

[9] *"Adonai's voice peals across"* Taken from Birnbaum. The Hebrew literally reads "is on," but the next line which is in apposition and thus parallel in meaning, refers to "thunder . . . across great water," suggesting that in both cases we have images of sound waves moving across an expanse. The English "peals across" thus best captures the poetic flavor of the Hebrew. Other possibilities, though less likely, are "Adonai's voice is above" or even "Adonai's voice is better than." *JPS* and *NRSV* both read, "The voice of the Lord is over the waters; the God of glory thunders, the Lord, over the mighty waters."

[12] *"Can break...can smash"* The modal verb "can" is often, as (p. 204)

¹¹Adonai's voice is glorious. ¹²Adonai's voice can break cedar trees, and Adonai can smash the cedar trees of Lebanon and make them dance like a calf, Lebanon and Sirion like a wild ox. ¹³Adonai's voice can carve out flames of fire. ¹⁴Adonai's voice can make the desert tremble. ¹⁵Adonai can make the Kadesh desert tremble. ¹⁶Adonai's voice can pierce oak trees, and strip forests. ¹⁷In his palace everything says "honor." ¹⁸Adonai reigned during the flood, and Adonai will reign supreme forever. ¹⁹Adonai will give strength to his people. ²⁰Adonai will bless his people with peace.

¹⁰קוֹל ¹¹ .קוֹל־יְיָ בַּכֹּחַ. ¹¹ קוֹל יְיָ בֶּהָדָר: ¹² קוֹל יְיָ שֹׁבֵר אֲרָזִים. וַיְשַׁבֵּר יְיָ אֶת־אַרְזֵי הַלְּבָנוֹן: וַיַּרְקִידֵם כְּמוֹ־עֵגֶל. לְבָנוֹן וְשִׂרְיוֹן כְּמוֹ בֶן־רְאֵמִים. ¹³ קוֹל־יְיָ חֹצֵב לַהֲבוֹת אֵשׁ. ¹⁴ קוֹל יְיָ יָחִיל מִדְבָּר. ¹⁵ יָחִיל יְיָ מִדְבַּר קָדֵשׁ. ¹⁶ קוֹל יְיָ יְחוֹלֵל אַיָּלוֹת. וַיֶּחֱשֹׂף יְעָרוֹת. ¹⁷ וּבְהֵיכָלוֹ כֻּלּוֹ אֹמֵר כָּבוֹד: ¹⁸ יְיָ לַמַּבּוּל יָשָׁב. וַיֵּשֶׁב יְיָ מֶלֶךְ לְעוֹלָם: ¹⁹ יְיָ עֹז לְעַמּוֹ יִתֵּן. ²⁰ יְיָ יְבָרֵךְ אֶת־עַמּוֹ בַשָּׁלוֹם.

J. HOFFMAN (TRANSLATION

here, merely implied in Hebrew. Literally, the verbs are imperfect, implying "will," but they are best translated as modal forms. The Hebrew for "smash" is closely related to the Hebrew for "break," creating a verbal pun we fail to capture in the English.

¹²*"Cedar trees of Lebanon"* The "cedar trees of Lebanon" were used symbolically to denote might and beauty.

¹²*"Make them dance"* "Them" refers to Lebanon and Sirion. The following line, "Lebanon and Sirion like a wild ox," is in apposition to "makes them dance like a calf," allowing us to identify "them" in the first line with "Lebanon and Sirion" in the second.

¹²*"Carve out"* Birnbaum: "strike." *JPS:* "kindles." *NRSV:* "flashes forth flames of fire."

¹⁵*"Kadesh"* The name of a place, with no relation to the prayer spelled identically. It occurs as part of the name of a biblical city, Kadesh Barnea (Num. 34:4), but usually as the name of a desert. The Rabbis identify it as another name for the Sinai (see Rashi to Ps. 29:8). Here, it is used in apposition to "the desert," possibly because the addition of the word *Kadesh* in the second half of the verse provides metric parallelism with the first half.

¹⁶*"Pierce oak trees [y'cholel ayalot]"* The Hebrew is hard to fathom. Our line is in parallelism with "strips the forests" *(yechesof y'arot).* JPS takes *y'cholel ayalot* to mean

"causes hinds to calve," seeing *ayalot* as the plural of *ayil,* "a hind [deer]." But then it has no parallelism, so it has to suggest an alternative reading of *y'cholel ayalot,* "brings ewes to early birth." *NRSV* isn't sure, so prefers "causes oaks to whirl" but supplies the alternative, "causes the deer to calve." Birnbaum follows the latter. Probably we have all missed something.

[17] *"Everything says [kulo omer]"* This is the most likely interpretation of the Hebrew, followed by *JPS* and *NRSV* ("all say"), but it's not immediately clear why the Hebrew is grammatical, raising the possibility that again we have missed something.

[18] *"Reigned"* Literally, "sat."

[20] *"Peace"* Or "peacefulness."

D. "And with its resting" (U'v'nuchoh yomar)

[Torah is placed in ark.]

[Torah is placed in ark.]

^{1} And with its resting, he would say: ^{2} "Adonai, return to the myriad families of Israel." ^{3} Adonai, rise up to your resting place, you and your mighty ark. ^{4} May your priests wear righteousness, and your faithful rejoice. ^{5} For the sake of David your servant, do not reject your anointed one. ^{6} For I have given you good instruction; do not abandon my Torah. ^{7} It is a tree of life to those who cling to it, and its supporters are happy. ^{8} Its ways are ways of pleasantness, and all its paths are peace. ^{9} Adonai, return us to You, that we might return. ^{10} Renew our days as of old.

^{1}וּבְנֻחֹה יֹאמַר ^{2}שׁוּבָה יְיָ רִבְבוֹת אַלְפֵי
יִשְׂרָאֵל. ^{3}קוּמָה יְיָ לִמְנוּחָתֶךָ אַתָּה
וַאֲרוֹן עֻזֶּךָ. ^{4}כֹּהֲנֶיךָ יִלְבְּשׁוּ־צֶדֶק
וַחֲסִידֶיךָ יְרַנֵּנוּ. ^{5}בַּעֲבוּר דָּוִד עַבְדֶּךָ
אַל תָּשֵׁב פְּנֵי מְשִׁיחֶךָ. ^{6}כִּי־לֶקַח טוֹב
נָתַתִּי לָכֶם תּוֹרָתִי אַל־תַּעֲזֹבוּ. ^{7}עֵץ
חַיִּים הִיא לַמַּחֲזִיקִים בָּהּ וְתֹמְכֶיהָ
מְאֻשָּׁר. ^{8}דְּרָכֶיהָ דַרְכֵי־נֹעַם וְכָל־
נְתִיבוֹתֶיהָ שָׁלוֹם: ^{9}הֲשִׁיבֵנוּ יְיָ אֵלֶיךָ
וְנָשׁוּבָה ^{10}חַדֵּשׁ יָמֵינוּ כְּקֶדֶם.

BRETTLER (BIBLE)

[1] *"With its resting"* The Torah liturgy began with a reference to the traveling of the ark of the covenant (see "With the moving of the ark," above); it ends with this companion verse, about the ark coming to a rest (Num. 10:36). It too emphasizes the role of the ark in Israelite wars.

[6-8] *"Good instruction...a tree of life...all its paths"* From Proverbs 4:2; 3:18,17. The earlier verses of this prayer focused on the ark; these focus on Torah. Thus, the ark and the Torah are brought together on the literary level, symbolizing their unification in the ritual of the return of the scroll to the ark.

(p. 210)

DORFF (THEOLOGY)

[7] *"It is a tree of life"* This verse is Proverbs 3:18. In its biblical context, the antecedent of "it," going back to 3:13, is not the Torah but Wisdom personified. In using these verses for returning the Torah to the ark, though, the author of our prayer (probably deliberately) has us applying the message of these verses to the Torah as the font of Jewish wisdom. This is somewhat of a liturgical sleight of hand, for Wisdom, as described in the biblical wisdom literature, is generally knowledge that comes not from study of God's Torah but from life experience. Still, this is not nearly as much of a theological leap as the one we saw earlier in the liturgist's cutting off the biblical verse in the middle, leaving out the part that describes God *(p. 210)*

FRANKEL (A WOMAN'S VOICE)

[10] *"Renew our days as of old"* Just as we began the Torah service with a paradox, so we end it with one. At the beginning, we acknowledged the paradox of Jewish space: that God reigns everywhere but especially in one particular place, and that the Jewish People lives everywhere, but calls one particular place home. Here we affirm the paradox of Jewish time: that we look always to the future, but the way there lies through our past: *chadesh yameinu k'kedem.* "Renew our days as of old."

D. "AND WITH ITS RESTING" *(U'V'NUCHOH YOMAR)*

[Torah is placed in ark.]

[1] And with its resting, he would say: [2] "Adonai, return to the myriad families of Israel." [3] Adonai, rise up to your resting place, you and your mighty ark. [4] May your priests wear righteousness, and your faithful rejoice. [5] For the sake of David your servant, do not reject your anointed one. [6] For I have given you good instruction; do not abandon

The final paragraph of the Torah service is a pastiche of biblical quotations from Numbers, Psalms, Proverbs, and Lamentations. Three of them touch on pivotal moments in Jewish history: the wilderness experience, the first commonwealth under the Davidic dynasty, and the destruction of the First Temple. Three defining moments: the Exodus, the establishment of an independent kingdom under David, the beginning of the first exile. Tellingly, the final line of this concluding prayer repeats the ending of the Book of Lamentations, the biblical *(p. 210)*

LANDES (HALAKHAH)

[1] *"And with its resting" Uv'nucho nomar* represents the successful completion of the Torah service. With the return of the Torah to the holy ark, everything is in its proper place. This prayer is therefore recited in a joyous but solemn tone.

[7] *"It is a tree of life to those who cling to it"* Those who hold onto the *atsei chayim*, the wooden rollers of the Torah, are promised life unending.

———

L. HOFFMAN (HISTORY)

WITH UNIVERSAL PRAISE CONCLUDING THE DRAMA, THE TORAH IS RETURNED TO THE ARK.

———

[Torah is placed in ark.]

[1]וּבְנֻחֹה יֹאמַר [2]שׁוּבָה יְיָ רִבְבוֹת אַלְפֵי יִשְׂרָאֵל. [3]קוּמָה יְיָ לִמְנוּחָתֶךָ אַתָּה וַאֲרוֹן עֻזֶּךָ. [4]כֹּהֲנֶיךָ יִלְבְּשׁוּ־צֶדֶק וַחֲסִידֶיךָ יְרַנֵּנוּ. [5]בַּעֲבוּר דָּוִד עַבְדֶּךָ אַל תָּשֵׁב פְּנֵי מְשִׁיחֶךָ. [6]כִּי־לֶקַח טוֹב נָתַתִּי לָכֶם

J. HOFFMAN (TRANSLATION)

[1] *"Its resting"* That is, the ark's. This line is biblical (Num. 10:36). It occurs immediately after "with the moving of the ark" (Num. 10:35), the line with which the Torah service began. The service is thus bracketed by two references to the ark, both from the same biblical section.

[1] *"He"* Moses.

[3] *"Resting place"* This phrase should not be confused with the English expression "final resting place."

———

my Torah. ⁷It is a tree of life to those who cling to it, and its supporters are happy. ⁸Its ways are ways of pleasantness, and all its paths are peace. ⁹Adonai, return us to You, that we might return. ¹⁰Renew our days as of old.

תּוֹרָתִי אַל־תַּעֲזֹבוּ. ⁷עֵץ חַיִּים הִיא לַמַּחֲזִיקִים בָּהּ וְתֹמְכֶיהָ מְאֻשָּׁר. ⁸דְּרָכֶיהָ דַרְכֵי־נֹעַם וְכָל־נְתִיבוֹתֶיהָ שָׁלוֹם: ⁹הֲשִׁיבֵנוּ יְיָ אֵלֶיךָ וְנָשׁוּבָה ¹⁰חַדֵּשׁ יָמֵינוּ כְּקֶדֶם.

BRETTLER (BIBLE)

⁹*"Return us"* The next to last verse of Lamentations (5:21), in which context it expresses hope for restoration and ultimately the return from exile and the reconstruction of the Temple. This wish serves as a fitting conclusion here as well. Additionally, the use of this verse here connects the return of the Torah to the ark to the return of Israel to its God and its restored land. This suggests that the ritual action of returning the Torah might help bring about a spiritual return and anticipated restoration.

DORFF (THEOLOGY)

as *not* wiping away our sins (see above, "Adonai, Adonai, merciful and gracious God"), for the Book of Proverbs regularly identifies the Torah as a primary source of wisdom: "Fear of Adonai is the beginning [or "best part"] of knowledge" (Prov. 1:7).

FRANKEL (A WOMAN'S VOICE)

chronicle of Jerusalem's destruction: "Cause us to return to You, God, and we shall return." We have never gotten over this ancient loss.

Only one biblical excerpt included in this prayer rises above historical reference: the three verses quoted from Proverbs, cited here in reverse sequence from their original context. In their new order, the verses build from divine prescription to messianic promise: Do not forsake my Torah, declares God, for it is good; it will make you happy; it will bring you peace. The cumulative effect is redemptive for both God and the Jewish People. We both yearn for this ultimate *shalom*. We both pledge, as we return the Torah to its hiding place, that we will return to its life-giving ways as of old.

About the Contributors

MARC BRETTLER

Marc Brettler, Ph.D., is Associate Professor of Hebrew Bible in the Department of Near Eastern and Judaic Studies at Brandeis University. His major areas of research are biblical historical texts, religious metaphors, and gender issues in the Bible. Brettler is author of *God Is King: Understanding an Israelite Metaphor* (Sheffield Academic Press) and *The Creation of History in Ancient Israel* (Routledge) as well as a variety of articles on the Hebrew Bible.

ELLIOT N. DORFF

Elliot N. Dorff, Ph.D., is Rector and Distinguished Professor of Philosophy at the University of Judaism in Los Angeles. His book *Knowing God: Jewish Journeys to the Unknowable* (Jason Aronson) includes an extensive analysis of the nature of prayer. Ordained a rabbi by The Jewish Theological Seminary of America, Dorff is a member of the Conservative Movement's Committee on Jewish Law and Standards, its Commission on the Philosophy of the Conservative Movement, and its Commission to write a new Torah commentary for the Conservative Movement.

DAVID ELLENSON

David Ellenson, Ph.D., is the I. H. and Anna Grancell Professor of Jewish Religious Thought at Hebrew Union College–Jewish Institute of Religion in Los Angeles. Ordained a rabbi by Hebrew Union College–Jewish Institute of Religion, he has served as a visiting professor at Hebrew University in Jerusalem, The Jewish Theological Seminary, and at the University of California at Los Angeles. Ellenson has also taught at the Pardes Instutute of Jewish Studies and at the Shalom Hartman Institute in Jerusalem. Ellenson has published and lectured extensively on diverse topics in modern Jewish thought, history, and ethics.

ELLEN FRANKEL

Dr. Ellen Frankel is currently the CEO and Editor-in-Chief of The Jewish Publication Society. A scholar of Jewish folklore, Frankel has published eight books, including *The Classic Tales; The Encyclopedia of Jewish Symbols,* co-authored with artist Betsy Teutsch; *The Five Books of Miriam: A Woman's Commentary on the Torah; The Jewish Spirit;* and

The Illustrated Hebrew Bible. Frankel travels widely as a storyteller and lecturer, speaking at synagogues, summer study institutes, Hillels, Jewish women's groups, Jewish community centers, museums, schools, retirement communities, and nursing homes, and to radio audiences.

JUDITH HAUPTMAN

Judith Hauptman, Ph.D., is the Rabbi Philip R. Alstat Professor of Talmud at The Jewish Theological Seminary in New York City. Her many publications focus on Talmud, Jewish feminism, and their points of intersection. The author of two books, *Development of the Talmudic Sugya: Relationship between Tannaitic and Amoraic Sources* (University Press of America) and *Rereading the Rabbis, A Woman's Voice* (Westview/HarperCollins), she is currently researching the relationship between halakhah and aggadah in the ancient rabbinic texts.

JOEL M. HOFFMAN

Joel M. Hoffman, Ph.D., teaches advanced Hebrew, translation, and the history of Hebrew at Hebrew Union College–Jewish Institute of Religion in New York; he has also taught at Brandeis University, and lectured in America, Europe, and Israel. He has served as Hebrew consultant to HarperSanFrancisco and Jewish Lights Publishing. Hoffman's research in theoretical linguistics brings him to a new approach to ancient Hebrew, viewing it not merely as a dead language, but as a spoken language of antiquity. In addition to his graduate-level teaching, Hoffman teaches youngsters at various Hebrew schools. He considers teaching his greatest joy.

LAWRENCE A. HOFFMAN

Lawrence A. Hoffman, Ph.D., has served for over two decades as Professor of Liturgy at Hebrew Union College–Jewish Institute of Religion in New York, where he was ordained a rabbi. Widely recognized for his liturgical scholarship, Hoffman has combined research in Jewish ritual, worship, and spirituality with a passion for the spiritual renewal of contemporary Judaism.

He has written and edited numerous books, including *The Art of Public Prayer, 2nd Edition: Not for Clergy Only* (SkyLight Paths), now used nationally by Jews and Christians as a handbook for liturgical planners in church and synagogue, as well as a revision of *What Is a Jew?*, the best-selling classic that remains the most widely read introduction to Judaism ever written in any language. He is also the author of *Israel — A Spiritual Travel Guide: A Companion for the Modern Jewish Pilgrim* and *The Way Into Jewish Prayer* (both Jewish Lights). Hoffman is currently a developer of Synagogue 2000, a transdenominational project designed to envision and implement the ideal synagogue of the spirit for the 21st century.

LAWRENCE KUSHNER

Lawrence Kushner is Rabbi-in-Residence at Hebrew Union College–Jewish Institute of Religion, New York. He served as spiritual leader of Congregation Beth El in Sudbury,

Massachusetts, for 25 years and is widely regarded as one of the most creative religious writers in America. Ordained a rabbi by Hebrew Union College–Jewish Institute of Religion, Kushner led his congregants in publishing their own prayer book, *V'taher Libenu (Purify Our Hearts)*, the first gender-neutral liturgy ever written. Through his lectures and nine books, including *Invisible Lines of Connection: Sacred Stories of the Ordinary; The Book of Letters: A Mystical Hebrew Alphabet; Honey from the Rock: An Introduction to Jewish Mysticism; God Was in This Place and I, i Did Not Know: Finding Self, Spirituality, and Ultimate Meaning;* and *Eyes Remade for Wonder: A Lawrence Kushner Reader,* all published by Jewish Lights, he has helped shape the Jewish community's present focus on personal and institutional spiritual renewal.

DANIEL LANDES

Daniel Landes is Director of the Pardes Institute of Jewish Studies in Jerusalem and was an adjunct Professor of Jewish Law at Loyola University Law School in Los Angeles. Ordained a rabbi by Rabbi Isaac Elchanan Theological Seminary, Landes was a founding faculty member of the Simon Wiesenthal Center and the Yeshiva of Los Angeles. He has lectured and written various popular and scholarly articles on the subjects of Jewish thought, social ethics, and spirituality.

RUTH LANGER

Ruth Langer, Ph.D., is Assistant Professor of Jewish Studies in the Theology Department at Boston College. She received her rabbinic ordination and her Ph.D. in liturgy from Hebrew Union College–Jewish Institute of Religion in Cincinnati. She has published many articles and a book titled *To Worship God Properly: Tensions between Liturgical Custom and Halakhah in Judaism* (Hebrew Union College Press). Her current research examines the history and meanings of the liturgies celebrating the reading of the Torah in the synagogue.

NEHEMIA POLEN

Nehemia Polen, Ph.D., is Associate Professor of Jewish Thought and Associate Dean of Students at Hebrew College in Boston. Ordained a rabbi by Ner Israel Rabbinical College, Polen, a prolific writer whose academic and popular articles have appeared in many journals, is the author of *The Holy Fire: The Teachings of Rabbi Kalonymos Shapira, the Rebbe of the Warsaw Ghetto* (Jason Aronson).

List of Abbreviations

Artscroll	*Siddur Kol Ya'akov,* 1984.
Birnbaum	*Daily Prayer Book: Hasiddur Hashalem,* 1949.
FOP	*Forms of Prayer,* 1997.
Fox	Everett Fox, *The Five Books of Moses* (New York: Schocken Books, 1995).
GOP	*Gates of Prayer,* 1975.
HS	*Ha'avodah Shebalev* (1982).
KH	*Kol Haneshamah,* 1994.
JPS	*Jewish Publication Society Bible* (Philadelphia: Jewish Publication Society, 1962).
NRSV	*New Revised Standard Bible,* 1989.
SLC	*Siddur Lev Chadash,* 1995.
SOH	*Service of the Heart,* 1967.
SSS	*Siddur Sim Shalom,* 1985; revised, 1998.
SVT	*Siddur Va'ani T'fillati* (1998).
UPB	*Union Prayer Book,* 1894–1895.

Glossary

The following glossary defines Hebrew words used regularly throughout this volume, and provides the way the words are pronounced. Sometimes two pronunciations are common, in which case the first is the way the word is sounded in proper Hebrew, and the second is the way it is sometimes heard in common speech, under the influence of Yiddish, the folk language of Jews in northern and eastern Europe (it is a combination, mostly, of Hebrew and German). Our goal is to provide the way that many Jews actually use these words, not just the technically correct version.

- The pronunciations are divided into syllables by dashes.
- The accented syllable is written in capital letters.
- "Kh" represents a guttural sound, similar to the German (as in "sprach").
- The most common vowel is "a" as in "father," which appears here as "ah."
- The short "e" (as in "get") is written either "e" (when it is in the middle of a syllable) or "eh" (when it ends a syllable).
- Similarly, the short "i" (as in "tin") is written either "i" (when it is in the middle of a syllable) or "ih" (when it ends a syllable).
- A long "o" (as in "Moses") is written "oe" (as in the English word "toe") or "oh" (as in the English word "Oh!").

See also page 16 for additional terms and definitions related to the reading of Torah.

Acharonim (pronounced ah-khah-roe-NEEM, or, commonly, ah-chah-ROE-nim): The name given to Jewish legal authorities from roughly the sixteenth century on. The word means, literally, "later ones," as opposed to the "earlier ones," authorities prior to that time who are held in higher regard and are called *rishonim* (pronounced ree-shoh-NEEM, or, commonly, ree-SHOH-nim). Singular: *acharon* (pronounced ah-chah-RONE) and *rishon* (pronounced ree-SHONE).

Adon Olam (pronounced ah-DOHN oh-LAHM): An early morning prayer of unknown authorship, but dating from medieval times, and possibly originally intended as a nighttime prayer, because it praises God for watching over our souls when we sleep. Nowadays, it is used also as a concluding song for which composers have provided a staggering variety of tunes.

Alenu (pronounced ah-LAY-noo): The first word and, therefore, the title of a major prayer compiled in the second or third century as part of the New Year *(Rosh Hashanah)* service, but from about the fourteenth century on, used also as part of the concluding section of every daily service. *Alenu* means "it is incumbent upon us…" and introduces the prayer's theme: our duty to praise God.

Amidah (pronounced either ah-mee-DAH or, commonly, ah-MEE-dah): One of three commonly used titles for the second of two central units in the worship service, the first being The *Sh'ma* and Its Blessings. It is composed of a series of blessings, many of which are petitionary, except on Sabbaths and holidays, when the petitions are removed out of deference to the holiness of the day. Also called *T'fillah* and *Sh'moneh Esreh*. *Amidah* means "standing," and refers to the fact that the prayer is said standing up.

Amora (pronounced ah-MOE-rah): A title for talmudic authorities and, therefore, living roughly from the third to the sixth centuries. Plural: *amoraim* (pronounced ah-moe-rah-EEM, or, commonly, ah-moe-RAH-yim). Often used in contrast to a *tanna* (pronounced TAH-nah), the title of authorities in the time of the Mishnah, that is, prior to the third century. Plural: *tannaim* (pronounced tah-nah-EEM, or, commonly, tah-NAH-yim).

Arvit (pronounced ahr-VEET, or, commonly, AHR-veet): From the Hebrew word *erev* (pronounced EH-rev) meaning "evening." One of two titles used for the evening worship service (also called *Ma'ariv*).

Ashkenazi (pronounced ahsh-k'-nah-ZEE, or, commonly, ahsh-k'-NAH-zee): From the Hebrew word *Ashkenaz,* meaning the geographic area of northern and eastern Europe; *Ashkenazi* is the adjective, describing the liturgical rituals and customs practiced there, as opposed to *Sefardi,* meaning the liturgical rituals and customs that are derived from *Sefarad,* Spain (see *Sefardi*).

Ashre (pronounced ahsh-RAY, or, commonly, AHSH-ray): The first word and, therefore, the title of a prayer said three times each day, composed primarily of Psalm 145. *Ashre* means "happy" and introduces the phrase "Happy are they who dwell in your [God's] house."

Avodah (pronounced ah-voe-DAH): Literally, "sacrificial service," a reference to the sacrificial cult practiced in the ancient Temple until its destruction by the Romans in the year 70 C.E.; also the title of the third to last blessing in the *Amidah,* a petition for the restoration of the Temple in messianic times. Many liberal liturgies either omit the blessing or reframe it as a petition for divine acceptance of worship in general.

Avot (pronounced ah-VOTE): Literally, "fathers" or "ancestors," and the title of the first blessing in the *Amidah*. The traditional wording of the blessing recollects the covenantal relationship between God and the patriarchs: Abraham, Isaac, and Jacob. Most liberal liturgies include also explicit reference to the matriarchs: Sarah, Rebekah, Rachel, and Leah.

[The] Bach (pronounced BAHKH): An acronym for Rabbi Joel Sirkes (Poland, 1561–1640), formed by juxtaposing the two Hebrew initials of his major legal work, *Bayit Chadash* (BaCH).

Bar'khu (pronounced bah-r'-KHOO, or, commonly, BOH-r'khoo): The first word and, therefore, the title of the formal call to prayer with which the section called The *Sh'ma* and Its Blessings begins. *Bar'khu* means "praise," and introduces the invitation to the assembled congregation to praise God.

Barukh k'vod (pronounced bah-RUKH k'-VOD): The first two words of a response in the third blessing of the *Amidah* taken from Ezekiel 3:12, meaning "the glory of Adonai is blessed from his place."

Barukh she'amar (pronounced bah-ROOKH sheh-ah-MAHR): Literally, "Blessed is the One by whose speech [the world came to be]," the first words, and, therefore, the title of the blessing that opens the *P'sukei D'zimrah*, the "warm-up" section to the morning service composed mainly of biblical material (chiefly psalms) that were intended to be sung as praise of God.

Benediction (also called **Blessing**): One of two terms used for the Rabbis' favorite prose formula for composing prayers. The worship service is composed of many different literary genres, but most of it is benedictions. Long benedictions end with a summary line that begins *Barukh atah Adonai...* "Blessed are You, Adonai..." Short blessings have only the summary line alone.

Ben Sirah (pronounced behn SIH-rah): Author of a book of wisdom similar in style to Proverbs, probably dating to 180 or 280 B.C.E., and containing, among other things, a moving description of the High Priest in the Jerusalem Temple. Though not included in the Jewish Bible, it is known because it became part of Catholic scripture. The book carries the author's name, but is called, by Catholics, Ecclesiasticus. A recently discovered Hebrew edition of Ben Sirah contains a prayer that some identify (probably incorrectly) as an early version of the *Amidah* (see *Amidah*).

Binah (pronounced bee-NAH, or, commonly, BEE-nah): Literally, "knowledge" or "understanding," and the title of the fourth blessing in the daily *Amidah*. It is a petition for human knowledge, particularly insight into the human condition, leading to repentance.

Birkat (pronounced beer-KAHT): Literally, "Blessing of..." The titles of many blessings are known as "Blessing of...," for example, "Blessing of Torah" and "Blessing of Jerusalem." Some titles are commonly shortened so that only the qualifying last words are used (such as "Jerusalem" instead of "Blessing of Jerusalem"), and they are listed in the glossary by the last words, e.g., *Y'rushalayim* instead of *Birkat Y'rushalayim* ("Jerusalem" instead of "Blessing of Jerusalem"). Those blessings that are more generally cited with the full title appear under *Birkat*.

Birkat Hashir (pronounced beer-KAHT hah-SHEER): Literally, "Blessing of song," and the title, therefore, of the final blessing to the *P'sukei D'zimrah,* the "warm-up" section to the morning service composed mainly of biblical material (chiefly psalms) that were intended to be sung as praise of God. Technically, a *Birkat Hashir* concludes any *Hallel* (see *Hallel*), in this case, the Daily Hallel, which is the central component of the *P'sukei D'zimrah.*

Birkat Hatorah (pronounced beer-KAHT hah-toe-RAH): Literally, "Blessing of Torah," the title for the second blessing in the liturgical section called The *Sh'ma* and Its Blessings; its theme is the revelation of the Torah to Israel on Mount Sinai.

Birkat Kohanim (pronounced beer-KAHT koe-hah-NEEM): Literally, "blessing of the priests," but usually referred to as "the priestly benediction," a reference to Numbers 6:24–25. Also the title of the final blessing of the *Amidah.* See also *Kohanim.*

Birkhot Hashachar (pronounced beer-KHOT hah-SHAH-khar): Literally, "Morning Blessings," the title of the first large section in the morning prayer regimen of Judaism; originally said privately upon arising in the morning, but now customarily recited immediately upon arriving at the synagogue. It is composed primarily of benedictions thanking God for the everyday gifts of health and wholeness, as well as study sections taken from the Bible and rabbinic literature.

B'rakhah (pronounced b'-rah-KHAH): The Hebrew word for "benediction" or "blessing." See *Benediction*. Plural ("benedictions") is *b'rakhot* (pronounced b'-rah-KHOTE).

Chanukah (pronounced KHAH-noo-kah): An eight-day festival beginning on the twenty-fifth day of the Hebrew month of Kislev, corresponding, usually, to some time in December. Chanukah celebrates the miraculous deliverance of the Jews as described in the books known as *Maccabees* (pronounced MA-kah-beez). Although not canonized in the Jewish Bible, Maccabees is carried in Catholic scripture and describes the heroic acts of a priestly family, known also as the Maccabees, or the Hasmoneans (pronounced has-moe-NEE-'ns), in 167 B.C.E.

Chasidism (pronounced KHAH-sih-dizm): The doctrine generally traced to an eighteenth-century Polish Jewish mystic and spiritual leader known as the Ba'al Shem Tov (called also the BeSHT, an acronym composed of the initials of his name B, SH, and T). Followers are called *Chasidim* (pronounced khah-see-DEEM or khah-SIH-dim; singular, *Chasid* pronounced khah-SEED, or, commonly, KHA-sid) from the Hebrew word *chesed* (pronounced KHEH-sed), meaning "loving-kindness" or "piety."

Chatimah (pronounced chah-tee-MAH): The final summary line of a benediction (see *Benediction*).

Cheshvan (pronounced KHESH-vahn): A Hebrew month corresponding to late October or November.

Daily Hallel (pronounced hah-LAYL, or, commonly, HAH-layl): English for *Hallel sheb'khol yom*. See *Hallel*.

David (pronounced dah-VEED): Literally, "David," a reference to the biblical King David, and the title of the fifteenth blessing of the daily *Amidah*, a petition for the appearance of the messianic ruler said by tradition to be a descendent of King David. Some liberal liturgies omit the blessing or reframe it to refer to a messianic age of perfection, but without the arrival of a human messianic ruler.

Doxology: Technical term for a congregational response to an invitation to praise God; generally a single line of prayer affirming praise of God forever and ever. Examples in The *Sh'ma* and Its Blessings are the responses to the Call to Prayer and to the *Sh'ma* itself. From the Greek word *doxa,* meaning "glory."

El Adon (pronounced ayl ah-DOHN): An early medieval (or, perhaps, ancient) poem celebrating God as a king enthroned on high; it is arranged as an acrostic, that is, each line begins with a different letter of the alphabet. Nowadays *El Adon* is a popular Sabbath morning hymn.

Eretz Yisrael (pronounced EH-retz yis-rah-AYL): Hebrew for "the Land of Israel."

Gaon (pronounced gah-OHN; plural: *Geonim,* pronounced g'-oh-NEEM): Title for the leading rabbis in Babylon (present-day Iraq) from about 750 to 1038. From a biblical word meaning "glory," which is equivalent in the title to saying "Your Excellence."

Genizah (pronounced g'-NEE-zah): A cache of documents, in particular, the one discovered at the turn of the twentieth century in an old synagogue in Cairo; the source of our knowledge about how Jews prayed in the Land of Israel and vicinity prior to the twelfth century. From a word meaning "to store or hide away," "to archive."

G'ulah (pronounced g'-oo-LAH): Literally, "redemption" or "deliverance," and the title of the seventh blessing of the daily *Amidah,* as well as the third blessing in The *Sh'ma* and Its Blessings; its theme affirms God's redemptive act of delivering the Israelites from Egypt, and promises ultimate deliverance from suffering and want at the end of time.

G'vurot (pronounced g'voo-ROTE): Literally, "strength" or "power," and the title of the second blessing in the *Amidah*. It affirms the power of God to bring annual rain and new growth in nature and, by extension, to resurrect the dead. Some liberal liturgies omit the belief in resurrection or replace it with wording that suggests other concepts of eternal life.

Haftarah (pronounced hahf-tah-RAH, or, commonly, hahf-TOE-rah): The section of Scripture taken from the prophets and read publicly as part of Shabbat and holiday worship services. From a word meaning "to conclude," since it is the "concluding reading," that is, it follows a reading from the Torah (the five books of Moses).

Haggadah (pronounced hah-gah-DAH, or, commonly, hah-GAH-dah): The liturgical service for the Passover eve Seder meal. From a Hebrew word meaning "to tell," since the *Haggadah* is a telling of the Passover narrative.

Hakafah (pronounced hah-kah-FAH): "Going around [the room]," a procession in which the Torah is not only taken from the ark but is carried to the *bimah* during the introductory prayers. As the procession winds its way to the *bimah,* people approach the Torah, even kiss it.

Halakhah (pronounced hah-lah-KHAH, or, commonly, hah-LAH-khah): The Hebrew word for "Jewish law." Used as an anglicized adjective, *halakhic* (pronounced hah-LAH-khic), meaning "legal." From the Hebrew word meaning "to walk, to go," so denoting the way on which a person should walk through life.

Hallel (pronounced hah-LAYL, or, commonly, HAH-layl): A Hebrew word meaning "praise," and by extension, the name given to sets of psalms that are recited liturgically in praise of God: Psalms 145–150, the Daily *Hallel,* is recited each morning; Psalm 136, the Great *Hallel,* is recited on Shabbat and holidays and is part of the Passover *Seder.* Psalms 113–118, the best-known *Hallel,* known more fully as the Egyptian Hallel, is recited on holidays and gets its name from Psalm 114:1, which celebrates the moment "when Israel left Egypt."

Hallel Sheb'khol Yom (pronounced hah-LAYL [or, commonly, HAH-layl] sheh-b'-khol YOHM): The Hebrew term for "The Daily *Hallel.*" See **Hallel.**

Halleluyah (pronounced hah-l'-loo-YAH, but sometimes anglicized as hah-l'-LOO-yah): A common word in psalms, meaning "praise God," and the final word of a congregational response within the third blessing of the *Amidah* (from Psalm 146:10).

Hat'fillah (pronounced hah-t'-fee-LAH): Literally, "the *T'fillah,*" another name for the *Amidah.* See *T'fillah.*

Hoda'ah (pronounced hoe-dah-AH): Literally, a combination of the English words "gratitude" and "acknowledgment," so translated here as "grateful acknowledgment." The title of the second to last blessing in the *Amidah,* an expression of our grateful acknowledgment to God for the daily wonders that constitute human existence.

Hoeche K'dushah (pronounced HAY-kh' k'DOO-shah): A Yiddish term combining German and Hebrew and meaning, literally, "the High *Kedushah.*" Refers to a way to shorten the time it takes to say the *Amidah* by avoiding the necessity of having the prayer leader repeat it all after it is said silently by the congregation.

Inclusio (pronounced in-CLOO-zee-oh): A rhetorical style common to biblical prayer, whereby the end of a composition reiterates the theme or words with which the composition began.

Kabbalah (pronounced kah-bah-LAH, or, commonly, kah-BAH-lah): A general term for Jewish mysticism, but used properly for a specific mystical doctrine that began in western Europe in the eleventh or twelfth centuries; recorded in the *Zohar* (see *Zohar*) in the thirteenth century, and then was further elaborated, especially in the Land of Israel (in Safed), in the sixteenth century. From a Hebrew word meaning "to receive" or "to welcome," and secondarily, "tradition," implying the receiving of tradition from one's past.

Kabbalat Shabbat (pronounced kah-bah-LAHT shah-BAHT): Literally, "welcoming Sabbath," and therefore a term for the introductory synagogue prayers that lead up to the arrival of the Sabbath at sundown Friday night.

Kaddish (pronounced kah-DEESH, or, more commonly, KAH-dish): One of several prayers from a Hebrew word meaning "holy," and therefore the name given to a prayer affirming God's holiness. This prayer was composed in the first century but later found its way into the service in several forms, including one known as the Mourners' *Kaddish* and used as a mourning prayer.

Kavvanah (pronounced kah-vah-NAH): From a word meaning "to direct," and therefore used technically to denote the state of directing one's words and thoughts sincerely to God, as opposed to the rote recitation of prayer.

K'dushah (pronounced k'-doo-SHAH, or, commonly, k'-DOO-shah): From the Hebrew word meaning "holy," and therefore one of several prayers from the first or second century occurring in several places and versions, all of which have in common the citing of Isaiah 6:3: *kadosh, kadosh kadosh...*, "Holy, holy, holy is the Lord of hosts. The whole earth is full of his glory."

K'dushat Hashem (pronounced k'-doo-SHAHT hah-SHEM): Literally, "sanctification of the name [of God]," and the full name for the prayer that is generally called *K'dushah* (see *K'dushah*). Best known as the third blessing in the *Amidah,* but found also prior to the morning *Sh'ma.* Used also in variant form *kiddush hashem* (pronounced kee-DOOSH hah-SHEM) as a term to describe dying for the sanctification of God's name, that is, martyrdom.

Keva (pronounced KEH-vah): A Hebrew word meaning "fixity, stability," and therefore the aspect of a service that is fixed and immutable: the words on the page, perhaps, or the time at which the prayer must be said. In the early years, when prayers were delivered orally and improvised on the spot, *keva* meant the fixed order in which the liturgical themes had to be expressed.

Kibbutz G'luyot (pronounced kee-BOOTS g'-loo-YOTE): Literally, "gathering the exiles," and the title of the tenth blessing of the daily *Amidah,* a petition for Jews outside the Land of Israel to return home to their land as a sign that messianic times are imminent. Some liberal liturgies omit the blessing or interpret it more broadly to imply universal messianic liberation, but without the literal belief that Jews outside the Land of Israel are in "exile," or that they need to or want to "return home."

Kiddush (pronounced kee-DOOSH, or, commonly, KIH-d'sh): Literally, "sanctification," the name given to the prayer recited over wine at the outset of Sabbaths and holy days, declaring the day in question sanctified. A shorter version is recited the next morning after services, at which time worshipers commonly share a meal or light refreshments together. By extension, *Kiddush* is sometimes used to designate that meal as well.

Kohanim (pronounced koe-hah-NEEM): Literally, "priests," plural of *kohen* (pronounced koe-HAYN), "priest," a reference to the priests who offered sacrifices in the ancient temple until its destruction by Rome in the year 70 C.E. Also the name of modern-day Jews who claim priestly descent, and who are customarily given symbolic recognition in various ritual ways — as, for instance, being called first to stand beside the Torah reader and to recite a blessing over the reading. It is also the title of the last blessing in the *Amidah,* which contains the priestly benediction from Numbers 6:24–25. Another more popular name for that blessing is *Shalom* (pronounced shah-LOME), "peace," because the priestly benediction requests peace. See also ***Birkat Kohanim***.

Kri'at Hatorah (pronounced k'ree-AHT hah-toe-RAH): The public reading of the Torah.

Kri'at Sh'ma (pronounced k'-ree-YAHT sh'-MAH): Literally, "reciting the *Sh'ma,"* and therefore a technical term for the liturgical act of reading the prayer known as the *Sh'ma* (See *Sh'ma*).

Liturgy Public worship, from the Greek word *leitourgia,* meaning "public works." Liturgy in ancient Greece was considered a public work, the act of sacrificing or praising the gods, from which benefit would flow to the body politic.

Ma'ariv (pronounced mah-ah-REEV, or, commonly, MAH-ah-reev): From the Hebrew word *erev* (pronounced EH-rev), meaning "evening": one of two titles used for the evening worship service (also called ***Arvit***).

Massekhet Sofrim (pronounced mah-SEH-khet sohf-REEM): Literally, "Tractate [dealing with issues relevant to] scribes," an eighth-century compilation (with some later interpolations) dealing with such matters as the writing of Torah scrolls, but also including much detail on the early medieval (and possibly ancient) prayer practice of Jews in the Land of Israel.

Mid'ora'ita (pronounced mee-d'-oh-RYE-tah): Strictly speaking, commandments derived directly from Torah, which are of a higher order than those rooted only in rabbinic ordinance (called *Mid'rabbanan*), but all are binding.

Mid'rabbanan (pronounced mee-d'-rah-bah-NAHN): Commandments rooted only in rabbinic ordinance. See *Mid'ora'ita.*

Midrash (pronounced meed-RAHSH, or, commonly, MID-rahsh): From a Hebrew word meaning "to ferret out the meaning of a text," and therefore a rabbinic interpretation of a biblical word or verse. By extension, a body of rabbinic literature that offers classical interpretations of the Bible.

Minchah (pronounced meen-KHAH, or, more commonly, MIN-khah): Originally the name of a type of sacrifice, then the word for a sacrifice offered during the afternoon, and now the name for the afternoon synagogue service usually scheduled just before nightfall. *Minchah* means "afternoon."

Minhag (pronounced meen-HAHG, or, commonly, MIN-hahg): The Hebrew word for custom and, therefore, used liturgically to describe the customary way that different groups of Jews pray. By extension, *minhag* means a "rite," as in *Minhag Ashkenaz,* meaning "the rite of prayer, or the customary way of prayer for Jews in *Ashkenaz*" — that is, northern and eastern Europe.

Minim (pronounced mee-NEEM): Literally, "heretics" or "sectarians," and the title of the twelfth blessing of the daily *Amidah,* a petition that heresy be eradicated, and heretics punished. Liberal liturgies frequently omit the blessing, considering it an inappropriate malediction, not a benediction at all, or reframe it as a petition against evil in general.

Minyan (pronounced meen-YAHN, or, commonly, MIN-y'n): A quorum, the minimum number of people required for certain prayers. *Minyan* comes from the word meaning "to count."

Mi sheberakh (pronounced, commonly, MEE sheh-BAY-rakh): A standard blessing beginning, "May the One who blessed [our ancestors]...," which could be adapted for any number of instances. This set of prayers requesting God's blessing on those who receive an *aliyah* or on their family members is perhaps the best known addition to the service.

Mishnah (pronounced meesh-NAH, or, commonly, MISH-nah): The first written summary of Jewish law, compiled in the Land of Israel about the year 200 C.E., and therefore our first overall written evidence for the state of Jewish prayer in the early centuries.

Mishpat (pronounced meesh-PAHT): Literally, "justice," and the title of the eleventh blessing of the daily *Amidah;* a petition for just rulership, a condition associated with the messianic age.

Mitzvah (pronounced meetz-VAH, or, commonly, MITZ-vah; plural, *mitzvot,* pronounced meetz-VOTE): A Hebrew word used commonly to mean "good deed," but in the more technical sense, denoting any commandment from God, and therefore, by extension, what God wants us to do. Reciting the *Sh'ma* morning and evening, for instance, is a *mitzvah.*

Modim D'rabbanan (pronounced moe-DEEM d'-rah-bah-NAHN): *Modim* is the first word of the second to last blessing of the *Amidah,* and therefore a shorthand way of referring to that prayer. *Modim D'rabbanan* is the name given to the form of the prayer that is reserved for congregational recitation during the repetition of the *Amidah* by the prayer leader. Literally, it means "the *Modim* of our Rabbis," and refers to the fact that the prayer is composed of what were once several alternative responses, each of which was the custom of one of the Rabbis of the Talmud.

Musaf (pronounced moo-SAHF, or, commonly, MOO-sahf): The Hebrew word meaning "extra" or "added," and therefore the title of the additional sacrifice that was offered in the Temple on Shabbat and holy days. It is now the name given to an added service of worship appended to the morning service on those days.

M'zuzah (pronounced m'-zoo-ZAH, or, commonly, m'-ZOO-zah): The Hebrew word in the Bible meaning "doorpost," and by extension, the term now used for a small casement that contains the first two sections of the *Sh'ma* (Deut. 6:4–9, 11:13–21) and is affixed to the doorposts of Jewish homes.

N'illah (pronounced n'-ee-LAH, or, commonly, n'-EE-lah): The concluding service for Yom Kippur.

Nishmat kol cha'i (pronounced nish-MAHT kohl KHA'i): A blessing mentioned in the Talmud as one of two benedictions in use as the *Birkat Hashir* (pronounced beer-KAHT hah-SHEER), the blessing that ends a psalm collection known as a *Hallel.* (See *Hallel.*) Nowadays, we use it 1) as part of a longer *Birkat Hashir* after the Daily *Hallel,* that constitutes the central section of the *P'sukei D'zimrah* for Sabbaths and festivals; and 2) to conclude a similar *Hallel* in the Passover Haggadah.

N'kadesh (pronounced n'kah-DAYSH): The *Amidah* is first recited silently by each worshiper individually and then repeated aloud by the prayer leader, at which time its third blessing appears in extended form. *N'kadesh* (literally, "Let us sanctify...") is the first Hebrew word of that extended blessing and is thus, by extension, a common way to refer to it.

Orach Chayim (pronounced OH-rakh CHA-yim): Abbreviated as O. Ch. Literally, "The Way of Life," one of four sections in the *Tur* and the *Shulchan Arukh,* two of Judaism's major law codes; the section containing the rules of prayer.

Payy'tan (pronounced pah-y'-TAHN; plural *Payy'tanim,* pronounced pah-y'-tah-NEEM): A poet; the name given particularly to classical and medieval poets whose work is inserted into the standard prayers for special occasions.

Perek (pronounced PEH-rek; plural, *p'rakim,* pronounced p'-rah-KEEM): Literally, a "section" or "chapter" of a written work, and used liturgically to mean the sections of the *Sh'ma.* Each of its three biblical sections is a different *perek.*

Piyyut (pronounced pee-YOOT; plural: pee-yoo-TEEM): Literally, "a poem," but used technically to mean liturgical poems composed in classical and medieval times, and inserted into the standard prayers on special occasions.

P'sukei D'zimrah (pronounced p'-soo-KAY d'-zeem-RAH, or, commonly, p'-SOO-kay d'-ZIM-rah): Literally, "verses of song," and therefore the title of a lengthy set of opening morning prayers that contain psalms and songs, and serve as spiritual preparation prior to the official call to prayer.

Purim (pronounced PU-rim, or, pu-REEM): A festival falling on the fourteenth day of the Hebrew month of Adar, generally corresponding to late February or early March. It celebrates the miraculous deliverance referred to in the biblical Book of Esther. Literally, *purim* means "lots," as in the phrase "drawing of lots," because the date on which the Jews were to have been killed was chosen by lot.

R'fuah (pronounced r'-foo-AH, or, commonly, r'-FOO-ah): Literally, "healing," and the title of the eighth blessing of the daily *Amidah,* a petition for healing.

Rosh Chodesh (pronounced rohsh CHOH-desh): Literally, "the head of the month," and therefore the Hebrew name for the one- or two-day new moon period with which lunar months begin. It is marked as a holiday in Jewish tradition, a period of new beginnings.

Rubric (pronounced ROO-brick): A technical term for any discrete section of liturgy, whether a prayer or a set of prayers. The *Sh'ma* and Its Blessings is one of several large rubrics in the service; within that large rubric, the *Sh'ma* or any one of its accompanying blessings may be called a rubric as well.

Seder (pronounced SEH-der, or, commonly, SAY-der): The Hebrew word meaning "order," and therefore 1) the name given to the ritualized meal eaten on Passover eve, and 2) an early alternative term for the order of prayers in a prayer book. The word *Siddur* (see *Siddur*) is now preferred for the latter.

Seder Rav Amram (pronounced SAY-dehr rahv AHM-rahm): First known comprehensive Jewish prayer book, emanating from Rav Amram Gaon, a leading Jewish scholar and head of Sura, a famed academy in Babylonia (modern-day Iraq), c. 860 C.E.

Sefardi (pronounced s'-fahr-DEE, or, commonly s'-FAHR-dee): From the Hebrew word *Sefarad* (pronounced s'-fah-RAHD), meaning the geographic area of modern-day Spain and Portugal. *Sefardi* is the adjective, describing the liturgical rituals and customs that are derived from *Sefarad* prior to the expulsion of Jews from there at the end of the fifteenth century, as opposed to *Ashkenazi* (see *Ashkenazi*), meaning the liturgical rituals and customs common to northern and eastern Europe. Nowadays, *Sefardi* refers also to the customs of Jews from North Africa and Arab lands, whose ancestors came from Spain.

S'firot (pronounced s'-fee-ROTE; singular: *s'firah*, pronounced s'-fee-RAH): According to the Kabbalah (Jewish mysticism, see *Kabbalah*), the universe came into being by a process of divine emanation, whereby the divine light, as it were, expanded into empty space, eventually becoming physical matter. At various intervals, this light was frozen in time, as if captured by containers, each of which is called a *s'firah*. Literally, *s'firah* means "number," because early theory conceptualized the stages of creation as primordial numbers.

Shabbat (pronounced shah-BAHT): The Hebrew word for "Sabbath," from a word meaning "to rest."

Shacharit (pronounced shah-khah-REET, or, commonly, SHAH-khah-reet): The name given to the morning worship service; from the Hebrew word *shachar* (SHAH-khar), meaning "morning."

Shalom (pronounced shah-LOME): Literally, "peace," and a popular title for the final benediction of the *Amidah*, more properly entitled *Kohanim* (pronounced koe-hah-NEEM), "priests," or, more fully, *Birkat Kohanim* (pronounced beer-KAHT koe-hah-NEEM), "blessing of the priests," "priestly benediction." See also *Birkat Kohanim*, *Kohanim*.

Shanim (pronounced shah-NEEM): Literally, "years," and the title of the ninth blessing of the daily *Amidah;* a petition for a year of agricultural abundance, such as is associated with messianic days.

Shirat Hayam (pronounced shee-RAHT hah-YAHM): Literally, "Song of the sea," the song of praise and gratitude sung by Israel after the splitting of the Red Sea, and, since the Middle Ages, a prominent constituent of the *P'sukei D'zimrah*, the "warm-up" section to the morning service composed mainly of biblical material (chiefly psalms) that were intended to be sung as praise of God.

Shivah d'n'chemta (pronounced shih-VAH d'-n'-KHEM-tah): "Seven weeks of comfort." The seven Sabbaths following Tisha B'av, which take us all the way to Rosh Hashanah, call for *Haftarot* that guarantee hope.

Sh'liakh Tsibbur (pronounced sh'-LEE-ahkh tsee-BOOR): Literally, the "agent of the congregation," and therefore the name given to the person who leads the prayer service.

Sh'ma (pronounced sh'-MAH): The central prayer in the first of the two main units in the worship service, the second being the *Amidah* (see *Amidah*). The *Sh'ma* comprises three citations from the Bible, and the larger unit in which it is embedded (called The *Sh'ma* and Its Blessings) is composed of a formal call to prayer (see *Bar'khu*) and a series of blessings on the theological themes that, together with the *Sh'ma,* constitute a liturgical creed of faith. *Sh'ma,* meaning "hear," is the first word of the first line of the first biblical citation, "Hear O Israel: Adonai is our God; Adonai is One," which is the paradigmatic statement of Jewish faith, the Jews' absolute commitment to the presence of a single and unique God in time and space.

Sh'mini Atseret (pronounced sh'-MEE-nee ah-TSEH-ret): Literally, "the eighth day of solemn assembly," and the name given to the eighth and final day of the Autumn festival of Sukkot.

Sh'moneh Esreh (pronounced sh'-MOE-neh ES-ray): A Hebrew word meaning "eighteen," and therefore a name given to the second of the two main units in the worship service that once had eighteen benedictions in it (it now has nineteen), known also as the *Amidah* (see *Amidah*).

Shulchan Arukh (pronounced shool-KHAN ah-ROOKH, or, commonly, SHOOL-khan AH-rookh): The name given to the best-known code of Jewish law, compiled by Joseph Caro in the Land of Israel and published in 1565. *Shulchan Arukh* means "The Set Table," and refers to the ease with which the various laws are set forth — like a table prepared with food ready for consumption.

Siddur (pronounced see-DOOR, or, commonly, SIH-d'r): From the Hebrew word *seder* (see *Seder*) meaning "order," and therefore, by extension, the name given to the "order of prayers," or prayer book.

S'lichah (pronounced s'lee-KHAH, or, commonly S'LEE-khah): Literally, "pardon" or "forgiveness," and the title of the sixth blessing of the daily *Amidah,* a petition for divine forgiveness of our sins.

Tachanun (pronounced TAH-khah-noon): A Hebrew word meaning "supplications," and therefore, by extension, the title of the large unit of prayer that follows the *Amidah,* and which is largely supplicatory in character.

Tallit (pronounced tah-LEET; plural: *talitot,* pronounced tah-lee-TOTE): The prayer shawl equipped with tassels (see *Tsitsit*) on each corner, and generally worn during the morning *(Shacharit)* and additional *(Musaf)* synagogue service.

Talmud (pronounced tahl-MOOD, or, more commonly, TAHL-m'd): The name given to each of two great compendia of Jewish law and lore compiled over several centuries, and ever since, the literary core of the rabbinic heritage. The *Talmud Yerushalmi* (pronounced y'-roo-SHAHL-mee), the "Jerusalem Talmud," is earlier, a product of the Land of Israel generally dated about 400 C.E. The better-known *Talmud Bavli* (pronounced BAHV-lee), or "Babylonian Talmud," took shape in Babylonia (present-day Iraq), and is traditionally dated about 550 C.E. When people say "the" Talmud without specifying which one they mean, they are referring to the Babylonian version. *Talmud* means "teaching."

Tetragrammaton: The technical term for the four-letter name of God that appears in the Bible. Treating it as sacred, Jews stopped pronouncing it centuries ago, so that the actual pronunciation has been lost; instead of reading it according to its letters, it is replaced in speech by the alternative name of God, Adonai.

T'fillah (pronounced t'-fee-LAH, or, commonly, t'-FEE-lah): A Hebrew word meaning "prayer," but used technically to mean a specific prayer, namely, the second of the two main units in the worship service. It is known also as the *Amidah* or the *Sh'moneh Esreh* (see *Amidah*). Also the title of the sixteenth blessing of the *Amidah,* a petition for God to accept our prayer.

T'fillin (pronounced t'-FIH-lin, or, sometimes, t'-fee-LEEN): Two cube-shaped black boxes containing biblical quotations (Exod. 13:1–10; 13:11–16; 6:4–9; Deut. 11:13–21) and affixed by means of attached leather straps to the forehead and left arm (right arm for left-handed people) during morning prayer.

T'hillah l'david (pronounced t'-hee-LAH l'-dah-VEED): Literally, "A psalm of David," and the first two words of Psalm 145; hence, the rabbinic name for Psalm 145, which eventually became known, more popularly, as *Ashre* (pronounced ahsh-RAY, or, commonly, AHSH-ray). See *Ashre.*

T'lata d'puranuta (pronounced t'-LAH-tah d'-poo-rah-NOO-tah): "The three readings of retribution." As the Rabbis saw it, God must have allowed, and perhaps even caused, the Temple to fall as punishment for Israel's sins. The three weeks prior to Tisha B'av, therefore, anticipate the fall, culminating in Shabbat *Chazon* (khah-ZOHN), ("The Sabbath of 'the Vision,'") which features Isaiah's premonitory vision of Jerusalem's fall and the expectation of ultimate recovery (Isa. 1:1–27).

Tsadikim (pronounced tsah-dee-KEEM): Literally, "the righteous," and the title of the thirteenth blessing of the daily *Amidah,* a petition that the righteous be rewarded.

Tsitsit (pronounced tsee-TSEET): A Hebrew word meaning "tassels" or "fringes" and used to refer to the tassels affixed to the four corners of the *tallit* (the prayer shawl, see *tallit*) as Numbers 15:38 instructs.

T'shuvah (pronounced t'shoo-VAH, or, commonly t'SHOO-vah): Literally, "repentance," and the title of the fifth blessing in the daily *Amidah,* a petition by worshipers that they successfully turn to God in heartfelt repentance.

Tur (pronounced TOOR): The shorthand title applied to a fourteenth-century code of Jewish law, compiled by Jacob ben Asher in Spain, and the source for much of our knowledge about medieval liturgical practice. *Tur* means "row" or "column." The full name of the code is *Arba'ah Turim* (pronounced ahr-bah-AH too-REEM), "The Four Rows," with each row (or *Tur*) being a separate section of law on a given broad topic.

V'hu rachum (pronounced v'HOO rah-KHOOM): Literally, "He [God] is merciful," and, because of its sentiment, a common introductory line to prayers lauding God's gracious beneficence. The best example is a seven-paragraph penitential prayer that makes up the bulk of the version of *Tachanun* (pronounced TAH-khah-noon) that is said Mondays and Thursdays.

Yigdal (pronounced yig-DAHL): A popular morning hymn that encapsulates the thirteen principles of faith composed by prominent medieval philosopher Moses Maimonides (1135–1204). These thirteen principles were arranged poetically as *Yigdal* in the fourteenth century by Daniel ben Judah Dayan (pronounced dah-YAHN) of Rome.

Yishtabach (pronounced yish-tah-BAKH): The first word, and, therefore, the title of the blessing used as the *Birkat Hashir* for weekdays (see *Birkat Hashir*). On Sabbaths and festivals, it is expanded by the addition of *Nishmat kol cha'i* (pronounced neesh-MAHT kohl KHA'i), a blessing mentioned in the Talmud (see *Nishmat kol cha'i*).

Yotser (pronounced yoe-TSAYR, or, commonly, YOE-tsayr): The Hebrew word meaning "creator," and by extension, the title of the first blessing in The *Sh'ma* and Its Blessings, which is on the theme of God's creation of the universe.

Y'rushalayim (pronounced y'roo-shah-LAH-yeem): Literally, "Jerusalem," and the title of the fourteenth blessing of the daily *Amidah;* a petition for the divine building up of Jerusalem, a condition associated with the imminence of the messianic age. Some liberal liturgies interpret it more broadly to include the restoration of modern-day Jerusalem, currently under way.

Zohar (pronounced ZOE-hahr): A shorthand title for *Sefer Hazohar* (pronounced SAY-fer hah-ZOE-hahr), literally, "The Book of Splendor," which is the primary compendium of mystical thought in Judaism; written mostly by Moses de Leon in

Spain near the end of the thirteenth century, and ever since, the chief source for the study of Kabbalah (see **Kabbalah**).

A Note on the Border

The border decoration used in this book is from the
Sarajevo Haggadah, one of the best-known Hebrew
illuminated manuscripts; Barcelona (?), Spain, 14th century.

Notes

Notes

Notes

Notes

Notes

About JEWISH LIGHTS Publishing

People of all faiths and backgrounds yearn for books that attract, engage, educate and spiritually inspire.

Our principal goal is to stimulate thought and help all people learn about who the Jewish People are, where they come from, and what the future can be made to hold. While people of our diverse Jewish heritage are the primary audience, our books speak to people in the Christian world as well and will broaden their understanding of Judaism and the roots of their own faith.

We bring to you authors who are at the forefront of spiritual thought and experience. While each has something different to say, they all say it in a voice that you can hear.

Our books are designed to welcome you and then to engage, stimulate and inspire. We judge our success not only by whether or not our books are beautiful and commercially successful, but by whether or not they make a difference in your life.

We at Jewish Lights take great care to produce beautiful books that present meaningful spiritual content in a form that reflects the art of making high quality books. Therefore, we want to acknowledge those who contributed to the production of this book.

Stuart M. Matlins, Publisher

PRODUCTION
Marian B. Wallace & Bridgett Taylor

EDITORIAL
Sandra Korinchak, Emily Wichland,
Martha McKinney & Amanda Dupuis

TEXT COMPOSITION
Douglas S. Porter, Desktop Services & Publishing
San Antonio, Texas

HEBREW TYPESETTING
Ronnie Serr, Alphabet House, Los Angeles, California

JACKET DESIGN
Glenn Suokko

JACKET PRINTING
John P. Pow Company, South Boston, Massachusetts

TEXT PRINTING & BINDING
Hamilton Printing Company, Rensselaer, New York

Spirituality

The Women's Torah Commentary: *New Insights from Women Rabbis on the 54 Weekly Torah Portions* Ed. by *Rabbi Elyse Goldstein*

For the first time, women rabbis provide a commentary on the entire Torah. More than 25 years after the first woman was ordained a rabbi in America, women have an impressive group of spiritual role models that they never had before. Here, in a week-by-week format, these inspiring teachers bring their rich perspectives to bear on the biblical text. A perfect gift for others, or for yourself. 6 x 9, 496 pp, HC, ISBN 1-58023-076-8 **$34.95**

Bringing the Psalms to Life
How to Understand and Use the Book of Psalms by *Rabbi Daniel F. Polish*

Here, the most beloved—and least understood—of the books in the Bible comes alive. This simultaneously insightful and practical guide shows how the psalms address a myriad of spiritual issues in our lives: feeling abandoned, overcoming illness, dealing with anger, and more. 6 x 9, 208 pp, HC, ISBN 1-58023-077-6 **$21.95**

Stepping Stones to Jewish Spiritual Living: *Walking the Path*
Morning, Noon, and Night by *Rabbi James L. Mirel* & *Karen Bonnell Werth*

Transforms our daily routine into sacred acts of mindfulness. Chapters are arranged according to the cycle of each day. "A wonderful, practical, and inspiring guidebook to gently bring the riches of Jewish practice into our busy, everyday lives. Highly recommended." —*Rabbi David A. Cooper.* 6 x 9, 240 pp, Quality PB, ISBN 1-58023-074-1 **$16.95**; HC, ISBN 1-58023-003-2 **$21.95**

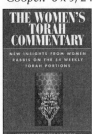 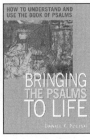 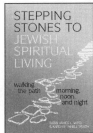 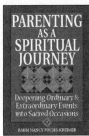 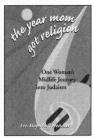

Parenting As a Spiritual Journey:
Deepening Ordinary & Extraordinary Events into Sacred Occasions
by Rabbi Nancy Fuchs-Kreimer 6 x 9, 224 pp, Quality PB, ISBN 1-58023-016-4 **$16.95**

The Year Mom Got Religion: *One Woman's Midlife Journey into Judaism*
by Lee Meyerhoff Hendler 6 x 9, 208 pp, Quality PB, ISBN 1-58023-070-9 **$15.95**;
HC, ISBN 1-58023-000-8 **$19.95**

Moses—The Prince, the Prophet: *His Life, Legend & Message for Our Lives*
by Rabbi Levi Meier, Ph.D. 6 x 9, 224 pp, Quality PB, ISBN 1-58023-069-5 **$16.95**;
HC, ISBN 1-58023-013-X **$23.95**

Ancient Secrets: *Using the Stories of the Bible to Improve Our Everyday Lives*
by Rabbi Levi Meier, Ph.D. 5½ x 8½, 288 pp, Quality PB, ISBN 1-58023-064-4 **$16.95**

Or phone, fax or mail to: JEWISH LIGHTS Publishing
Sunset Farm Offices, Route 4 • P.O. Box 237 • Woodstock, Vermont 05091
Tel: (802) 457-4000 • Fax: (802) 457-4004 • www.jewishlights.com
Credit card orders: (800) 962-4544 (9AM–5PM ET Monday–Friday)
Generous discounts on quantity orders. SATISFACTION GUARANTEED. Prices subject to change.

Spirituality

My People's Prayer Book: *Traditional Prayers, Modern Commentaries*
Ed. by *Dr. Lawrence A. Hoffman*

This momentous, critically-acclaimed series is truly a people's prayer book, one that provides a diverse and exciting commentary to the traditional liturgy. It will help modern men and women find new wisdom and guidance in Jewish prayer, and bring liturgy into their lives. Each book includes Hebrew text, modern translation, and commentaries *from all perspectives* of the Jewish world. Vol. 1—*The Sh'ma and Its Blessings*, 7 x 10, 168 pp, HC, ISBN 1-879045-79-6 **$23.95**
Vol. 2—*The Amidah*, 7 x 10, 240 pp, HC, ISBN 1-879045-80-X **$23.95**
Vol. 3—*P'sukei D'zimrah* (Morning Psalms), 7 x 10, 240 pp, HC, ISBN 1-879045-81-8 **$23.95**
Vol. 4—*Seder K'riyat Hatorah* (Shabbat Torah Service), 7 x 10, 240 pp, ISBN 1-879045-82-6 **$23.95**

Voices from Genesis: *Guiding Us through the Stages of Life*
by *Dr. Norman J. Cohen*

In a brilliant blending of modern *midrash* (finding contemporary meaning from biblical texts) and the life stages of Erik Erikson's developmental psychology, the characters of Genesis come alive to give us insights for our own journeys. 6 x 9, 192 pp, HC, ISBN 1-879045-75-3 **$21.95**

  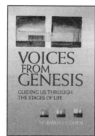 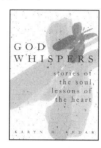 

God Whispers: *Stories of the Soul, Lessons of the Heart*
by Rabbi Karyn D. Kedar 6 x 9, 176 pp, Quality PB, ISBN 1-58023-088-1 **$15.95**;
HC, ISBN 1-58023-023-7 **$19.95**

Being God's Partner: *How to Find the Hidden Link Between Spirituality and Your Work*
by Rabbi Jeffrey K. Salkin; Intro. by Norman Lear AWARD WINNER!
6 x 9, 192 pp, Quality PB, ISBN 1-879045-65-6 **$16.95**; HC, ISBN 1-879045-37-0 **$19.95**

ReVisions: *Seeing Torah through a Feminist Lens* AWARD WINNER!
by Rabbi Elyse Goldstein 5½ x 8½, 208 pp, HC, ISBN 1-58023-047-4 **$19.95**

Soul Judaism: *Dancing with God into a New Era*
by Rabbi Wayne Dosick 5½ x 8½, 304 pp, Quality PB, ISBN 1-58023-053-9 **$16.95**

Finding Joy: *A Practical Spiritual Guide to Happiness* AWARD WINNER!
by Rabbi Dannel I. Schwartz with Mark Hass
6 x 9, 192 pp, Quality PB, ISBN 1-58023-009-1 **$14.95**; HC, ISBN 1-879045-53-2 **$19.95**

**The Empty Chair: *Finding Hope and Joy—
Timeless Wisdom from a Hasidic Master, Rebbe Nachman of Breslov* AWARD WINNER!**
Adapted by Moshe Mykoff and the Breslov Research Institute
4 x 6, 128 pp, Deluxe PB, 2-color text, ISBN 1-879045-67-2 **$9.95**

The Gentle Weapon: *Prayers for Everyday and Not-So-Everyday Moments*
Adapted from the Wisdom of Rebbe Nachman of Breslov by Moshe Mykoff and
S. C. Mizrahi, with the Breslov Research Institute
4 x 6, 144 pp, Deluxe PB, 2-color text, ISBN 1-58023-022-9 **$9.95**

"Who Is a Jew?" *Conversations, Not Conclusions* by Meryl Hyman
6 x 9, 272 pp, Quality PB, ISBN 1-58023-052-0 **$16.95**; HC, ISBN 1-879045-76-1 **$23.95**

Spirituality—The Kushner Series

Honey from the Rock, Special Anniversary Edition
An Introduction to Jewish Mysticism
by *Lawrence Kushner*

An insightful and absorbing introduction to the ten gates of Jewish mysticism and how it applies to daily life. "The easiest introduction to Jewish mysticism you can read."
6 x 9, 176 pp, Quality PB, ISBN 1-58023-073-3 **$15.95**

Eyes Remade for Wonder
The Way of Jewish Mysticism and Sacred Living
A Lawrence Kushner Reader

Intro. by *Thomas Moore*

Whether you are new to Kushner or a devoted fan, you'll find inspiration here. With samplings from each of Kushner's works, and a generous amount of new material, this book is to be read and reread, each time discovering deeper layers of meaning in our lives.
6 x 9, 240 pp, Quality PB, ISBN 1-58023-042-3 **$16.95**; HC, ISBN 1-58023-014-8 **$23.95**

Invisible Lines of Connection
Sacred Stories of the Ordinary
by *Lawrence Kushner* AWARD WINNER!

Through his everyday encounters with family, friends, colleagues and strangers, Kushner takes us deeply into our lives, finding flashes of spiritual insight in the process.
6 x 9, 160 pp, Quality PB, ISBN 1-879045-98-2 **$15.95**; HC, ISBN 1-879045-52-4 **$21.95**

The Book of Letters
A Mystical Hebrew Alphabet AWARD WINNER!
by Lawrence Kushner
Popular HC Edition, 6 x 9, 80 pp, 2-color text, ISBN 1-879045-00-1 **$24.95**; *Deluxe Gift Edition,* 9 x 12, 80 pp, HC, 2-color text, ornamentation, slipcase, ISBN 1-879045-01-X **$79.95**; *Collector's Limited Edition,* 9 x 12, 80 pp, HC, gold-embossed pages, hand-assembled slipcase. With silkscreened print. Limited to 500 signed and numbered copies, ISBN 1-879045-04-4 **$349.00**

The Book of Words
Talking Spiritual Life, Living Spiritual Talk AWARD WINNER!
by Lawrence Kushner 6 x 9, 160 pp, Quality PB, 2-color text, ISBN 1-58023-020-2 **$16.95**; 152 pp, HC, ISBN 1-879045-35-4 **$21.95**

God Was in This Place & I, i Did Not Know
Finding Self, Spirituality & Ultimate Meaning
by Lawrence Kushner 6 x 9, 192 pp, Quality PB, ISBN 1-879045-33-8 **$16.95**

The River of Light: *Jewish Mystical Awareness*
by Lawrence Kushner 6 x 9, 192 pp, Quality PB, ISBN 1-879045-03-6 **$14.95**

Spirituality & More

These Are the Words: *A Vocabulary of Jewish Spiritual Life*
by *Arthur Green*

What are the most essential ideas, concepts and terms that an educated person needs to know about Judaism? From *Adonai* (My Lord) to *zekhut* (merit), this enlightening and entertaining journey through Judaism teaches us the 149 core Hebrew words that constitute the basic vocabulary of Jewish spiritual life. 6 x 9, 304 pp, HC, ISBN 1-58023-024-5 **$21.95**

The Enneagram and Kabbalah: *Reading Your Soul*
by *Rabbi Howard A. Addison*

Combines two of the most powerful maps of consciousness known to humanity—The Tree of Life (the *Sefirot*) from the Jewish mystical tradition of *Kabbalah*, and the nine-pointed Enneagram—and shows how, together, they can provide a powerful tool for self-knowledge, critique, and transformation. 6 x 9, 176 pp, Quality PB, ISBN 1-58023-001-6 **$15.95**

Embracing the Covenant
Converts to Judaism Talk About Why & How
Ed. and with Intros. by *Rabbi Allan L. Berkowitz* and *Patti Moskovitz*

Through personal experiences of 20 converts to Judaism, this book illuminates reasons for converting, the quest for a satisfying spirituality, the appeal of the Jewish tradition and how conversion has changed lives—the convert's, and the lives of those close to them.
6 x 9, 192 pp, Quality PB, ISBN 1-879045-50-8 **$15.95**

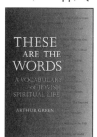 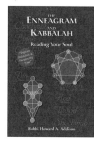   

Shared Dreams: *Martin Luther King, Jr. and the Jewish Community*
by Rabbi Marc Schneier; Preface by Martin Luther King III
6 x 9, 240 pp, HC, ISBN 1-58023-062-8 **$24.95**

Mystery Midrash: *An Anthology of Jewish Mystery & Detective Fiction*
Ed. by Lawrence W. Raphael; Preface by Joel Siegel, ABC's *Good Morning America*
6 x 9, 304 pp, Quality PB, ISBN 1-58023-055-5 **$16.95**

The Jewish Gardening Cookbook: *Growing Plants & Cooking for Holidays & Festivals*
by Michael Brown 6 x 9, 224 pp, HC, Illus., ISBN 1-58023-004-0 **$21.95**

Wandering Stars: *An Anthology of Jewish Fantasy & Science Fiction* Ed. by Jack
Dann; Intro. by Isaac Asimov 6 x 9, 272 pp, Quality PB, ISBN 1-58023-005-9 **$16.95**

More Wandering Stars
An Anthology of Outstanding Stories of Jewish Fantasy and Science Fiction
Ed. by Jack Dann; Intro. by Isaac Asimov 6 x 9, 192 pp, Quality PB, ISBN 1-58023-063-6 **$16.95**

A Heart of Wisdom: *Making the Jewish Journey from Midlife through the Elder Years*
Ed. by Susan Berrin; Foreword by Harold Kushner
6 x 9, 384 pp, Quality PB, ISBN 1-58023-051-2 **$18.95**; HC, ISBN 1-879045-73-7 **$24.95**

Sacred Intentions: *Daily Inspiration to Strengthen the Spirit, Based on Jewish Wisdom*
by Rabbi Kerry M. Olitzky and Rabbi Lori Forman
4½ x 6½, 448 pp, Quality PB, ISBN 1-58023-061-X **$15.95**

Life Cycle

Jewish Paths toward Healing and Wholeness
A Personal Guide to Dealing with Suffering
by *Rabbi Kerry M. Olitzky*; Foreword by *Debbie Friedman*

"Why me?" Why do we suffer? How can we heal? Grounded in the spiritual traditions of Judaism, this book provides healing rituals, psalms and prayers that help readers initiate a dialogue with God, to guide them along the complicated path of healing and wholeness.
6 x 9, 192 pp, Quality PB, ISBN 1-58023-068-7 **$15.95**

Mourning & Mitzvah: *A Guided Journal for Walking the Mourner's Path through Grief to Healing*
by *Anne Brener, L.C.S.W.*; Foreword by *Rabbi Jack Riemer*; Intro. by *Rabbi William Cutter*

For those who mourn a death, for those who would help them, for those who face a loss of any kind, Brener teaches us the power and strength available to us in the fully experienced mourning process. 7½ x 9, 288 pp, Quality PB, ISBN 1-879045-23-0 **$19.95**

Tears of Sorrow, Seeds of Hope
A Jewish Spiritual Companion for Infertility and Pregnancy Loss
by *Rabbi Nina Beth Cardin*

A spiritual companion that enables us to mourn infertility, a lost pregnancy, or a stillbirth within the prayers, rituals, and meditations of Judaism. By drawing on the texts of tradition, it creates readings and rites of mourning, and through them provides a wellspring of compassion, solace—and hope. 6 x 9, 192 pp, HC, ISBN 1-58023-017-2 **$19.95**

Lifecycles
V. 1: *Jewish Women on Life Passages & Personal Milestones* AWARD WINNER!
Ed. and with Intros. by Rabbi Debra Orenstein
V. 2: *Jewish Women on Biblical Themes in Contemporary Life* AWARD WINNER!
Ed. and with Intros. by Rabbi Debra Orenstein and Rabbi Jane Rachel Litman
V. 1: 6 x 9, 480 pp, Quality PB, ISBN 1-58023-018-0 **$19.95**; HC, ISBN 1-879045-14-1 **$24.95**
V. 2: 6 x 9, 464 pp, Quality PB, ISBN 1-58023-019-9 **$19.95**; HC, ISBN 1-879045-15-X **$24.95**

Grief in Our Seasons: *A Mourner's Kaddish Companion*
by Rabbi Kerry M. Olitzky 4½ x 6½, 448 pp, Quality PB, ISBN 1-879045-55-9 **$15.95**

A Time to Mourn, A Time to Comfort: *A Guide to Jewish Bereavement and Comfort*
by Dr. Ron Wolfson 7 x 9, 336 pp, Quality PB, ISBN 1-879045-96-6 **$16.95**

When a Grandparent Dies
A Kid's Own Remembering Workbook for Dealing with Shiva and the Year Beyond
by Nechama Liss-Levinson, Ph.D.
8 x 10, 48 pp, HC, Illus., 2-color text, ISBN 1-879045-44-3 **$15.95**

So That Your Values Live On: *Ethical Wills & How to Prepare Them*
Ed. by Rabbi Jack Riemer & Professor Nathaniel Stampfer
6 x 9, 272 pp, Quality PB, ISBN 1-879045-34-6 **$17.95**

Life Cycle & Holidays

How to Be a Perfect Stranger, In 2 Volumes
A Guide to Etiquette in Other People's Religious Ceremonies
Ed. by *Stuart M. Matlins* & *Arthur J. Magida*   AWARD WINNER!

What will happen? What do I do? What do I wear? What do I say? What should I avoid doing, wearing, saying? What are their basic beliefs? Should I bring a gift? In question-and-answer format, *How to Be a Perfect Stranger* explains the rituals and celebrations of America's major religions/denominations, helping an interested guest to feel comfortable, participate to the fullest extent possible, and avoid violating anyone's religious principles. It is not a guide to theology, nor is it presented from the perspective of any particular faith.
Vol. 1: *America's Largest Faiths,* 6 x 9, 432 pp, HC, ISBN 1-879045-39-7 **$24.95**
Vol. 2: *Other Faiths in America,* 6 x 9, 416 pp, HC, ISBN 1-879045-63-X **$24.95**

Putting God on the Guest List, 2nd Ed.
How to Reclaim the Spiritual Meaning of Your Child's Bar or Bat Mitzvah
by *Rabbi Jeffrey K. Salkin*   AWARD WINNER!

The expanded, updated, revised edition of today's most influential book (over 60,000 copies in print) about finding core spiritual values in American Jewry's most misunderstood ceremony.
6 x 9, 224 pp, Quality PB, ISBN 1-879045-59-1 **$16.95**; HC, ISBN 1-879045-58-3 **$24.95**

For Kids—Putting God on Your Guest List
How to Claim the Spiritual Meaning of Your Bar or Bat Mitzvah
by Rabbi Jeffrey K. Salkin 6 x 9, 144 pp, Quality PB, ISBN 1-58023-015-6 **$14.95**

Bar/Bat Mitzvah Basics
A Practical Family Guide to Coming of Age Together
Ed. by Cantor Helen Leneman 6 x 9, 240 pp, Quality PB, ISBN 1-879045-54-0 **$16.95**;
HC, ISBN 1-879045-51-6 **$24.95**

The New Jewish Baby Book AWARD WINNER!
Names, Ceremonies, & Customs—A Guide for Today's Families
by Anita Diamant 6 x 9, 336 pp, Quality PB, ISBN 1-879045-28-1 **$16.95**

Hanukkah: The Art of Jewish Living
by Dr. Ron Wolfson 7 x 9, 192 pp, Quality PB, Illus., ISBN 1-879045-97-4 **$16.95**

The Shabbat Seder: The Art of Jewish Living
by Dr. Ron Wolfson 7 x 9, 272 pp, Quality PB, Illus., ISBN 1-879045-90-7 **$16.95**
Also available are these helpful companions to *The Shabbat Seder*: Booklet of the Blessings and Songs, ISBN 1-879045-91-5 **$5.00**; Audiocassette of the Blessings, DN03 **$6.00**; Teacher's Guide, ISBN 1-879045-92-3 **$4.95**

The Passover Seder: The Art of Jewish Living
by Dr. Ron Wolfson 7 x 9, 352 pp, Quality PB, Illus., ISBN 1-879045-93-1 **$16.95**
Also available are these helpful companions to *The Passover Seder*: Passover Workbook, ISBN 1-879045-94-X **$6.95**; Audiocassette of the Blessings, DN04 **$6.00**; Teacher's Guide, ISBN 1-879045-95-8 **$4.95**

Children's Spirituality

A Prayer for the Earth
The Story of Naamah, Noah's Wife
by *Sandy Eisenberg Sasso*
Full-color illus. by *Bethanne Andersen*

For ages 4 & up

NONDENOMINATIONAL, NONSECTARIAN

This new story, based on an ancient text, opens readers' religious imaginations to new ideas about the well-known story of the Flood. When God tells Noah to bring the animals of the world onto the ark, God also calls on Naamah, Noah's wife, to save each plant on Earth.

"A lovely tale. . . . Children of all ages should be drawn to this parable for our times."
—*Tomie dePaola*, artist/author of books for children

9 x 12, 32 pp, HC, Full-color illus., ISBN 1-879045-60-5 **$16.95**

  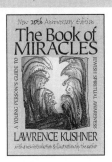

The 11th Commandment: Wisdom from Our Children
by *The Children of America*

For all ages

MULTICULTURAL, NONDENOMINATIONAL, NONSECTARIAN

"If there were an Eleventh Commandment, what would it be?" Children of many religious denominations across America answer this question—in their own drawings and words. "A rare book of spiritual celebration for all people, of all ages, for all time."—*Bookviews*
8 x 10, 48 pp, HC, Full-color illus., ISBN 1-879045-46-X **$16.95**

Sharing Blessings: Children's Stories for Exploring the Spirit of the Jewish Holidays
by *Rahel Musleah* and *Rabbi Michael Klayman*
Full-color illus. by *Mary O'Keefe Young*

For ages 6 & up

What is the spiritual message of each of the Jewish holidays? How do we teach it to our children? Many books tell children about the historical significance and customs of the holidays. Now, through engaging, creative stories about one family's preparation, *Sharing Blessings* explores ways to get into the *spirit* of 13 different holidays. "Lighthearted, and yet thorough—allows all Jewish parents (even those with very little Jewish education) to introduce the spirit of our cherished holiday traditions." —*Shari Lewis*, creator and star of PBS' *Lamb Chop's Play-Along*
8½ x 11, 64 pp, HC, Full-color illus., ISBN 1-879045-71-0 **$18.95**

The Book of Miracles
A Young Person's Guide to Jewish Spiritual Awareness
by *Lawrence Kushner*

For ages 9 & up

From the miracle at the Red Sea to the miracle of waking up this morning, this intriguing book introduces kids to a way of everyday spiritual thinking to last a lifetime. Kushner, whose award-winning books have brought spirituality to life for countless adults, now shows young people how to use Judaism as a foundation on which to build their lives. "A well-written, easy to understand, very lovely guide to Jewish spirituality. I recommend it to all teens as a good read." —*Kimberly Kirberger*, co-author, *Chicken Soup for the Teenage Soul* 6 x 9, 96 pp, HC, 2-color illus., ISBN 1-879045-78-8 **$16.95**

Children's Spirituality

In Our Image
God's First Creatures
by *Nancy Sohn Swartz*
Full-color illus. by *Melanie Hall*

For ages 4 & up

NONDENOMINATIONAL, NONSECTARIAN

A playful new twist on the Creation story—from the perspective of the animals. Celebrates the interconnectedness of nature and the harmony of all living things. "The vibrantly colored illustrations nearly leap off the page in this delightful interpretation." —*School Library Journal*

"A message all children should hear, presented in words and pictures that children will find irresistible." —*Rabbi Harold Kushner*, author of *When Bad Things Happen to Good People*

9 x 12, 32 pp, HC, Full-color illus., ISBN 1-879045-99-0 **$16.95**

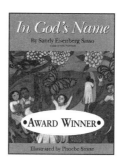

God's Paintbrush
by *Sandy Eisenberg Sasso*; Full-color illus. by *Annette Compton*

For ages 4 & up

MULTICULTURAL, NONDENOMINATIONAL, NONSECTARIAN

Invites children of all faiths and backgrounds to encounter God openly in their own lives. Wonderfully interactive; provides questions adult and child can explore together at the end of each episode. "An excellent way to honor the imaginative breadth and depth of the spiritual life of the young." —*Dr. Robert Coles*, Harvard University

11 x 8½, 32 pp, HC, Full-color illus., ISBN 1-879045-22-2 **$16.95**

Also available: **A Teacher's Guide: A Guide for Jewish & Christian Educators and Parents**
8½ x 11, 32 pp, PB, ISBN 1-879045-57-5 **$6.95**

God's Paintbrush Celebration Kit 9½ x 12, HC, Includes 5 sessions/40 full-color Activity Sheets and Teacher Folder with complete instructions, ISBN 1-58023-050-4 **$21.95**

In God's Name
by *Sandy Eisenberg Sasso*; Full-color illus. by *Phoebe Stone*

For ages 4 & up

MULTICULTURAL, NONDENOMINATIONAL, NONSECTARIAN

Like an ancient myth in its poetic text and vibrant illustrations, this award-winning modern fable about the search for God's name celebrates the diversity and, at the same time, the unity of all the people of the world. "What a lovely, healing book!" —*Madeleine L'Engle*

9 x 12, 32 pp, HC, Full-color illus., ISBN 1-879045-26-5 **$16.95**

What Is God's Name? (A Board Book)
An abridged board book version of the award-winning *In God's Name*.

For ages 0–4

5 x 5, 24 pp, Board, Full-color illus., ISBN 1-893361-10-1 **$7.95**

Children's Spirituality

ENDORSED BY CATHOLIC, PROTESTANT, AND JEWISH RELIGIOUS LEADERS

God Said Amen
by *Sandy Eisenberg Sasso*
Full-color illus. by *Avi Katz*

For ages 4 & up

MULTICULTURAL, NONDENOMINATIONAL, NONSECTARIAN

A warm and inspiring tale of two kingdoms: Midnight Kingdom is overflowing with water but has no oil to light its lamps; Desert Kingdom is blessed with oil but has no water to grow its gardens. The kingdoms' rulers ask God for help but are too stubborn to ask each other. It takes a minstrel, a pair of royal riding-birds and their young keepers, and a simple act of kindness to show that they need only reach out to each other to find God's answer to their prayers.

9 x 12, 32 pp, HC, Full-color illus., ISBN 1-58023-080-6 **$16.95**

For Heaven's Sake
by *Sandy Eisenberg Sasso*; Full-color illus. by *Kathryn Kunz Finney*

For ages 4 & up

MULTICULTURAL, NONDENOMINATIONAL, NONSECTARIAN

Everyone talked about heaven: "Thank heavens." "Heaven forbid." "For heaven's sake, Isaiah." But no one would say what heaven was or how to find it. So Isaiah decides to find out, by seeking answers from many different people. "This book is a reminder of how well Sandy Sasso knows the minds of children. But it may surprise—and delight—readers to find how well she knows us grown-ups too." —*Maria Harris*, National Consultant in Religious Education, and author of *Teaching and Religious Imagination* 9 x 12, 32 pp, HC, Full-color illus., ISBN 1-58023-054-7 **$16.95**

But God Remembered: Stories of Women from Creation to the Promised Land
by *Sandy Eisenberg Sasso*; Full-color illus. by *Bethanne Andersen*

For ages 8 & up

NONDENOMINATIONAL, NONSECTARIAN

A fascinating collection of four different stories of women only briefly mentioned in biblical tradition and religious texts. Award-winning author Sasso vibrantly brings to life courageous and strong women from ancient tradition; all teach important values through their actions and faith. "Exquisite. . . . A book of beauty, strength and spirituality." —*Association of Bible Teachers* 9 x 12, 32 pp, HC, Full-color illus., ISBN 1-879045-43-5 **$16.95**

God in Between
by *Sandy Eisenberg Sasso*; Full-color illus. by *Sally Sweetland*

For ages 4 & up

MULTICULTURAL, NONDENOMINATIONAL, NONSECTARIAN

If you wanted to find God, where would you look? A magical, mythical tale that teaches that God can be found where we are: within all of us and the relationships between us. "This happy and wondrous book takes our children on a sweet and holy journey into God's presence." —*Rabbi Wayne Dosick, Ph.D.*, author of *Golden Rules* and *Soul Judaism*
9 x 12, 32 pp, HC, Full-color illus., ISBN 1-879045-86-9 **$16.95**

Healing/Wellness/Recovery

Jewish Pastoral Care
A Practical Handbook from Traditional and Contemporary Sources
Ed. by *Rabbi Dayle A. Friedman*

This innovative resource builds on the classic foundations of pastoral care, enriching it with uniquely Jewish traditions and wisdom. Gives today's Jewish pastoral counselors practical guidelines based in the Jewish tradition. 6 x 9, 352 pp, HC, ISBN 1-58023-078-4 **$34.95** (Avail. Jan. 2001)

Healing of Soul, Healing of Body
Spiritual Leaders Unfold the Strength & Solace in Psalms
Ed. by *Rabbi Simkha Y. Weintraub, CSW*, for The National Center for Jewish Healing

A source of solace for those who are facing illness, as well as those who care for them. Provides a wellspring of strength with inspiring introductions and commentaries by eminent spiritual leaders reflecting all Jewish movements. 6 x 9, 128 pp, Quality PB, Illus., 2-color text, ISBN 1-879045-31-1 **$14.95**

Self, Struggle & Change: *Family Conflict Stories in Genesis and Their Healing Insights for Our Lives*
by *Dr. Norman J. Cohen*

How do I find wholeness in my life and in my family's life? Here a modern master of biblical interpretation brings us greater understanding of the ancient text and of ourselves in this intriguing re-telling of conflict between husband and wife, father and son, brothers and sisters. 6 x 9, 224 pp, Quality PB, ISBN 1-879045-66-4 **$16.95**; HC, ISBN 1-879045-19-2 **$21.95**

Twelve Jewish Steps to Recovery: *A Personal Guide to Turning from Alcoholism & Other Addictions . . . Drugs, Food, Gambling, Sex . . .* by Rabbi Kerry M. Olitzky & Stuart A. Copans, M.D. Preface by Abraham J. Twerski, M.D.; Intro. by Rabbi Sheldon Zimmerman; "Getting Help" by JACS Foundation 6 x 9, 144 pp, Quality PB, ISBN 1-879045-09-5 **$13.95**

One Hundred Blessings Every Day: *Daily Twelve Step Recovery Affirmations, Exercises for Personal Growth & Renewal Reflecting Seasons of the Jewish Year* by Rabbi Kerry M. Olitzky, with selected meditations prepared by Rabbi James Stone Goodman, Danny Siegel, and Gordon Tucker. Foreword by Rabbi Neil Gillman, The Jewish Theological Seminary of America; Afterword by Dr. Jay Holder, Director, Exodus Treatment Center 4½ x 6½, 432 pp, Quality PB, ISBN 1-879045-30-3 **$14.95**

Recovery from Codependence: *A Jewish Twelve Steps Guide to Healing Your Soul* by Rabbi Kerry M. Olitzky; Foreword by Marc Galanter, M.D., Director, Division of Alcoholism & Drug Abuse, NYU Medical Center; Afterword by Harriet Rossetto, Director, Gateways Beit T'shuvah 6 x 9, 160 pp, Quality PB, ISBN 1-879045-32-X **$13.95**; HC, ISBN 1-879045-27-3 **$21.95**

Renewed Each Day: *Daily Twelve Step Recovery Meditations Based on the Bible* by Rabbi Kerry M. Olitzky & Aaron Z. *Vol. I: Genesis & Exodus*; Intro. by Rabbi Michael A. Signer; Afterword by JACS Foundation. *Vol. II: Leviticus, Numbers and Deuteronomy*; Intro. by Sharon M. Strassfeld; Afterword by Rabbi Harold M. Schulweis
Vol. I: 6 x 9, 224 pp, Quality PB, ISBN 1-879045-12-5 **$14.95**
Vol. II: 6 x 9, 280 pp, Quality PB, ISBN 1-879045-13-3 **$14.95**

Jewish Meditation

Discovering Jewish Meditation
Instruction & Guidance for Learning an Ancient Spiritual Practice
by *Nan Fink Gefen*

Gives readers of any level of understanding the tools to learn the practice of Jewish meditation on your own, starting you on the path to a deep spiritual and personal connection to God and to greater insight about your life. 6 x 9, 208 pp, Quality PB, ISBN 1-58023-067-9 **$16.95**

Meditation from the Heart of Judaism: *Today's Teachers Share Their Practices, Techniques, and Faith*
Ed. by *Avram Davis*

A "how-to"guide for both beginning and experienced meditators, drawing on the wisdom of 22 masters of meditation who explain why and how they meditate. A detailed compendium of the experts' "best practices" offers advice and starting points. 6 x 9, 256 pp, Quality PB, ISBN 1-58023-049-0 **$16.95**; HC, ISBN 1-879045-77-X **$21.95**

The Way of Flame
A Guide to the Forgotten Mystical Tradition of Jewish Meditation
by *Avram Davis* 4½ x 8, 176 pp, Quality PB, ISBN 1-58023-060-1 **$15.95**

  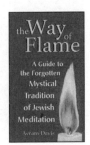 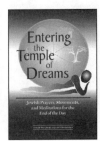 

Entering the Temple of Dreams: *Jewish Prayers, Movements, and Meditations for the End of the Day* by *Tamar Frankiel* and *Judy Greenfeld*
Nighttime spirituality is much more than bedtime prayers! Here, you'll uncover deeper meaning to familiar nighttime prayers—and learn to combine the prayers with movements and meditations to enhance your physical and psychological well-being.
7 x 10, 192 pp, Illus., Quality PB, ISBN 1-58023-079-2 **$16.95**

Minding the Temple of the Soul: *Balancing Body, Mind, and Spirit through Traditional Jewish Prayer, Movement, and Meditation*
by *Tamar Frankiel* and *Judy Greenfeld*

This new spiritual approach to physical health introduces readers to a spiritual tradition that affirms the body and enables them to reconceive their bodies in a more positive light. Focuses on traditional Jewish prayers, with exercises, movements, and meditations. 7 x 10, 184 pp, Quality PB, Illus., ISBN 1-879045-64-8 **$16.95**; Audiotape of the Blessings, Movements and Meditations (60-min. cassette), JN01 **$9.95**; Videotape of the Movements and Meditations (46-min. VHS), S507 **$20.00**

Theology/Philosophy

Torah of the Earth: *Exploring 4,000 Years of Ecology in Jewish Thought*

In 2 Volumes Ed. by *Rabbi Arthur Waskow*

Major new resource offering us an invaluable key to understanding the intersection of ecology and Judaism. Leading scholars provide us with a guided tour of ecological thought from four major Jewish viewpoints. Vol. 1: *Biblical Israel & Rabbinic Judaism*, 6 x 9, 272 pp, Quality PB, ISBN 1-58023-086-5 **$19.95**; Vol. 2: *Zionism & Eco-Judaism*, 6 x 9, 336 pp, Quality PB, ISBN 1-58023-087-3 **$19.95**

Broken Tablets: *Restoring the Ten Commandments and Ourselves*

Ed. by *Rabbi Rachel S. Mikva*; Intro. by *Rabbi Lawrence Kushner*;
Afterword by *Rabbi Arnold Jacob Wolf* **AWARD WINNER!**

Twelve outstanding spiritual leaders each share profound and personal thoughts about these biblical commands and why they have such a special hold on us.
6 x 9, 192 pp, HC, ISBN 1-58023-066-0 **$21.95**

Evolving Halakhah: *A Progressive Approach to Traditional Jewish Law*

by *Rabbi Dr. Moshe Zemer*

Innovative and provocative, this book affirms the system of traditional Jewish law, *halakhah*, as flexible enough to accommodate the changing realities of each generation. It shows that the traditional framework for understanding the Torah's commandments can be the living heart of Jewish life for all Jews. 6 x 9, 480 pp, HC, ISBN 1-58023-002-4 **$40.00**

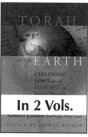    

God & the Big Bang
Discovering Harmony Between Science & Spirituality **AWARD WINNER!**
by Daniel C. Matt
6 x 9, 216 pp, Quality PB, ISBN 1-879045-89-3 **$16.95**; HC, ISBN 1-879045-48-6 **$21.95**

Israel—A Spiritual Travel Guide **AWARD WINNER!**
A Companion for the Modern Jewish Pilgrim
by Rabbi Lawrence A. Hoffman 4¾ x 10, 256 pp, Quality PB, ISBN 1-879045-56-7 **$18.95**

Godwrestling—Round 2: *Ancient Wisdom, Future Paths* **AWARD WINNER!**
by Rabbi Arthur Waskow
6 x 9, 352 pp, Quality PB, ISBN 1-879045-72-9 **$18.95**; HC, ISBN 1-879045-45-1 **$23.95**

Ecology & the Jewish Spirit: *Where Nature & the Sacred Meet* Ed. and with Intros. by
Ellen Bernstein 6 x 9, 288 pp, Quality PB, ISBN 1-58023-082-2 **$16.95**;
HC, ISBN 1-879045-88-5 **$23.95**

Israel: *An Echo of Eternity* by Abraham Joshua Heschel; New Intro. by
Dr. Susannah Heschel 5½ x 8, 272 pp, Quality PB, ISBN 1-879045-70-2 **$18.95**

The Earth Is the Lord's: *The Inner World of the Jew in Eastern Europe*
by Abraham Joshua Heschel 5½ x 8, 112 pp, Quality PB, ISBN 1-879045-42-7 **$13.95**

A Passion for Truth: *Despair and Hope in Hasidism* by Abraham Joshua Heschel
5½ x 8, 352 pp, Quality PB, ISBN 1-879045-41-9 **$18.95**

Theology/Philosophy

A Heart of Many Rooms
Celebrating the Many Voices within Judaism
by *Dr. David Hartman*   AWARD WINNER!

Named a *Publishers Weekly* "Best Book of the Year." Addresses the spiritual and theological questions that face all Jews and all people today. From the perspective of traditional Judaism, Hartman shows that commitment to both Jewish tradition and to pluralism can create understanding between people of different religious convictions.
6 x 9, 352 pp, HC, ISBN 1-58023-048-2 **$24.95**

A Living Covenant: *The Innovative Spirit in Traditional Judaism*
by *Dr. David Hartman*   AWARD WINNER!

Winner, National Jewish Book Award. Hartman reveals a Judaism grounded in covenant—a relational framework—informed by the metaphor of marital love rather than that of parent-child dependency.   6 x 9, 368 pp, Quality PB, ISBN 1-58023-011-3 **$18.95**

The Death of Death: *Resurrection and Immortality in Jewish Thought*
by *Dr. Neil Gillman*   AWARD WINNER!

Does death end life, or is it the passage from one stage of life to another? This National Jewish Book Award Finalist explores the original and compelling argument that Judaism, a religion often thought to pay little attention to the afterlife, not only offers us rich ideas on the subject—but delivers a deathblow to death itself.   6 x 9, 336 pp, Quality PB, ISBN 1-58023-081-4 **$18.95**; HC, ISBN 1-879045-61-3 **$23.95**

   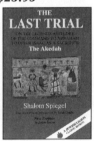 

Aspects of Rabbinic Theology by Solomon Schechter; New Intro. by Dr. Neil Gillman
6 x 9, 448 pp, Quality PB, ISBN 1-879045-24-9 **$19.95**

The Last Trial: *On the Legends and Lore of the Command to Abraham to Offer Isaac as a Sacrifice* by Shalom Spiegel; New Intro. by Judah Goldin
6 x 9, 208 pp, Quality PB, ISBN 1-879045-29-X **$17.95**

Judaism and Modern Man: *An Interpretation of Jewish Religion* by Will Herberg; New Intro. by Dr. Neil Gillman 5½ x 8½, 336 pp, Quality PB, ISBN 1-879045-87-7 **$18.95**

Seeking the Path to Life AWARD WINNER!
Theological Meditations on God and the Nature of People, Love, Life and Death
by Rabbi Ira F. Stone
6 x 9, 160 pp, Quality PB, ISBN 1-879045-47-8 **$14.95**; HC, ISBN 1-879045-17-6 **$19.95**

The Spirit of Renewal: *Finding Faith after the Holocaust* AWARD WINNER!
by Rabbi Edward Feld
6 x 9, 224 pp, Quality PB, ISBN 1-879045-40-0 **$16.95**

Tormented Master: *The Life and Spiritual Quest of Rabbi Nahman of Bratslav*
by Dr. Arthur Green
6 x 9, 416 pp, Quality PB, ISBN 1-879045-11-7 **$18.95**

Your Word Is Fire: *The Hasidic Masters on Contemplative Prayer*
Ed. and Trans. with a New Introduction by Dr. Arthur Green and Dr. Barry W. Holtz
6 x 9, 160 pp, Quality PB, ISBN 1-879045-25-7 **$14.95**

The Way Into... Series

A major 14-volume series to be completed over the next several years, *The Way Into...* provides an accessible and usable "guided tour" of the Jewish faith, its people, its history and beliefs—in total, an introduction to Judaism for adults that will enable them to understand and interact with sacred texts. Each volume is written by a major modern scholar and teacher, and is organized around an important concept of Judaism.

The Way Into... will enable all readers to achieve a real sense of Jewish cultural literacy through guided study. Forthcoming volumes include:

  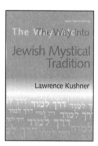 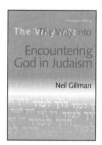

The Way Into Torah

by *Dr. Norman J. Cohen*

What is "Torah"? What are the different approaches to studying Torah? What are the different levels of understanding Torah? For whom is the study intended? Explores the origins and development of Torah, why it should be studied and how to do it.
6 x 9, 160 pp, HC, ISBN 1-58023-028-8 **$21.95**

The Way Into Jewish Prayer

by *Dr. Lawrence A. Hoffman*

Opens the door to 3,000 years of the Jewish way to God by making available all you need to feel at home in Jewish worship. Provides basic definitions of the terms you need to know as well as thoughtful analysis of the depth that lies beneath Jewish prayer.
6 x 9, 224 pp, HC, ISBN 1-58023-027-X **$21.95**

The Way Into Jewish Mystical Tradition

by *Rabbi Lawrence Kushner*

Explains the principles of Jewish mystical thinking, their religious and spiritual significance, and how they relate to our lives. A book that allows us to experience and understand the Jewish mystical approach to our place in the world.
6 x 9, 176 pp, HC, ISBN 1-58023-029-6 **$21.95**

The Way Into Encountering God in Judaism

by *Dr. Neil Gillman*

Explains how Jews have encountered God throughout history—and today—by exploring the many metaphors for God in Jewish tradition. Explores the Jewish tradition's passionate but also conflicting ways of relating to God as Creator, relational partner, and a force in history and nature.
6 x 9, 176 pp, HC, ISBN 1-58023-025-3 **$21.95**

Or phone, fax or mail to: **JEWISH LIGHTS Publishing**
Sunset Farm Offices, Route 4 • P.O. Box 237 • Woodstock, Vermont 05091
Tel: (802) 457-4000 • Fax: (802) 457-4004 • www.jewishlights.com
Credit card orders **(800) 962-4544** (9AM–5PM ET Monday–Friday)
Generous discounts on quantity orders. SATISFACTION GUARANTEED. Prices subject to change.